# BORIS KARLOFF
## The Man Remembered

# BORIS KARLOFF
## The Man Remembered

by Gordon B. Shriver

BearManor Media
2021

*Boris Karloff: The Man Remembered*

© 2021 Gordon B. Shriver

All rights reserved.

No portion of this publication may be reproduced, stored, and/or copied electronically (except for academic use as a source), nor transmitted in any form or by any means without the prior written permission of the publisher and/or author.

Published in the United States of America by:

BearManor Media
1317 Edgewater Dr #110
Orlando FL 32804

bearmanormedia.com

Printed in the United States.

ISBN—978-1-62933-822-4

*To*
*My Mother*
*and*
*My Father*

# Contents

Foreword .................................................................ix

Early Stages ............................................................ 1

"It's Alive! It's Alive!" ............................................. 7

An Actor Prospers ................................................. 29

Haunting the Airwaves ......................................... 49

Photos .................................................................. 81

The Last Decade ................................................. 123

Credits ............................................................... 151

Bibliography ....................................................... 219

# Foreword

**THE GENESIS OF THIS BOOK** took place in the early '70's, when I was in high school, and spent hours on end in libraries, looking for whatever information I could find on a British actor whose work I had seen only on television. Great thanks and appreciation go out to those who graciously took time to respond to my letters, e-mails, and phone calls over the years, and told me how Boris Karloff touched their lives and what he meant to them.

I must single out the late Evelyn Karloff, Boris' widow, with whom I corresponded between 1983 and 1992. Her personal memories and comments as this project came together were of immense help, as well as her assistance in contacting friends of hers and her husband. Regrettably, she did not live to see this book completed, as she died in 1993. Similarly, I'm indebted to Sara Jane Karloff, the actor's daughter, for her friendship, remarks, and support. It is my hope that this opus captures the spirit and achievements of her father and adds something more to the body of work he left behind.

Friends, associates, and others who crossed paths with Karloff who have contributed in some way are Robert Anderson, Peter Asher, Edward Asner, Orson Bean, Douglas Benton, Theodore Bikel, Robert Bloch, Paul Bogart, Peter Bogdanovich, Adrian Booth, Tom Bosley, Ray Bradbury, Frank and MaryJo Brink, Himan Brown, Kirk Browning, Frank Cady, Booth Colman, Patrick Curtis, Melvyn Douglas, Frances Drake, Ralph Edwards, Denholm Elliott, John Elliott, Maurice Evans, Norman Felton, Bramwell Fletcher, Robert Florey, William Frye, Eva Gabor, John Gay, Bruce Gordon, Richard Gordon,

Julie Harris, Mother Dolores Hart, Kristin Helmore, Tom Helmore, Douglas Heyes, Pat Hingle, Barbara Holdridge, Norris Houghton, Norman Jewison, Lamont Johnson, Henry Jones, Nathan Juran, Yousuf Karsh, Arthur Kennard, Walter Kerr, Buzz Kulik, Christopher Lee, Eva LeGallienne, June Lockhart, Roddy MacDowall, George Maharis, Delbert Mann, Martin Manulis, Fletcher Markle, Richard Matheson, Mercedes McCambridge, Dorothy McGuire, Martin Milner, Paul Monash, Robert Mulligan, Mildred Natwick, Ralph Nelson, Anthony Newley, William F. Nolan, Dan O'Herlihy, Gregory Peck, Nehemiah Persoff, Daniel Petrie, Tony Randall, and President Ronald Reagan.

Also, Chita Rivera, Joseph Robinette, Edward G. Robinson, Hubbell Robinson, Mark Robson, William Ross, Donald Sanford, Alvin Sapinsley, Gerald Savory, George Schaefer, John Schlesinger, Daniel Selznick, James Sheldon, Stirling Silliphant, Stewart Stern, Roger L. Stevens, Dorothy Stickney, Susan Strasberg, Herbert L. Strock, Gloria Stuart, Inga Swenson, Phyllis Thaxter, Wendy Toye, Shirley Ulmer, Russell Wade, Eli Wallach, Betty White, Jonathan Winters, Robert Wise, Joseph Wiseman, Ian Wolfe, Teresa Wright, Jane Wyatt, Dana Wynter, James Yaffe, and Barry Yellen.

In addition, I thank the staffs of the Academy of Motion Picture Arts and Sciences and its Margaret Herrick Library, the American Federation of Television and Radio Artists, the Atlanta Historical Society, the Broadcast Pioneers Library, the California Historical Society, the Los Angeles Public Library, the Museum of the City of New York, the Paley Center For Media, the Mystery Writers of America, the Performing Arts Research Center at the New York Public Library, the State Historical Society of Wisconsin, the U.S. Air Force Band, the University of California at Los Angeles and its Television Archives, and the Wisconsin Center for Film and Theater Research. And, for their own special efforts, I thank Kenneth Carr, Richard Cooper, Gary Dorst, Lieutenant Colonel Arnold D. Gabriel, Harry Gleeson, D'Arcy More, Major Jack Oswald, Jame Riley, Bradley G. Stanley, and Tom Weaver. Finally, thanks to my family and friends for their interest and indulgence in hearing about this project over the decades, and seeing it come to be after such a long but wonderful journey.

# Early Stages

**In 1887, Queen Victoria** had ruled England for fifty years, *A Study in Scarlet*, the first Sherlock Holmes story, was published, and on November 23rd in the London suburb of Camberwell, Boris Karloff entered the world.

His birth name was William Henry Pratt, the youngest of nine children born to Edward John Pratt, an employee of the British Indian Civil Service, and Eliza Sara Millard Pratt, his third wife. Mr. Pratt's intention was that all of his eight sons (there was one daughter, Julia) would follow him into the consular service. When Billy, as the newest member of the family was called, had grown up to become Boris Karloff he recalled that each brother would address him about his reluctance in pursuing the family trade.

The elder Pratt, who was about sixty when Billy was born, died in 1892, and Mrs. Pratt, still in her teens when she got married, followed him in death two years later. Childhood was a difficult time for Billy, a shy, stammering boy having to deal with a father who was rarely home (and very strict when he was), a mother in poor health, and being bullied by his brothers, who were frequently gone, too, to India or China. Nevertheless, he sought enjoyment in games and the theater. At the time of his mother's passing, the Pratts had relocated to Middlesex, where Billy was raised by a half-sister Emma, from his father's second marriage. He was all of nine years when he discovered his life's calling. This came about in 1896, when he was cast as the Demon King in a church production of *Cinderella*. Having attended the Enfield Grammar School, Billy went on to Merchant Taylors' School in London for four years, and from there to the prestigious Uppingham School, where his pursuits included choir, cricket, playing the piano, and rugby.

During his teens, Billy was more interested in theater than schoolwork. Part of that was due to his brother George, who for a time had acted under the name of George Marlow, but abandoned the craft and eventually went into business. However, he maintained his interest by assisting at the Enfield Amateur Dramatic Society, staging an annual show at the Enfield Cricket Club, and coaching acting.

When Billy was nineteen, he completed his education at King's College in London. Disregarding the strong discipline and tradition of his family, who urged him to abandon the acting interest and follow them into the consular service, he decided to leave England. Based on the flip of a coin, Billy headed for Canada, the other option being Australia. With some money left to him by his half-sister when she died, he sailed at twenty-one from Liverpool in May of 1909.

The ship took him to Montreal, a stop on the way to Toronto where he planned to work as a farmer. He was assigned to a farm in Hamilton, Ontario, stayed for a few months, and moved on to Banff and Vancouver, trying to make a living at starvation wages by breaking horses, selling real estate, and as a laborer. Billy approached stock theater companies in Vancouver, yet his efforts went unrewarded. Fate stepped in for the better when a letter arrived from Walter Kelly, a Seattle theatrical agent he'd contacted. Kelly referred him to the Jean Russell company in Kamloops, so Billy, who said he was an experienced actor and was not, boarded the train to the small British Columbia town. Figuring he couldn't be an actor with the name Pratt, he chose the stage name of Boris Karloff. Its origin is still cryptic. After achieving fame, he would say that Karloff came from his mother's side of the family, but his genealogy doesn't confirm it. Boris was his own conception.

The Jean Russell players saw through his supposed acting background, but took him on anyway, and his first role was that of a sixty year-old banker in Ferenc Molnar's *The Devil*. His debut was not an auspicious one, as his salary was cut in half before the curtain was rung down. Still, they liked him and he stayed, learning his craft and touring western Canada until 1912. As he would in years to come, he become popular playing villains.

The company ended up in Regina, Saskatchewan, where a cyclone hit, devastating the town. All of the actors assisted in cleaning up the damage, but the troupe, which had run out of money, dissolved. Karloff worked briefly as a baggage handler and moved on to Prince Albert. There, he joined the Harry St. Clair repertory group, which needed a young leading man, and had responded to a letter of application Karloff sent. Throughout Canada and the northern United States, Karloff played 106 parts and, being a fast learner of lines, got the best casting in plays such as *East Lynne, Charley's Aunt,* and *Way Down East.*

After close to two years in Prince Albert and with some money saved, Karloff believed he had enough experience to make a go of it in a larger theater town, so he went to Chicago. When he found work, his finances had dwindled to practically nothing, and he had to go to Virginia for a ten-week run with another stock company. After that, he returned to the Windy City. He had tried enlisting in the British army at the start of World War I in 1914 and was rejected for a supposed heart murmur.

On the road then was the Billie Bennett theater company staging *The Virginian.* Karloff hooked up with them, playing in several states, until they made it to Los Angeles in December of 1917. That was temporary, and it was on to three other repertory troupes, playing northern California stops as San Francisco and Vallejo and eventually coming back to Los Angeles. Amidst all that touring, he spent two months pulling sacks of flour and loading trucks, when a flu epidemic destroyed the theater business, closing venues and disbanding the players.

Regarding his personal life at this point, and ever after, Karloff kept it private. He was married a total of six times. The first four were brief, beginning in 1910 to a Grace Harding and ending three years later. The second from 1915 to 1919 to Olive de Wilton, a stage actress in Canada and the northeastern United States. The third was from 1920 to 1922 to Montena Lorena Williams, a musician from New Mexico, and the fourth to Helen Vivian Soule, an actress from Maine, from 1924 to 1928.

Hollywood was in its infancy, and silent pictures were taking their hold on America. Karloff's entry into the world of moviemaking, he said, was at Universal Pictures in a crowd scene directed by Frank Borzage, who won Academy Awards for *Seventh Heaven* (1927) and *Bad Girl* (1931). The name of the film, if in fact Karloff was correct, is unknown. *The Dumb Girl of Portici* (1916) and, with Douglas

Fairbanks, *His Majesty, the American* (1919) have both been said to be Karloff's first film, further complicating the research process into his career, so it may never be known exactly what was his maiden voyage onto the screen.

Karloff appeared as an extra initially and on to bit parts such as heavies and such of various ethnic origin as a French-Canadian trapper or a Mexican half-breed. His first featured role, Douglas Benton (associate producer of Karloff's TV series *Thriller*) told me, was at Paramount. He said, "They were putting the railroad tracks down Melrose, and he was working as a day laborer laying ties, and one of the assistant directors came out of the front gate, and shouted they needed one hundred actors for a battle scene.

"Boris said everybody on the streetcar track laying detail dropped their hammers, rails, ties, and raced for the gate. He said there must have been 400 people fighting to get in, and the toughest one hundred who were left standing were the ones they hired. In those days, an extra got five dollars a day and a box lunch, which was awfully good. Working on the railroad, he was lucky to make five dollars and didn't get the box lunch. But he got in, somebody liked the look of him, and put him in a toga and handed him a spear and got a close-up and he was on his way."

Not quite. Yes, there was work, but it was intermittent. To put food on the table, Karloff hauled cement, gravel, and rock at a building material yard. That led to the equally grueling task of driving a truck which he had to load and unload with sacks of cement and lime putty, weighing hundreds of pounds.

Karloff's roles in silent films were not noteworthy, though over time the parts grew, with more of them as villains, and laying out a path of sorts for his career. One of the most significant was in *The Bells* (1926) with Lionel Barrymore, who would direct him a few years later in *The Unholy Night* (1929). Karloff played a mesmerist who haunts Barrymore's character of a murder and thief. Still, he was disappointed at his slow progress, when he encountered none other than one of cinema's most famous performers Lon Chaney, the Man of a Thousand Faces.

Introduced by another actor, Chaney and Karloff went to watch boxing, with Karloff often standing outside the arena because he couldn't afford the admission. Chaney, who would greet Karloff by name, gave him a ride home one night and advised, "Find something no one else can or will do, and they'll begin to take notice of you. Hollywood is full of competent actors. What the screen needs is individuality!". Karloff certainly had no idea when he heard those words how loudly their truth was to ring.

On April 20,1930, Karloff was married at the Hollywood Presbyterian Church to Dorothy Stine, a librarian for the city of Los Angeles. When they met, he was doing his extra roles, and living in Laurel Canyon, the first of several locations they lived in over time.

# "It's Alive! It's Alive!"

**By the early Thirties,** Universal Pictures had been in operation for close to two decades, having been founded by Carl Laemmle in 1912. By producing the classics *The Hunchback of Notre Dame* and *The Phantom of the Opera*, both starring Lon Chaney (who was under contract to MGM), Universal had begun to realize the hold that horror pictures were beginning to have on the moviegoing public.

Once the talkies began, Universal put out *Dracula*, which became a hit, simultaneously seducing and thrilling audiences. Bela Lugosi, an emigrant from Lugos, Hungary (his real name was Bela Blasko), had played the vampire to great success on Broadway and on a national tour. It was not long before the powers that be decided to make a film based on Mary Shelley's 1818 novel *Frankenstein*, the incredible story of a dedicated, young scientist named Victor Frankenstein, who dares to go beyond the limit of medical science, and create a human being by using his own, unorthodox methods.

*Frankenstein* had also been adapted for the stage, and in the spring of 1931, Universal bought the rights to that adaptation by Peggy Webling for $200,000, including one percent of the world gross. A screenplay was the next step, with the inevitable question arising of who would play Frankenstein's monster. Had Lon Chaney not died the year before, he might have been a possiblity, despite his agreement with MGM. John Carradine, soon to begin his career as one of Hollywood's best character actors, was then a classically trained performer, but still unknown. Universal called him in to see Jack Pierce, the head of their make-up division. When Pierce told the actor all he would have to do to play the Monster was grunt, Carradine turned it down, but would figure prominently in other Universal horror films. In 1930, when he and Karloff were beginning stage actors, they appeared together in a production of *Window Panes*. Karloff was the heavy and Carradine the comic. While all of this was going on, entering the picture was Universal's hot directorial property, James Whale, a thirty-eight year--old Englishman with experience as a cartoonist, and from the theater, where his duties included acting, directing, and designing sets. In England, he had staged the war drama *Journey's End*, starring Colin Clive and Maurice Evans to great acclaim, and took it to the United States. Whale directed the subsequent film version, with Clive repeating his role, and it had such an impact on Carl Laemmle, Jr., put in charge of general production at Universal when he was just twenty-one, that Laemmle signed Whale to work for the studio, where his next work was *Waterloo Bridge*.

*Dracula* had been such a hit that Universal had Bela Lugosi, who would forever be associated with that role, test for *Frankenstein*. Some accounts have said that director Robert Florey, who met Karloff several years prior during work on *Omar the Tentmaker* (1924), suggested Lugosi play the Monster. In 1973, 1 asked Florey about that and this was his response:

"I did not suggest Boris for the role. I directed several sequences--about two reels--of the first *Frankenstein* script with Bela as the Monster. While writing the adaptation of Shelley's story, my idea was to give the role of Dr. Frankenstein to Lugosi. I told Dick Schayer [head of production at Universal] that any tall bit player could play the Monster, but apparently my suggestion was rejected."

James Whale replaced Florey (who brought *Frankenstein* to Laemmle, and thought he would also direct it, but Florey's contract didn't say that), revising his script, and going over the adaptation by John L. Balderston, one of the five writers who received screen credit.

Boris Karloff was still alternating between bit parts in films, the theater, and driving a truck. Hollywood was starting to become aware of and use him for such films as Howard Hawks' *The Criminal Code*, repeating the role he played on stage in Los Angeles. Written by Martin Flavin, it was the story of a tough yet fair-minded prison warden whose daughter falls in love with an inmate, and starred Walter Huston and Constance Cummings. Karloff's part as a prison trustee named Galloway, though small, is significant. In a memorable scene where he kills a fellow inmate, one can see how closely related Karloff's physical stance and movements are to those of the Frankenstein monster.

There were other notable pictures for Karloff in 1931, putting him opposite several fellow ascending stars. Among these were *Smart Money* with James Cagney and Edward G. Robinson, *Young Donovan's Kid* with Jackie Cooper, *The Mad Genius* with John Barrymore (Karloff thought Lionel was the better actor), and in *Five Star Final*, again with Edward G. Robinson, he gave a fine performance as T. Vernon Isopod, a sleazy reporter for a sensationalist newspaper. Robinson considered the film, a portrait of yellow journalism, one of his personal favorites, and told me Karloff was one of the most intelligent actors he'd ever been associated with. Karloff was finally being noticed and one in particular who did was James Whale.

Whale became aware of Karloff from seeing him in *Graft*, a gangster picture from Universal. One day, while dining in the studio commissary, Karloff was invited to join Whale at his table. The director expressed the desire that Karloff test for the role of the Monster in his upcoming film *Frankenstein*. At first, Karloff was taken aback, but given Whale's high status as Universal, he accepted. Movie history and magic would soon be made.

Later on, Whale told *The New York Times* why the film appealed to him: "I chose *Frankenstein* because it was the strongest meat and gave me a chance to dabble in the macabre. I thought it would be an amusing thing to try and make what everybody knows to be a physical impossibility into the almost believable for sixty minutes. A director must be pretty bad if he can't get a thrill out of a war, murder, and robbery. *Frankenstein* was a sensational story and had a chance to become a sensational picture. It offered fine pictorial possibilities, had two grand characterizations, and dealt with a subject which might go anywhere, and that is part of the fun of making pictures."

In the same interview, Whale went on to say, "To make this old tale fresh for the screen, modern intriguing and gruesome details were added to the story in the belief that most of the picture goers believe what they see (with their very own eyes). I never intended this picture for children, but would like to make a children's version. It is an adult subject and I tried to make it seem as real as possible." His comments take on greater meaning when one considers how many children seeing *Frankenstein* sympathized with the Monster, due to Karloff's unforgettable acting.

Added to the cast were Colin Clive as Dr. Henry Frankenstein (Leslie Howard was the Laemmles' choice, but Whale rejected him for Clive), Mae Clarke as his fiance Elizabeth, Dwight Frye as Fritz, the doctor's hunchbacked assistant, and Edward Van Sloan (Dr. Van Helsing in *Dracula*) as Dr. Waldman, Frankenstein's university professor.

In her novel, Mary Shelley described the Monster this way: "His yellow skin scarcely covered the work of muscles and arteries beneath. His hair was of lustrous black and flowing; his teeth of a pearly whiteness; but these luxuriances only formed a more horrid contrast with his, watery eyes, that seemed almost as the same color as the dun-white sockets in which they were set, his shriveled complexion, and straight black lips." In addition, he had, in the text, beautiful features, so the celluloid version is far more of a monster in the true sense of the word.

Transforming a middle-aged character actor into a close approximation of that literary description was entrusted to Jack Pierce. He and Karloff collaborated under a veil of secrecy, as Pierce kept his work to himself, not even trusting his staff. From a medical reference, he learned there were six methods of cutting open a human skull and decided to implement the most simple, given that Henry Frankenstein was not a practicing surgeon. That would require removing the entire top of the head, by which the doctor could insert a new brain, taken from a corpse, then close it up with metal clamps. To achieve that effect, Pierce constructed a headpiece made of layered cotton, and applied with collodion to make the skin look burned.

Because lightning is what gave the Monster life, metal studs were put on Karloff's neck. His face was covered with blue-green greasepaint (which photographed as gray), his fingernails were blackened with shoe polish, cheesecloth was used to simulate pores of the skin, and (the result of an observation by Karloff that his eyes appeared too normal), his eyelids were veiled with mortician's wax.

Then there was the costume. The sleeves of the Monster's coat were shortened to make his arms look longer, steel struts made Karloff's legs stiffer, he was fitted with an artificial spine, and on his feet he wore thirteen-pound asphalt-spreader's boots. The entire procedure took between four to six hours every day. When it was completed, Karloff was over seven feet tall and had taken on forty-eight pounds.

If being made up wasn't enough of an ordeal for Karloff, there was the weather to deal with. *Frankenstein* was filmed in the middle of summer. He was also wearing a double-quilted undersuit and, after just an hour's work, would be drenched with perspiration. When the production broke for lunch, Karloff retreated to his dressing room to eat alone, put on fresh underwear, and don the costume again. Jack Pierce was always there on the set with him, for a touch-up if necessary.

Playing the Monster was a very physical task for Karloff. For the film's climax at a windmill, where Henry has been taken by the Monster, Whale had Karloff run uphill, carrying Clive, for numerous takes. Once inside, when Henry tries to escape, Karloff and Clive were forced to wrestle at great length and strain.

*Frankenstein* shared with its first two sequels many impressive scenes that sear into the viewer's mind. From the bleak and somber opening in which Henry and Fritz rob a fresh grave in search of a body, to the dramatic finale inside the burning windmill where the Monster struggles with its creator only to have his brief existence apparently snuffed out, *Frankenstein* was remarkable. While it seemed melodramatic in places, its visual impact was nonetheless a strong one. Karloff's superb performance reinforced the strength of watching the Monster make his entrance at Henry's request, discover things like sunlight and fire, and toss flowers into a lake to watch them float. He accurately termed the Monster as "a pathetic, child-like waif who does not understand what is going on around him." That Karloff conveyed the Monster's range of emotions so well and without a word of dialogue is testament to his skill, his personal sensitivity, and James Whale's direction.

Karloff's work did not slight or diminish the performances of the other cast members. Colin Clive and Dwight Frye were equally fine, as a contrasting and unlikely pair of accomplices. Clive, who died at thirty-seven just six years after *Frankenstein* was released, was perfect as Henry, whose bizarre notion of bringing the dead to life becomes an obsession gone horribly wrong. His almost manic reaction, for example, at seeing the Monster's hand move, revealing its first sign of life, to which he responds, "It's alive! It's alive!" added a crescendo to the entire creation scene. For his part, Frye made Fritz a hateful wretch, exemplified by his use of fire and a whip against the Monster, which ultimately brings about his own demise. Also adding to the film's impact were Arthur Edeson's photography and Kenneth Strickfaden's electrical effects.

A press showing of the almost-finished film took place in November, which resulted in some editing. Excised was the shot of the Monster tossing the little girl into the lake (and, early in the film's release, Colin Clive's line "Oh, in the name of God--now I know what it feels like to be God!"). Both of those cuts were restored for home video in 1987. Additionally, a prologue in which Edward Van Sloan addresses the audience about the film it is about to see, and a revised ending in which Henry survived the fire became part of the final product.

On December 4, 1931, *Frankenstein* premiered in New York, and from that day forward, Boris Karloff would become a household name, and synonymous for all time with a particular kind of movie and for the creature developed in the mind of an eighteen year-old girl.

Reaction to *Frankenstein* was overwhelming. The public flocked to see it, making it a blockbuster which grossed more than a million dollars, and among *The New York Times*' list of the year's ten best pictures. Oddly enough, Mordaunt Hall in his review for that paper, wrote, "Boris Karloff undertakes the Frankenstein creation and his make-up can be said to suit anybody's demands", while at the same time noting that it was "an artistically conceived work". The *New York Daily News* said *Frankenstein* "clutches at you icily and holds you until the romantic ending guarantees satisfaction after an hour's worth of gripping, intriguing horrors", while *Variety* said the film was "handled in production with, supreme craftsmanship", adding that Karloff as the Monster was a fascinating acting bit of mesmerism." His role, said *Film Weekly*, was an astonishing piece of work", although the reviewer believed *Frankenstein* had "no theme and points no moral, but is simply a shocker beside which the Grand Guignol was a kindergarten."

While Karloff's Monster chilled adult moviegoers and had their children feeling sorry for him, there was a very memorable response on the part of screenwriter Stewart Stern, who vividly recalled for me this story from his childhood, the first of three experiences he had with Karloff over time:

"He was my beloved monster in my growing up years, and my first image of him came from our wonderful black doorman at the apartment house where I used to live in New York, who had just seen *Frankenstein*. While I would be putting on my roller skates on the bench in the lobby, Eddie would turn around and turn his face into the Monster's face and turn back and try to scare me to death. He was not very successful, but it was a warning of things to come.

"My uncle was Adolph Zukor, the founder of Paramount Pictures, and he had an enormous estate about thirty miles up the Hudson River. His neighbor was Sam Katz, later an executive at MGM. He had brought from Scotland, brick by brick and stone by stone, a great manor house, which had been reassembled on a mountain. It had a huge portcullis, a cobblestone courtyard, and an enormous automatic pipe organ, which churned out music night and day in a very ghostly fashion.

"I was taken there one weekend as a little boy, and put to bed in his son's room, his son being away at boarding school, and that room had been built like the hold of a ship, great curved ribs plunged out from the floor and there were leaded windows and the door was a sea door. I was put to bed at a reasonable hour, and it was one of those freak nights when, in the middle of winter, with the snow falling. The moon was out and there was thunder. I woke up, not knowing where I was. Nothing was where it should have been in my room at home and I'd forgotten that I'd come away.

"In terror, I got myself out of bed and began treading across this plank floor to a wall where I found the door handle, somehow got this door open, and peered out. Far, far in the distance, down what seemed to be a long, damp tunnel, I saw a figure lurching away from me. I stepped out on the balcony, fascinated by this apparition, and suddenly I was borne closer and closer to it, not knowing how it was happening until there was only an enormous head which turned and looked at me. It was the head of Boris Karloff as Frankenstein's monster, and I let out a yell which could have been heard in New York City and, I think, fainted. What had happened was that they had gotten an early print of *Frankenstein* before its release. Mr. Katz was running it for friends after dinner, and it was not appropriate for a boy my age, so I'd been shipped off and woke up in the middle of the screening."

With the huge success of *Frankenstein*, Universal had a new star in its company of players, and didn't hesitate to make full use of Karloff, often billed then by just his last name. Following *Frankenstein*, Karloff was seen in a few pictures, the best being Howard Hawks' classic gangster saga *Scarface*, produced by Howard Hughes. Starring Paul Muni in the title role, based on the infamous Al Capone, and George Raft, it was, for its time, an unflinching and strong portrayal of the underworld, which met with resistance from censors at first because of what they saw as a portrayal of Tony Camonte, Muni's character, that was too sympathetic. The violence was also something that up to that point hadn't been seen on screen: gunfights, car chases, and graphic deaths. Several endings also were shot in a move to appease the censors, but eventually Hawks' final cut was released.

Karloff, working with Hawks for the second time, played Gaffney, a rival hood whom Camonte kills in a bowling alley. Some critics faulted Karloff for his British accent, which to them seemed out of place in such an American setting. However, Karloff's character was based on an actual British gangster named Owney Madden, who played a role in the New York crime scene. This same part was played by Bob Hoskins in Francis Ford Coppola's *The Cotton Club* in 1984.

That fall, horror fans whetted by *Frankenstein* had their chance to see Karloff in the type of role that became his trademark. In James Whale's quirky melodrama *The Old Dark House*, adapted from J.B. Priestley's *Benighted*, Karloff, decked out in heavy make-up and wearing a padded suit underneath his costume, was Morgan, a hulking, inarticulate brute of a butler in a strange household run by the Femms, an eccentric brother and sister, played by Ernest Thesiger and Eva Moore. In the midst of a thunderstorm one night, they are forced to put up three travelers (Melvyn Douglas, Raymond Massey, and Gloria Stuart) seeking shelter. As a British couple, equally forced to stay there, were Charles Laughton and Lillian Bond.

As the plot unfolds, the guests have to cope with Morgan's drunken rage, the sister's religious fanaticism, the family's bedridden patriarch, and the eldest son, a murderer and firestarter, who's locked away. Karloff has his moments of menace and sympathy, as did his Frankenstein monster, but *The Old Dark House* is an ensemble piece, with oddities and tongue-in-cheek humor (which Whale also would insert in *The Bride of Frankenstein* three years later) that suggest the film is not to be taken entirely seriously. On a point of cinema history, it was their first picture made in America for both Laughton and Canadian-born Massey.

Gloria Stuart, who appeared a year later opposite Claude Rains in *The Invisible Man*, told me, "Everyone in the film was professional, taking their cues from James Whale, a most serious, involved, and particular director. He missed nothing, and all of us were at our best with him. Boris was soft-spoken, a very private person, agreeable, no tricks. Charles was very self-involved, not very communicative. Melvyn and Raymond charming and earnest. Everyone was happy to be in the film and we all worked very hard. Lots of backlot shooting with wind, rain, and mud machines at night, and many, many days in the cobwebby, dusty old house. The imported English actors had tea with James every afternoon. That group was quite apart from the Americans!"

Karloff was loaned out to MGM to star in *The Mask of Fu Manchu*, the Asian villain created by writer Sax Rohmer, with Myrna Loy as his daughter. Director Charles Vidor began the film and was replaced by Charles Brabin, who scuttled much of Vidor's footage, and altered the script. Karloff scarcely had an opportunity to study the material held been given, which was taken back and overhauled. What emerged was a hokey B picture in which Fu Manchu seeks Genghis Khan's ceremonial mask and sword, and in so doing, to become Khan's descendant, eliminate the Caucasian race, and rule the world.

Both Karloff and Loy, who was often seen in exotic and vampish parts at the time, played their parts with appropriate relish, and together made *The Mask of Fu Manchu* more entertaining than it deserved to be.

For Karloff, it was back to the Universal lot for his next assignment, and what an assignment it was. Cinematographer Karl Freund, who had worked for German directors Fritz Lang and F. W. Murnau, directed him in *The Mummy*, with a script by John D. Balderston, one of *Frankenstein*'s screenwriters. Karloff played Im-Ho-Tep, a High Priest who was buried alive with a magic scroll he intended to use to revive a dead Egyptian princess he had loved. A team from the British Museum discovers the mummy and the scroll 3700 years later. While reading the scroll's magic text aloud, one of the team, played by stage actor Bramwell Fletcher, unintentionally revives Im-Ho-Tep and goes mad from the shock of seeing him. The mummy and the scroll vanish for a decade, until Im-Ho-Tep assumes the guise of Ardath Bey, an Egyptian archaeologist. During an expedition to the tomb of the princess, he learns she has been reincarnated as the daughter (Zita Johann) of the British governor of Sudan. He plans to end her new life in order that they be together again for eternity.

Making Karloff look the part was as involved and detailed a process as it was for Frankenstein's monster. His ears were glued back, and strips of cotton were put on his face, and dried. Beauty clay was smeared into his slick-backed hair. When it hardened, rubber cement was put on it. After that, linen which had been rotted with acid and oven-baked, was wrapped around him, to simulate the mummy's ancient and rotting bandages. His face and hands were covered with greasepaint to match the bandages' color. Next, he was coated with Fuller's earth, giving the effect of clay. For his scenes as Ardath Bey, his skin was stretched, and the cotton strips used again. When the skin was relaxed, deep wrinkles appeared to set in.

Up to eight hours was the length of time it took Jack Pierce to do the procedure. Bramwell Fletcher, whose film career was short, was under contract with Samuel Goldwyn and farmed out for *The Mummy*. About Karloff, he told me, "He came on after being in the make-up room and was popped into the coffin lying against the wall, and he fell face out. Everybody was very concerned and they sent for the studio doctor. He said, 'Well, you damn fools. This fellow, he's not breathing. You've got him all taped up. The man has to breathe through his skin as well as his nose.' They brought him around, and I was able to suggest that they split the back of the surgical bandages they put around him."

Of his scene in which Im-Ho-Tep awakened, Fletcher added, "They said to me, 'When he starts toward you, reaching out his hand, the shadow falls on the old papyrus that you're reading. Then you turn around and you see the mummy.' I said, 'Well, then what do I do?' The director said, 'You scream like hell and run like mad.' I thought it over, and said, 'No, I don't think he'd do that. When you see a mummy alive reaching towards you, you're frozen. He said, 'Show me what you think ought to be done.' I sat, frozen, staring, and I started that low long laugh which reached finally a scream of hysteria. I went laughing mad was the idea."

Fletcher, who told me he did not regard himself as a film actor, explained, "I got a release out of my contract with Goldwyn and came back to the theater where I started, which was at Stratford-on-Avon. I like audiences, not just the crowd of technicians." Later in his career, he was the first actor sanctioned by the estate of George Bernard Shaw to impersonate Shaw, whom he played in a one-man show on Broadway that he took on the road for several years.

Not only was his make-up an ordeal for Karloff, so was working for Karl Freund, who had his cast work up to eighteen hours a day. As she and Karloff were shooting one night, Zita Johann collapsed from exhaustion.

It was this form of treatment actors were subjected to at times that prompted Karloff, and some of his fellow performers, to lay the groundwork for a union, which became the Screen Actors Guild. The seeds for the Guild were planted, in terms of Karloff's participation, in May of 1933 at a dance put on by the Hollywood Cricket Club, which he was an active member of. Annually, as the cricket season was beginning, a fund-raiser of some type was held, and on that particular evening, Karloff was asked whether he'd be interested in an organization for film actors to be affiliated with Actors' Equity, the union for stage performers founded in 1913.

Karloff expressed his interest and began attending meetings in secret with people such as Frank Morgan, Ralph Morgan, C. Aubrey Smith, Lyle Talbot, and Richard Tucker. Gradually, more people trickled in to listen, the goal being to form such a group, and the hope that the producers would attempt something which would make the actors realize they had to start a union. In time, that happened when the producers tried to cut actors' salaries under the National Recovery Administration Code.

As Karloff recalled later, telegrams went out to every major star in Hollywood, and after everyone assembled at Frank Morgan's home, as he put it, "the Guild was off to the races." Karloff was one of the original founders and remained a strong voice in Guild matters from then on. Ian Wolfe, one of his fellow cast in both *The Raven* (1935) and *Bedlam* (1946) told me, "Karloff was a very kind and cooperative big pussycat, and always defended actors in general. I also worked with him in a pilot for a series. The pilot did not sell, and I don't think we would ever have been paid a cent, had Boris not seen to it." Guild leaders during Karloff's involvement, which lasted until the early '50's, included James Cagney, Robert Montgomery, and George Murphy.

With two stars of horror films on its hands, it was only a matter of time until Universal put Karloff and Bela Lugosi opposite each other. The first of their several collaborations was *The Black Cat*, Edgar G. Ulmer's 1934 tale of modern-day witchcraft. Karloff played Hjalmar Poelzig, a former Army engineer living in the Hungarian countryside whom Lugosi's Dr. Vitus Verdegast comes to visit. Arriving with a young couple he met en route, Lugosi seeks the location of his wife and daughter whom Poelzig had kidnapped. As the story unfolds, Poelzig is revealed to be a Satanist, in command of a coven of Devil-worshippers. From the beginning, *The Black Cat* was a risky venture in many aspects. Karloff's character was inspired by real-life Satanist Aleister Crowley, and the story had no connection with Edgar Allan Poe. Intertwined with the macabre plot were such taboos as black magic, necrophilia, and sadism. It was also one of the first movies to use classical music exclusively. When Carl Laemmle, Sr. learned of this move, shortly before it was released, he hit the roof, and took it up with Carl Jr., but the younger Laemmle backed up Ulmer, and won out.

Not only did *The Black Cat* sound different from the garden variety horror film, it looked different, from the make-up to the sets. Jack Pierce used white pancake and lip rouge on Karloff, who wore a headpiece, giving him a sharp, angular, Satanic-like hairstyle. The geometric set design was revolutionary, what with digital clocks, a curved staircase, and glass tables, giving Poelzig's home a very futuristic ambience. In this regard, it looked like the setting for a science fiction, and not horror, picture. Techniques such as backlighting, dissolves, and offbeat camera angles added greatly to *The Black Cat*, shot in less than three weeks at a total cost of $95,745.

Shirley Ulmer, the director's wife who was script girl on the picture, told me Karloff and Lugosi didn't immediately warm up to each other on this film, the first of their several pairings, but in time they did, although they were never good friends. Still, the two men were alike in both a personal and professional sense. They both came from overseas, started performing in the theater, played some of the same parts, reached stardom in their '40's, married several times, and each had one child.

When *The Black Cat* was released, it was a hit, grossing $140,000. *The New York Times*, which appears hard-pressed to have praised any horror film during the genre's heyday, called the film "more foolish than horrible", and also said, "The story and dialogue pile the agony on too thick." *Variety*'s review said, "A certain eeriness has been achieved" and that "Karloff and Lugosi are sufficiently sinister and convincingly demented."

Before he continued work with Lugosi, Karloff changed his style briefly by appearing in two straight pictures, John Ford's desert drama *The Lost Patrol* for RKO, where he played a religious fanatic, and then portrayed the anti-Semitic Count Ledrantz in Alfred Werker's *The House of Rothschild* for United Artists. Both were good films with Karloff in challenging roles, and the critics responded in like fashion.

Universal called Karloff back for another round as the Monster in what was meant to be *The Return of Frankenstein*. Its new title was *The Bride of Frankenstein*, with Karloff again excellent at the Monster, and most of the original's major players before and behind the camera. With a bigger budget on his hands, James Whale crafted a more fluid film, with less of a melodramatic air and which has become regarded as even better than *Frankenstein*.

*The Bride of Frankenstein* began with a prologue, in which Lord Byron, Percy Shelley, and Mary Shelley gather in Lake Geneva on a night beset by a thunderstorm. At the urging of Percy, Mary (Elsa Lanchester, also in the title role) continues her story from where the novel ended. The film picks up at the burned remains of the windmill, as the villagers cheer what they believe is the Monster's swan song. A floor gives way, and one of those remaining falls into the watery cellar. His wife offers a hand to help him out, only to see that the hand extended to hers is that of the Monster, who survived, and does away with both of them. The creature then stalks off into the darkness.

Colin Clive again played Henry, whom his wife, played by Valerie Hobson this time, had thought was dead, only to find that he, too, survived the fiery ordeal. While recovering, Henry is visited by a Dr. Pretorius, who relates his experience in creating life, and wants to collaborate with him. Frankenstein's first reaction is to refuse the offer, but the film was just getting started.

Karloff again coped with the task of being made up once more as the Monster, with some slight variations, so he appeared visibly burned and further scarred in the sequel. Beginning at 7 a.m., five hours were required to apply Karloff's make-up. When it reached afternoon, he put on a costume weighing sixty-two pounds. Shooting started at 2:00. He lost twenty pounds during filming and dislocated his hip.

As *The Bride of Frankenstein* progresses, the Monster is captured in the forest by townspeople, and made prisoner in the local dungeon. He escapes, and then finds refuge in the cottage of a blind hermit, whose violin music has attracted the Monster. In a touching sequence, the man welcomes the injured Monster, to end their mutual loneliness and become friends. The Monster is taught to speak, a move Karloff always thought was a mistake, and enjoy the simple pleasures of cigars, food, music, and wine. Karloff was no less moving than he was in the first film, and made the Monster again a creature worthy of pity and sympathy, alone in a world in which he had little control. Eventually, the Monster meets up with Pretorius and requests a woman be created for him. Elizabeth Frankenstein is kidnapped by the Monster, and Henry is forced to cooperate with Pretorius to make another person from the remains of the dead.

Elsa Lanchester's make-up took three to four hours, and her relatively brief appearance on screen as the hissing, scarred female Monster became one of her most famous roles. At the sight of her fellow creature, she screams in horror. The Monster, on the verge of blowing up the laboratory, tells the reunited Henry and Elizabeth to leave, but to Pretorius, he says, "You stay. We belong dead!" The Frankensteins leave the laboratory, and at the pull of a lever, the Monsters and Pretorius perish as the structure explodes.

Once again. the public flocked to see the Karloff Monster, making *Bride* as successful as its predecessor, and the critics' response was warm. *The Bride of Frankenstein* was "a first-rate horror film", said the *New York Times*. The paper's view was that Whale had "done another excellent job", and said, "Mr. Karloff is so splendid in the role that all one can say is, 'he is the Monster.'" In its summation, *Variety* called the film an "imaginative and outstanding" one, adding that "Karloff is in top form as the Monster." For their work, the other cast members, particularly Ernest Thesiger, and cinematographer John Mescall received justified high praise, too.

The Thirties being the zenith of his work in films, Karloff stayed busy, being offered respectable scripts, and starring in a continuing variety of parts, even within the confines of typecasting. He had no qualms about being typed, figuring that all actors were in one way or another. The horror roles marked him for life, yet the skill and dimension he brought to them was frequently overlooked.

Roy William Neill, who did many of the Sherlock Holmes pictures with Basil Rathbone, directed Karloff in *The Black Room,* with the star doing a challenging and excellent turn as a pair of brothers, one good and the other evil. The story involved Gregor and Anton de Berghman, who carried with them a curse, that twins born into the family will be separated by death, when the younger one murders the older one in the black room of their home. As adults, Anton, realizing his tyrannical sibling Gregor has committed a murder, is pushed by Gregor into a pit in the black room, and dies with a knife clutched in his hand. Gregor proceeds to impersonate Anton and, when his ruse becomes evident, commits another murder. In the end, he is pursued into the black room, only to fall into the pit himself and be impaled by the knife still in the dead Anton's grasp.

Karloff did some of his best work in *The Black Room,* a good, unpretentious thriller, unworthy of the dismissive review from *Variety* that referred to its "lengthy, dull proceedings" and thought Karloff was "his usual self." England's *Kinematograph Weekly* did see the merit in the actor's virtuoso playing when it said, "Karloff differentiates well between the two brothers, and gives a sound performance."

Away from the studio, the Karloffs lived comfortably in the Coldwater Canyon section of Beverly Hills, their house one of Mexican-style architecture with two acres of gardens, which Karloff enjoyed working in, and many fruit trees. Boris and Dorothy shared their home with several dogs and a small menagerie that included chickens, ducks, and a pig named Violet. They played tennis and grew their own fruits and vegetables. He liked rugby and field hockey, and his consuming athletic pursuit for life was cricket. At the Hollywood Cricket Club, Karloff was one of the British Colony (as many of England's actors living and working in America were known) who played there. Joining him were such other stars as Clive Brook, Ronald Colman, Errol Flynn, Cary Grant, David Niven, and the two leads of Universal's Sherlock Holmes series, Basil Rathbone and Nigel Bruce. Karloff also loved literature, and edited two collections of short stories, *Tales of Terror* (1943) and, three years later, *And the Darkness Falls.* The second volume developed while he was touring in *Arsenic and Old Lace,* and he'd go through books sent to him by the publishers. He personally made the selections, and wrote introductions not only to both books, but each story and poem, too. Among the authors represented were Joseph Conrad (his personal favorite), Algernon Blackwood, August Derleth, Conan Doyle, William Faulkner, Edgar Allan Poe, Jonathan Swift, and Dorothy Sayers. His assessment of Sayers, noted for her Lord Peter Wimsey mysteries, in *And the Darkness Falls* is evidence of his scholarly side and foresight:

"If I may presume to make a guess, Miss Sayers will have a permanent place in the literature of relaxation, for her sense of humor, her ability to include comedy, love, exciting drama, and enough erudition to excite the sophisticated reader, but never burden him--as well as for her excellent English style, and her genius in creating surprising situations."

This excerpt from his lead-in to *Tales of Terror* spoke to the telling of the macabre onscreen and in print: "It has always grieved me professionally that the two words 'horror' and 'terror' are used indiscriminately for stories designed to stir the imagination and tingle the spine. The terms are literally poles apart in their true meaning and impact. Horror carries with it a connotation of revulsion, which has nothing to do with clean terror. If we are not careful, we will end by giving simple terror a bad name."

Two more pictures with Bela Lugosi, *The Raven* and *The Invisible Ray*, were next on Karloff's schedule at Universal. In the former film, Lugosi had the main role as a surgeon with an Edgar Allan Poe obsession, whose house has been fitted with devices taken from the author's writings, such as a descending pendulum. His Dr. Vollin saves the life of a young woman, whom he wants to marry, but she is engaged to another. Karloff was Bateman, a bank robber and murderer who comes to Vollin, asking for the doctor to perform plastic surgery on his features, in order to evade the law. Lugosi agrees but disfigures the fugitive's face, leaving it grossly deformed. In order to have his features restored, Karloff cooperates with the doctor in his revenge against the woman and her loved ones. Lugosi plays his part over the top, as his character gleefully proclaims, toward the climax, "Poe, you are avenged!" whereas Karloff in more of a supporting role is restrained by comparison, though he was billed above Lugosi. *Variety* called *The Raven* "a good horror flicker", but it was overwrought and a lesser film than the next Karloff/Lugosi outing *The Invisible Ray*, an early foray into science fiction territory. Karloff was the lead, as Janos Rukh, a scientist visiting the site of a meteorite containing an unknown element. He becomes contaminated by its radioactive elements, making him phosphorescent and causing anything he touches to die. Lugosi, a fellow man of science, develops a temporary antidote. Rukh creates a weapon, the title's invisible ray, but with his brain in a poisoned state, believes his discovery has been stolen by Lugosi and Sir Francis Stevens, another scientist. As in many Karloff films, his character brings death to those he believed had wronged him.

Directed by Lambert Hillyer, who had done many Westerns in the silent era, *The Invisible Ray* was a good, well-made film in almost all ways. Playing Karloff's wife was Frances Drake, who had appeared opposite Colin Clive and Peter Lorre in another admirable horror film, *Mad Love* (1935). Miss Drake told me, "Boris was a very intelligent, rather serious man, and a very effective actor. During the making of *The Invisible Ray*, he was interested in establishing the Screen Actors Guild. Very pleasant to work with, no temperament on the set, and seemed to get on well with Bela Lugosi.

"In fact, the whole picture went very smoothly. We had an extremely efficient cast and director. I think that if Boris had not become an actor, he might have gone into politics, and he would have done well with his good voice and beautiful eyes." *The Invisible Ray* was panned as Universal's "newest penny dreadful" by the *New York Times* while *Variety* noted, "Karloff and Lugosi stand out" in a picture their critic called "fairly entertaining."

Other strong Karloff films followed. *The Walking Dead*, directed by the versatile Michael Curtiz, *The Man Who Lived Again*, and *Charlie Chan at the Opera*. His other association with an Asian detective was as Mr. Wong in a series of pictures done for Monogram, a studio whose low-budget output consisted primarily of Westerns, serials, and action pictures, and which later became Allied Artists. The Mr. Wong aeries was weak compared to those featuring Charlie Chan, and with Karloff the only saving grace.

The medium of radio was in its heyday in the 30's and '40's, and Karloff appeared behind the microphone often. In early 1938, he went to Chicago for several episodes of Arch Oboler's mystery show *Lights Out*. It began as a local broadcast, airing at midnight on account of its often gruesome content, and had such a following that NBC went nationwide with it. At one point, the network dropped *Lights Out*, bringing forth listeners' demands that it come back, and it did.

One of the highlights of radio was certainly the use of sound effects, and on *Lights Out* a number of techniques were utilized to capture the show's macabre mood. The sound of a body splattering on payment, for example, was made by throwing a wet rag onto a concrete slab. The crushing of human bones was created by breaking spareribs with a pipe wrench. A head being slashed or cut off would be made by slicing a head of cabbage, and flesh being eaten was reproduced by squashing cooked spaghetti and smacking one's lips. And, the sound of an electrocution required the use of bacon sizzling in a frying pan on a grill and the sparks made by using a telegraph key and a dry-cell battery.

*Lights Out* was revived in 1947 on ABC, lasting just a month, and was no less horrible in content, as it recycled stories from the original version. On one episode, Karloff was a doctor whose success in bringing a dead woman back to life backfires when her whole nature is altered and she becomes a murderer. Reviewing the show, *Variety* said, "Why anyone without a barely latent thirst for blood would care to inflict these ghoulish goings-on on themselves is hard to understand", but conceded the show and Karloff were fine, "aside from the question whether such grisliness is good entertainment."

While the witty Karloff didn't like the Frankenstein monster being the target of humor, he had no qualms about poking fun at his own image, witnessed by his many appearances on radio and TV doing so. As a guest on Jack Benny's radio show, Karloff had this exchange:

BENNY: You look so much like Boris Karloff.

KARLOFF: Thanks, and you're looking well yourself.

Universal was not about to let a good thing go, given their smash re-release of *Dracula* and *Frankenstein* as a double feature. Thus, in October of 1938, *Son of Frankenstein* began shooting, the last of Karloff's three film portrayals of the Monster. Rowland V. Lee occupied the director's chair and his previous works included *The Guilty Generation* with Karloff, *The Count of Monte Cristo* with Robert Donat, and *Cardinal Richelieu* with George Arliss. For the title role, Lee went with Basil Rathbone, and as the broken-necked blacksmith Ygor, Bela Lugosi in one of his best parts. In support were Lionel Atwill, another fine movie villain, as Krogh, the local chief of police, and Josephine Hutchinson as Rathbone's wife. This time around, Wolf von Frankenstein comes to the village, which endured the consequences of his father Henry's experiments with life and death. While staying at Castle Frankenstein, Wolf is visited by Krogh, who tells him about the earlier horrors and of a number of recent murders in the community. The following day, Ygor leads Wolf to what is left of the Frankenstein laboratory, and then to a catacomb where the Monster is suspended on a stone slab.

Wolf is persuaded by Ygor to restore the Monster to life, and tries to, but the creature is revived only fleetingly. Later, acting on his young son's report of seeing a giant, Wolf quickly returns to the lab, encountering the very much alive Monster, who does Ygor's bidding and continues to murder the members of the jury that found Ygor guilty of body snatching and sentenced him to be hanged. Karloff had his memorable scenes as the Monster, displaying its child-like quality, as he examines Wolf's face during their first meeting, and his heart-rending pain, when he discovers Ygor has been killed. *Son of Frankenstein*, however, was dominated by Lugosi's rich characterization of Ygor, who plays Wolf and the Monster to his advantage as though they were chess pieces. Karloff wasn't the only one with time-consuming make-up, as Lugosi's took four hours to complete.

One striking aspect of the film were Jack Otterson's sets, reminiscent of early German films, with sharp angles, high ceilings, and deep shadows. With such strong elements from the cast down to the soundtrack, *Son of Frankenstein* measured up in its own original way to James Whale's work.

During the production, on November 23, 1938, two happy events occurred for Karloff. Not only did he celebrate his fifty-first birthday on the set, but that same day, he and his wife Dorothy became parents of a newborn daughter whom they named Sara Jane.

*Son of Frankenstein* opened in January of 1939. The reviews were primarily good. *The Hollywood Reporter* called it "a knockout of its type for production, acting, and effects" and *Motion Picture Herald* said, from an acting standpoint, "the picture is outstanding, because of the manner in which Basil Rathbone, Boris Karloff, Bela Lugosi, and Lionel Atwill, as well as members of the supporting cast, sink their teeth into their roles." The *New York Daily News* commented,

"Rowland V. Lee has created an eerie atmosphere for the story, and he has put into the working out of the plot enough horror to send the chills and shivers racing up and down the spectators' backs."

And, still again, *The New York Times* took a tongue-in-cheek and dismissive tone. Its review said, "If *Son of Frankenstein* isn't the silliest picture ever made, it's a sequel to the silliest picture ever made, which is even sillier." Further, it said the film had been "perpetrated by a good director in the best tradition of cinematic horror. so that even while you laugh at its nonsense, perhaps that's as good a way of enjoying oneself at a movie as any."

Rowland V. Lee again directed Rathbone and Karloff in *Tower of London*, the historical drama of Richard III, the humpbacked Duke of Gloucester, played by Rathbone, ruthlessly seeking the throne of England. Karloff--with his head shaved, ears taped back, and wearing padding to give his character a clubfooted gait--filled the role of Mord, the king's executioner, who does Richard's bidding. Cast as the Duke of Clarence, Richard's brother was a young stage actor from St. Louis, just starting out in Hollywood, after a successful Broadway run opposite Helen Hayes in *Victoria Regina*. His name was Vincent Price.

All three of them became good friends for life. One scene they shared was when Richard and Clarence have a drinking match, ending with a drunk Clarence being drowned in a vat of wine by Richard and Mord. Inside the vat to simulate wine was water--no divine intervention here--so Price had to suffer the indignity of being dunked by Rathbone and Karloff. Making it worse was that between takes, Price's co-stars used the vat as a receptacle for cigarette butts and empty Coke bottles (Coke was used to look like wine when photographed). As a gift for his troubles, Rathbone and Karloff rewarded Price with a beautifully wrapped carton of Coke.

Of *Tower of London*, *Variety* said, "As a horror picture, it's one of the most broadly etched, but still so strong it may provide disturbing nightmares as aftermath." Said the *New York Daily News*, "Although the picture is not without its weaknesses, lack of thrills is not one of them", and added, "Rathbone and Karloff are savage enough to please the most bloodthirsty." The *New York Times* thought it was "less than thrilling as pageantry, less than thrilling as drama, and less than satisfactory as drama" and added, "Karloff can't be taken seriously."

Around this time, Karloff started a succession of roles as doctors attempting a medical breakthrough of some type, such as curing cancer, developing artificial hearts, or contacting the dead. *The Devil Commands*, *The Man They Could Not Hang*, and *The Man with Nine Lives* were good examples of these, and some of his better pictures. Adrian Booth, who appeared in *The Man They Could Not Hang* under the name of Lorna Gray, told me, "Working with Mr. Karloff remains a great memory. We had English tea almost every afternoon. One day, we unexpectedly had to move from outside the studio to a courtroom scene inside. Mr. Karloff had nearly two pages of solid dialogue, which he glanced at and said he was ready. They shot it and printed it in one take!"

Karloff's next big assignment came not out of Hollywood, but from a couple of playwright/producers in New York, and earned him a place in theatrical history.

# An Actor Prospers

IN NOVEMBER OF 1940, rehearsals began on the East Coast for a new play by a former actor and music teacher named Joseph Kesselring. Originally called *Bodies In Our Cellar*, the plot dealt with two gentle spinsters, both sisters and living together in Brooklyn, who have spent their twilight years poisoning lonely men and burying them downstairs. Kesselring had sent the play to actress Dorothy Stickney, in the event she left the Broadway show *Life with Father*, produced by her husband Howard Lindsay and his partner Russel Crouse. Her reaction was she told Lindsay it was the funniest play she'd ever read, but needed some overhaul.

He agreed, and after reaching an agreement with Kesselring, began the task with Crouse of editing the play, retitled *Arsenic and Old Lace*. Figuring it would be either a hit or a massive flop, they deleted sections that were in questionable taste, as when one of the characters opened the cellar door and pointed out the smell. Lindsay and Crouse gave Kesselring full credit for writing the play and took credit as simply the producers.

Within a few months, the script was complete. As Abby and Martha Brewster, the ladies with a distinctive elderberry wine for their gentleman visitors, Lindsay and Crouse cast stage veterans Josephine Hull, so memorable as James Stewart's sister in *Harvey*, and Jean Adair, who appeared in *Ah, Wilderness!* and *On Borrowed Time*. Two of three nephews were played by Allyn Joslyn as Mortimer, a New York theater critic, and John Alexander as Teddy, who thinks he's Teddy Roosevelt. Further adding to the outrageous family was the remaining nephew

Jonathan, a homicidal maniac who, following plastic surgery, looks like Boris Karloff. In a masterstroke of casting, Lindsay and Crouse offered the part to Karloff himself. Persuading him to make his Broadway debut proved difficult.

At the outset, Karloff politely turned it down, saying he wasn't a Broadway actor, adding he wouldn't do it unless there were at least three other roles larger than his. Assured of that, Karloff accepted, yet what clinched the deal was the passage when Jonathan is told he shouldn't have killed someone, he replies, "He said I looked like Boris Karloff." He went to New York, only to find himself paralyzed with stage fright, and as a result, pronounced stuttering for three days. Karloff considered withdrawing but told himself he had to go through with it and he did.

Playing one of the policemen in the show was Bruce Gordon, noted for playing Frank Nitti in TV's *The Untouchables* (1959-1963). He remembered Karloff's first reaction to being onstage after many years: "The first rehearsal was always a reading. Everyone sits on long benches with cigarette buckets around. Everyone was smoking in those days. I was sitting on a bench, and he was sitting on the other end with people in between, and this bench would be shaking. Quivering. This man was so frightened. He'd light a cigarette and his hand would be shaking. When he got nervous, his stammer would become very pronounced. We would kid about it later, saying, 'This man's a big Hollywood star and he's so nervous. What's he so nervous about?' We were nervous about his being there, and he about not having been on the stage for a long time. He was with New York actors and was scared to death."

*Arsenic* had twenty-three investors, among them writer Clare Booth Luce, actress Nedda Harrigan (Mrs. Joshua Logan), journalist Frank Sullivan, and Katharine B. Day, whose family inspired *Life with Father*, as well as Russel Crouse and Boris Karloff. Each of them put up five hundred dollars, with the exception of one who pledged seventy-five hundred. When the play opened, the cost was $35,000. (By contrast, the Broadway revival in 1986 cost $700,000.) Lindsay and Crouse took delight in writing letters to the backers and addressing them as "angels" or "cherubs" when sending checks for the play's returns. A few years later, Karloff was one the backers of Lindsay and Crouse's *State of the Union*.

One read, "Enclosed you will find our first statement. We think it is a charming document and we hope that others more charming will follow. If there is anything in this about which you wish to complain, we shall be glad to hear from you. Just address us in care of the Dead Letter Office, Washington D.C." In part, another letter said, "We have received requests for its performance both in Denmark and in Spain, but we are refusing to allow its production in any country controlled by the Nazis or the Fascists on the grounds that it's too good for them."

More than sixty years later, Bruce Gordon still had strong memories of the show and its beginnings. He said, "Before we got to opening night, we were on tryouts in Baltimore. Howard Lindsay was playing *Life with Father* and we had a run-through on a Sunday. He came down, and tore us apart, we were so terrible. Oh, it was awful, and he set us on the right path. We came to New York and opening night was unbelievable, just unbelievable. And the notices the next morning. Wow! I never read anything like that in my life. I realized I had a job for at least a year."

The critics' response to the premiere at the Fulton Theatre on Jan. 10, 1941 was amazing. Brooks Atkinson of the *New York Times* said *Arsenic and Old Lace* was "so funny that none of us will ever forget it", while the *Herald-Tribune* called it "the most riotously hilarious comedy of the season" and the *Post* observed, "just when it is threatening to make you scream with terror, it compels you to scream with laughter." The cast took ten curtain calls and *Arsenic* was on its way to become, and still is, one of the longest-running shows in Broadway history (1,444 performances) and an American classic.

Bruce Gordon, who forced director Bretaigne Windust to give him an audition, became good friends with Karloff, and both of them were with the national tour. Said Gordon, "In the beginning, we weren't sure what sort of fellow he was. We knew he was an important star, but after all, we were New York actors and weren't going to be too impressed by him. We waited to see what kind of sense of humor he had. When we did, we began a campaign. I got together with the stage manager Walter Wagner, who was Howard Lindsay's nephew, and we devised a long letter with a legal stamp at the end as to why Boris Karloff should not be permitted in the city of New York or in the theater. He was all wrong for the part, and there were other actors who could have played the part.

"We posted it on the call board, and this went on for quite some time. He would have an answer to each one of them that he'd put up. Finally, he sent his secretary down to Chinatown, and had an answer written in Chinese red. That, of course, was the clincher because nobody could translate it. That was it.

"I was with the show twenty-seven months. Something like that. In light of today's grosses, it's kind of amusing. I remember walking back to the hotel one night someplace in the Midwest. We played some big hall, and Boris said, 'You know what the gross was tonight? Five thousand.'

"We stayed in touch. I was in boot camp in Idaho, and he made it possible for me to come to Los Angeles on my liberty by sending me $50. Not that I had any money. We were only getting about sixty dollars a month maybe. That was something. Bowled me over."

It was during the run of *Arsenic* that future screenwriter Stewart Stern would encounter Karloff, this time in person, ten years after Stern's unintended look at *Frankenstein* when he was a child. Frustrated in his search for a summer job in New York, the nineteen year-old Stern decided to go to a matinee and, while perusing the newspaper's theater section, noticed a small ad. It said the Rollins Studio School of the theater, located on Long Island, was having public auditions for the Josephine Hull Scholarship. Layton Rollins had named it in her honor because she wanted it to exist and was a member of his board. Stern called Rollins and was told to come in for an interview. Rollins' school was seeking a boy and girl to be awarded a full scholarship.

Stern told me, "I applied to be one of those who auditioned and went home and learned Richard's soliloquy from *Ah, Wilderness!*. We each had five minutes and there were 300 contestants. I was so frightened when I walked out on that stage, staring into the faces in front of me, and they all sat in the front row. Antoinette Perry, for whom the Tony Awards were named, Josephine Hull, Boris Karloff, and Layton Rollins. I literally couldn't stand and asked the stage manager for a chair and I sat.

"My knees were still shaking, so I lay down full-length on the floor, and propped my chin up on my fists, did the speech, and left, certain that my career had lasted thirty seconds. Went back up into the balcony to watch the other people, all of whom impressed me enormously. There were so many that the reading had to go on into the next day.

"I came back and sat in the balcony again, and then it all came to an end. Mr. Rollins stood and said they would now adjourn to come to their decision. Before he got the words out, Boris Karloff, Antoinette Perry, and Josephine Hull got their heads together. Mr. Karloff rose, and looked into the vast, grim hall and said, as only as he could, 'Is Mr. Stern there?' with his great lisp. He announced that I had been selected as the male winner that year of the Josephine Hull Scholarship. I shook his hand and that was the extent of our contact." Seventeen years later, the budding actor and the professional one would work together in television.

Between performances of *Arsenic*, Karloff found time to appear several times on radio's popular *Inner Sanctum Mysteries*, which opened each week with the sound of a creaking door, followed by the voice of the mysterious host Raymond. The show was produced by Himan Brown, whose credits included *Bulldog Drummond, Dick Tracy,* and *The Thin Man*. Over half a century later, Brown shared these memories:

"I did many shows with him on *Inner Sanctum* when it first began. Whenever he was between pictures, he would call me and I'd fit him in. He was very popular with my audience and I didn't always play him 'to type'.

"One of the most poignant I can remember was a script in which he played the small town's undertaker. A tiny New England community where the citizens kind of shunned him because he was an undertaker. He felt duty bound to bury the dead, and how he managed to bring the townspeople to accept him for himself rather than for the work he felt destined to perform.

"He was the easiest actor to work with and he could play anything. Unfortunately, he was always cast as *Frankenstein* in the casting agent's mind. I trusted him with everything. He was distinctive in voice, accent, and style. Whenever he was on the show, we would go out for dinner afterwards. In those days, we had no tape and the repeat performance for the Coast, which came three hours later, had to be live. I always looked forward to those dinners before we returned for the repeat performance. He had a rich, full life and I was enjoying the world he had already lived so fully.

"I miss his very special talents, his friendship, and his warmth." When this author, then a college student, first met Brown in 1978, his reaction when I asked him about Karloff was, "The most wonderful man who ever lived."

*Arsenic and Old Lace* took Karloff across the country. His friend Maurice Evans, an American citizen since 1941, was given the rank of major and assigned to oversee the Central Pacific Theater of the Army Entertainment Section. In the process, he began working with George Schaefer, a graduate of the Yale Drama School, and then a sergeant directing shows for the troops. Others comprising the section were Carl Reiner, Howard Morris, and lyricist Hal David, known for his collaborations with composer Burt Bacharach. The productions that were particularly fun were those in which name performers joined an all-soldier cast. Karloff was the first to do so and had a great time doing it.

Schaefer told me, "Boris came out to the Pacific and played his original part in *Arsenic*, which I directed and in which I played Teddy. We became very close friends and remained such until his death. We worked together on TV in *The Lark* and *Arsenic and Old Lace*, both very satisfactory experiences. Boris was a fine actor, particularly in films, and had the personality that made him a great star. There were limitations to his acting talent, but he seemed to know them, and would never reach out and play classics, for example. As a man, he had no limitations, and was one of the great minds and liberal souls of our time."

His production of *Arsenic* went to such islands as Christmas, Johnson, and Midway. When he was appearing in Schaefer's 1962 TV version of the play, Karloff pointed out, that not only did Schaefer direct the wartime show, "he drove the bloody truck." Karloff told his interviewer, "Which put us on the horns of a dilemma. Schaefer loved Gilbert and Sullivan, and the only way we could keep him awake was to bellow out Gilbert and Sullivan at the top of our lungs.

"Reminds me of the time we played Kwajalein. The Seabees had asked us to play their end of the island and said they'd build us a stage. They were marvels. They built the stage and in a couple of hours erected the set. A Victorian living room. And then the most astounding thing happened on that dreary, wasted island. A cat emerged from the kitchen door of the set. He looked around the living room and, bless me, walked out as if he'd lived there all his life."

After the war, a young actor just out of the Army and who then joined Maurice Evans' theater company was Booth Colman, who came to know and work with Karloff. He had just one Broadway credit and producer/director Margaret Webster arranged for him to meet Evans. He was cast as Guildenstern in *Hamlet*, which Evans starred in. He told me, "It was a great experience. Evans was a wonderful 'chief' and I learned much about style and stagecraft from him. During rehearsals, I met Boris, who was there much of the time as he was courting Evelyn Helmore, Evans' associate. When the company was in Philadelphia prior to the New York opening, Boris and Evelyn were married. Our Osric, Morton DaCosta, sent them a congratulatory wire on behalf of all of us. The wire read, 'Don't let him scare you out of bed!'" DaCosta later directed the Broadway and film versions of *Auntie Mame* and *The Music Man*.

"In later years, I played with Boris on TV. During one live show, a group of us were chatting during a break and were talking about our agents. Boris joined us and said, 'I'm with MCA, you know, and they have offices all over the world. And when I'm out of work, I'm out of work all over the world!'"

In the mid-40's, when his film output consisted largely of B-pictures such as *The Ape* (1940) and *You'll Find Out* (1942), Karloff teamed with producer Val Lewton, who believed, as Karloff put it, "the audience is the best actor in the theater, if you give it a chance". By that, Lewton meant it was better to put the suggestion of horror into the audience's minds instead of showing it outright. The first of three pictures Karloff did for Lewton was *The Body Snatcher*, based on the story by Robert Louis Stevenson, and directed by a young Robert Wise. Wise, a former editor who had worked on *Citizen Kane* (1941) and *The Magnificent Ambersons* (1942) made the picture in 1943. It wasn't released until 1945 so it wouldn't clash with other Lewton films.

Significantly, *The Body Snatcher* not only featured Karloff in one of his best performances, but it was his eighth and last film with Bela Lugosi. Wise, who would go on to such work as *The Set-Up* (1949), *The Day the Earth Stood Still* (1951), *West Side Story* (1961), *The Sound of Music* (1965), and *The Haunting* (1963), his tribute to Lewton, told me, "It was a great pleasure working with Mr. Karloff, whom I found to be a thorough professional. He was most intrigued and caught up in the challenge of playing the character of *The Body Snatcher* for he felt it would give him an opportunity to show his quality as an actor that went far beyond the monster roles he was so associated with. He recognized that in coming up against Henry Daniell, he was going to be playing opposite one of the finest character actors Hollywood had at that time, and he was anxious to show that he could hold his own with Daniell. I think the final results in the picture proved that he did just that."

Indeed, Karloff subtly underplayed the supplier of bodies for Daniell's medical school classes (a practice Daniell has concealed for some time) and, although Daniell was actually the lead, walked off with the film in a wonderfully modulated performance. Lugosi had a relatively small part as Daniell's servant Joseph, who learns of the grave robbing and, after trying to blackmail Karloff, ends up being murdered by him. Wise adds, "As far as I remember, Karloff got along well enough with Bela. Mr. Lugosi was a fairly quiet man and certainly not very outgoing. He had been ill for some time before we made the film and wasn't at his best, either physically or mentally. It was somewhat of a struggle to get the scenes out of Bela, because his memory wasn't strong and he had difficulty remembering his lines. Boris, professional and gentleman that he was, was very patient in all the scenes that he was in with Mr. Lugosi and helped him in every way he could to make the scene come off as well as possible."

*The Body Snatcher*, an RKO production, was followed by *Isle of the Dead* (1945), which was to have been Karloff's first picture for Lewton, but production was postponed while the actor underwent back surgery and subsequently recuperated. It was a much more moody, atmospheric film than *The Body Snatcher* with Karloff as a general from the Balkan War visiting his wife's grave on a Greek island, which was quarantined and may have a vampire in its midst.

Mark Robson, as was Robert Wise, a former editor (in fact, he and Wise collaborated on *Citizen Kane* and *The Magnificent Ambersons*, but Robson only got screen credit for the latter) was Lewton's choice as director. In addition to several other Lewton pictures, Robson went on to make *Champion* (1949), *The Bridges at Toko-Ri* (1954), *From the Terrace* (1960), and *Von Ryan's Express* (1965), among others. He told me, "Working with Mr. Karloff was a great pleasure for me. He had become an institution by that time, a trademark, a unique personality. He was gentle, warm, and a man with a rare sense of humanity. He was a generous man, a quiet man, a liberal man, in every sense of the word.

"As an actor, he had complete control of his instrument. This instrument he had tuned by and large to function within the framework of those horrendous characters he was fated to play. Mr. Karloff was very generous to me, who at the time was a young director still in his twenties, and extremely helpful and tolerant. It goes without saying that he was also a man of extraordinary erudition.

"To the very end, he was a man who loved the simple, earthy, beautiful things in life. He was a courageous man for he performed for the better part of his career under excruciating and severe pain to his back. Yet, at the time of performance and on the stage, he would never complain. It is with great pride that I can say that I had worked with Boris Karloff."

Robson would also direct *Bedlam* (1946, again with Karloff, who emphasized they were making an historical film, not a horror film. Robson co-wrote the script with Val Lewton, using the pseudonym Carlos Keith, telling the story of a young woman, played by Anna Lee, in the second of two films she made with Karloff, who seeks reform in London's famous asylum, St. Mary's of Bethlehem, which is referred to as Bedlam. She is repelled by the conditions, and deals with Master George Sims, the warden played by Karloff. In the process, Sims has her committed to the asylum before she could reveal the truth. Sims is later apprehended by the inmates and judged in a kangaroo court where he is found guilty. He is stabbed, but not killed by one of the inmates, and then was walled up inside Bedlam. In the end, a better situation for the asylum was forthcoming.

Similar to his John Gray in *The Body Snatcher*, Karloff's Master Sims is seemingly cordial and well-meaning, qualities that masked his cold-bloodedness and sadism. His work for Lewton was some of his best, and timely, following merely adequate performances in films such as *The Boogie Man Will Get You* (1942) a comedy with Peter Lorre, and *The Climax* (1944), in a too-small role slated originally for Charles Boyer. Of *Bedlam*, the *New York Times* merely said, "Karloff is completely at home and is his usual sinister self". *Variety* called the picture "morbid and depressing, but fascinating at the same time" and said, "Karloff plays with great finesse." Lewton had planned another Karloff film, *Blackbeard*, about the infamous pirate, but RKO scuttled the project.

In England, moviegoers were denied the chance to see *Bedlam*. Although historically accurate, its depiction of St. Mary's of Bethlehem prompted it to be banned by the British censors.

Offscreen, Karloff's personal life was taking on a new chapter. On April 10th, 1946, he divorced Dorothy, who received custody of their daughter Sara Jane. The following day, in Boulder City, Nevada, he married Evelyn Hope Helmore, an assistant story editor for David O.

Selznick, and who had assisted Maurice Evans when he was in charge of the Army Entertainment Section for the Central Pacific Theater during World War II. She had been married previously to theater and film actor Tom Helmore, who understudied Rex Harrison in *My Fair Lady* (1956) and was the first to succeed him on Broadway.

Evelyn took a great interest in her husband's career and had proved herself to be an able businesswoman. When she and Helmore were married, and both young actors, they operated a dry cleaners in London to make some extra money. Called 1980 Cleaners, it was the first of its kind to offer same day service. Kristin Helmore, daughter of Helmore and his wife, actress and playwright Mary Drayton, says, "Back in the twenties, that was meant to sound so futuristic. Their phone number was 1980. They had these dark green delivery vans with gold lettering, and on the side, it said '1980 Cleaners. Our Name's Our Number.' This was all very modern and very chic.

"There was a Scotsman who invented this method of cleaning. This revolutionized everybody's life. Before this, it would take several weeks to get something cleaned. They guaranteed that you could get your suit back the next day. The incredible part was they sent everything to Scotland. And the trains were so good and so fast that they could still promise it would be back the next day. It went up from London to Edinburgh to be cleaned."

The Helmores and the Karloffs continued to be friends, and when the Helmores first went to California, it was an occasion to be remembered. Kristin Helmore explained,

"Daddy's agent met them at the train and said, 'Well, the war's just over, every hotel is booked. The only place I can put you is the Miramar in Santa Monica.' My parents happened to know that the Miramar was where Boris and Evie were staying on their honeymoon. This is my parents' first meeting with Boris and Evie after they were all married to each other respectively.

"So, they knew that Boris and Evie were at the Miramar, too. They said, 'Oh my gosh, well, you know it's bound to happen. We're bound to run into them. We might as well make the best of it.' They went to the hotel, checked in, and settled in their room. I guess, at that point, Daddy said, 'Let's not run the risk of an awkward meeting in the lobby where they might be taken by surprise or embarrassed or whatever. Let's take the offensive as it were and invite them for dinner.' Daddy called up the desk and said, 'Would you give me Mr. and Mrs. Karloff's room?' The room rang, and Evie answered. Daddy said, 'Evie, guess what? Surprise! It's Tom.'

"She said, 'Oh, how wonderful! You're here in California. Where are you?' 'Well, as a matter of fact, we're at the Miramar.' And Evie said, 'Oh, I can hear you through the wall.' They were next door to each other. It was really like *Private Lives*, the Noel Coward play. Evie said, 'Let me put Boris on.' Boris got on the phone. He immediately said, 'There's nothing to be done about this, but for all of us to go out to dinner.' That was the beginning."

Around that same time, another funny instance took place when the two couples had gone to see tennis and were preparing to leave. Miss Helmore added, "They were waiting for their car to be brought around. Daddy happened to be standing by Evie by chance, and my mother happened to be standing with Boris. Along comes Rex Harrison, an old friend from England. 'Oh, the Helmores!', he says, seeing Daddy and Evie. 'My goodness, I haven't seen you in years. I didn't even know you were out here. How are you? What's been happening?' Evie got a little embarrassed and said, 'Well, Rex, a lot has happened.' She said, 'Mary here is now married to Tom, and Boris is married to Mary.' She got it all confused and said my mother was married to both of them. At that moment, Rex's car was brought around and he just sort of said, 'Well, it all sounds very delightful!' and went on and never got it straight."

The Helmores went on to live partly in California and partly in New York, as did the Karloffs, who, Kristin Helmore told me, "were a constant presence in our lives and in our families." Her parents also rented apartments at the Dakota in New York, which she says was a wonderful place for a child to grow up, with its large units, central courtyard, hand-cranked elevators with leather seats, and lots of parties. "I can remember trick-or-treating there on Halloween and not having to wear a coat because you were always in the building." Later, her mother wrote a thriller set in the Dakota, *The Playroom* (1967) starring her husband, as well as then-unknowns Bonnie Bedelia, Karen Black, and Richard Thomas that briefly ran on Broadway.

Tom Helmore had met Karloff several years before. He told me, "It was back in 1940. 1 was in Hollywood with Evie, and I remember going to his home off Coldwater, where Dorothy was sitting by the pool, and Sara Jane was floating in it on a rubber raft. He came later, and there was a Screen Actors Guild meeting, to which Mary Pickford came. I remember thinking that America's Sweetheart was a bit bossy!

"I saw Boris onstage, once in *Arsenic and Old Lace*, but also in Los Angeles in *On Borrowed Time*, in which he was very good. Boris and I worked together in a Theater Guild radio show, *Great Expectations*, and again on television where we were both lawyers in some courtroom drama.

"Mary and I were very fond of Boris. He was the warmest, wisest, most generous, fun-to-be-with man that I have known." The TV show Helmore referred to was a 1962 adaptation of Alfred Hitchcock's *The Paradine Case* (1946). Helmore's best-known film role was probably that of Kim Novak's husband in *Vertigo* (1958).

The production of *On Borrowed Time*, Paul Osborn's fantasy of an old man turning the tables on death, who has taken on human form as Mr. Brink, and is made prisoner in an apple tree, opened at the El Patio Theater in Los Angeles on Nov. 5, 1946. With Karloff in the lead role as Gramps, it was among a series of shows put on by Players Productions, a local group whose goal was to bring first-class theater to the Hollywood community. Among his fellow cast members were Beulah Bondi, Margaret Hamilton, and, as Mr. Brink, Ralph Morgan. A review by critic Patterson Greene in the *Los Angeles Herald-Examiner* said, in part, "Of the countless plays which have personified death, *On Borrowed Time* has been one of the few to take a place in the standard repertoire of the stage. It still makes magic, thanks to its skilled counterpoint of fantasy against homely reality; and, at El Patio, thanks also to shining honesty of performance and sensitized taste in direction.

"Boris Karloff brings charm and earthly vigor to the role of Gramps, whose love for his grandson leads him eventually to liberate death from his tree. He plays with never a note of false emotion or calculated comedy." For years afterwards, Karloff said it was his favorite role and one of his most enjoyable working experiences.

In a minor part was Frank Cady, later a regular on TV's *Petticoat Junction* (1963-1970). He remembered, "Nineteen forty-six was my first year in Hollywood, and when I met Karloff at the first rehearsal, it was the first time I had ever seen him without the bolts in his neck.

I was quickly impressed by his gentle affability, and shortly thereafter, with his no-nonsense approach to the job. It was obvious a first-rate performer was at work.

"The real pros in this business have one thing in common, and that is that they really listen to, and thoroughly absorb, everything another actor is saying to them. They are not just remaining silent and waiting for their turn to speak. Karloff had that attribute and, at the end of a scene with him, one would come away with the feeling that a great rapport had been achieved, and that something worthwhile had been given to the audience. At least I certainly felt that way." The show's limited engagement was extended until Nov. 24.

The Screen Actors Guild remained one of Karloff's most important causes, and among those he worked with on it was future Guild President Ronald Reagan. Toward the end of his second term as Governor of California, the former President told me, "My friendship with Boris was based on years of association as board members and officers of the Guild. He was public spirited and a stalwart in Guild activities on behalf of our fellow actors.

"As a person, he was one of the finest men I've ever known. He was a quiet man. He had a rich sense of humor and great intelligence. Add to this high standards of morality and you have quite a man."

In 1947, Maurice Evans and George Schaefer, as producer and director respectively, prepared to bring to Broadway *The Linden Tree* by J.B. Priestley, following the play's successful run in London. It dealt with a college history professor celebrating his sixty-fifth birthday who resists his family's and the college authorities' wish that he retire. Professor Robert Linden is of the belief that, despite his work being taken away from him, he will persevere, for those urging him to step down are, in his opinion, running away from life. The play was also a metaphor for postwar England, with Linden's study representing a country short on hope, and struggling to restore itself.

Evans offered the lead to his friend Boris Karloff, yet Priestley was opposed to such casting. In a letter dated Nov. 2 to Harold Freedman, president of Brandt and Brandt (Priestley's agents representing him in New York), Evans said, "I feel I ran into a brick wall with the Karloff idea. Please give it serious consideration and make full inquiries about him. I know the notion is startling at first hearing, but it is really no more revolutionary than my own departure from Shakespeare to Shaw. I believe that my connection with the production would eliminate any suspicion of its being a stunt, and it is my sincere conviction that Boris would play the part beautifully. It is just a fantastic accident that he has become identified with the horror stuff, and his personality is the exact opposite of the junk he has been doomed to be identified with in Hollywood.

"As Howard Lindsay said to me on the phone today, Boris is really miscast as 'the menace'. He has a solid background of theatre and I know positively from my association with him in the Pacific what his tastes and capabilities are. His inherent warmth and quiet dignity, his English speech, and his own political beliefs all point to his fundamental suitability for Professor Linden."

George Schaefer went to London to try and change Priestley's mind about Karloff. Referring to Cedric Hardwicke, Schaefer sent the following cablegram on Dec. 17 to Evans: "Freedman telephoned Priestley protesting Karloff – stop - Priestley now only approves Karloff providing Hardwicke remain adamant but Priestley disapproves pandering – stop - suggest you telephone any developments."

That same day, Evans cabled his reply to Schaefer: "Freedman confirming cable Priestley that Hardwicke will not give adequate guarantees play next season we are proceeding definitely Karloff - stop - we are signing contracts on this basis and want you to proceed urgently." In response, Harold Freedman sent a cable to Priestley: "Evans proceeding definitely with Karloff as Cedric will not concede sufficiently for Evans on guaranteeing to play into next season – stop - signing your contract tomorrow."

After Schaefer's meeting with Priestley, Karloff, with his wry humor, sent the playwright this message, "I promise you I would not have eaten the baby in the last act." Priestley, who had been hesitant because of Karloff's horror image, relented. On Dec. 30, Maurice Evans wrote to Howard Lindsay,

"You may have seen in the papers that we finally won the Karloff battle. I am most anxious that you should realize how big a contribution you made to the tipping of the scale, and how deeply grateful I am for your assistance. If you don't hear similarly from Boris, it will be because I don't want to embarrass him by making him too anxious of the brick wall which had to be vaulted."

The production of *The Linden Tree* was one in which Evie Karloff took great interest, from the casting to the set design. In a letter to

Walter Williams, who worked for Maurice Evans, she referred to the choice of Una O'Connor, the hysterical screecher in *The Bride of Frankenstein*, as the Lindens' Cockney maid. "George Schaefer talked about Una O'Connor this morning and will tell you what we felt. Simply that we were afraid she might be too comic, but no doubt direction will take care of that. I think she has an unpleasantish personality and is not the perfect one perhaps, but I am sure will be all right." Evie said she would have preferred, among others, Gladys Cooper or Mildred Natwick in the role. O'Connor remained in the show.

Writing from California, Evie had this to say to Williams about the role of one of Professor Linden's daughters and mentioned Mildred Natwick again: "Although she is not English, how about Jane Wyatt for Jean? We saw her as Mrs. Antrobus in *The Skin of Our Teeth* at a theatre here, and she was excellent. I would say her voice is as English as Millie's and I think she would be interested (she played in *Lost Horizon* opposite Colman and I think her last picture was *Boomerang*)."

Williams replied, "I met the Wyatt girl at Malibu with you and have seen her on stage and in pictures. I think that she would probably be very good as Jean, but way beyond our salary budget, and we have already read several girls who could play the part quite decently." He added, "Freedman of Brandt and Brandt thinks that all the human interest stories about Boris we can possibly dream up would be valuable. I told him the story about Boris being mistaken for a minister in the Hawaii hospital ward, which seemed to delight his soul. Will you please make poor Boris dream up some more sugar-coated pills."

The London production of *The Linden Tree*, starring Lewis Casson and Sybil Thorndike, was in its sixth month as of Jan. 28, 1948. In America, it opened on Feb. 4 in New Haven, Connecticut, and moved as of Feb. 9 for a two-week run in Philadelphia. In New Haven, the show drew lukewarm reaction and box office returns were just fair. While in Philadelphia, the critics were more appreciative, but business again was poor, dropping off the second week. Another preview took place in Washington, D.C., and then the play opened March 12 at the Music Box Theater in New York.

*The Daily News*' critic John Chapman, referring to Priestley's earlier work *An Inspector Calls* (1945), said "the second Priestley play this season is more quiet and undramatic than the first", but added he enjoyed "an excellent performance by Boris Karloff."

Similar thoughts were expressed by Richard Watts in the *New York Post* who termed *The Linden Tree* "thoughtful, intelligent, and theatrically unexhilirating" and wrote, "Mr. Karloff does a great deal to uphold the play's dramatic phases with his honestly sympathetic playing." *The New York World Telegram*'s William Hawkins wrote, "For the most part, it is performed as if it were the first reading of a script, when none of the actors have any notion of what the author is getting at." Robert Coleman, writing for the *Daily Mirror*, dismissed the play as "a pretentious, windy bore" but about Karloff, he said the actor "wrings all the emotion possible out of Priestley's surface chatter." *The New York Times*' Brooks Atkinson praised Karloff's work and called him "an extraordinarily winning actor." Interestingly enough, almost all the critics praised the performance of Una O'Connor.

*The Linden Tree* closed on March 6 after just seven performances. Forty years later, Maurice Evans told me, "The swift withdrawal pained me as much as it did Boris. The theatre owners insisted that the absence of any substantial advance booking proved that his motion picture fame was not the magnet we were relying upon." George Schaefer gave me his viewpoint also: "*The Linden Tree*, which I considered a beautiful play and which caught perfectly the various undercurrents running through postwar London, did not succeed in this country simply because the American public was not turned on to their problems. The production and the acting were first-rate, and I am convinced that if the London production, which ran for a couple of seasons, had opened instead in New York, it would have had the same fate. Moreover, there has always been a strong antipathy on the part of both critics and audiences to J.B. Priestley. I do not share this view, but it accounts for his lack of success on these shores."

Karloff was in just one film that year, George Marshall's *Tap Roots* (1948) in which he again played a Native American, and in 1949, instead of being above the title, he was part of it for *Abbott and Costello Meet the Killer, Boris Karloff*, originally conceived as a vehicle for Bob Hope. Weak in comparison to *Abbott and Costello Meet Frankenstein* (1948), *Killer* was a moderately amusing outing for the comedy team. With Abbott as a hotel detective and Costello as a bellboy, they encounter Karloff as one of several suspects in the murder of a guest. Karloff as a phony hypnotist contributed little to the plot, and despite the title, wasn't even the guilty party. On some theater marquees, Karloff's name was deleted so the title would fit.

That year, Broadway beckoned again, when Karloff took the lead in Edward Percy's thriller *The Shop at Sly Corner* (1949), directed by Margaret Perry, daughter of theater luminary Antoinette Perry. Under the title *Play with Fire*, the melodrama played in Boston and Princeton in 1941 starring Henry Hull, who played the title character in *The Werewolf of London* (a role at one point intended for Karloff). Four years later, renamed *The Shop at Sly Corner*, it opened in London and ran for two years. Percy's earlier work *Ladies in Retirement* (1940), which he co-wrote with Reginald Denham had been a success and made into a film with Ida Lupino and Louis Hayward.

Karloff played Descius Heiss, a former prisoner of Devil's Island, operating an antique shop in London where he receives stolen goods. His slimy shop assistant learns what Heiss is up to and blackmails him only to end up being strangled. Afterwards, when a police inspector shows up, Heiss, thinking that he has been found out, kills himself with a poisoned dart and dies laughing when he realizes the inspector simply wanted to buy a suit of armor.

The material at the outset appeared to be just made for Karloff, but he was defeated by a weak script and subsequent critical pounding. Of him, Brooks Atkinson said in the *New York Times*, "He has the shoulders, arms, and hands of an expert at natural homicide. His eyes are baleful. He walks like a panther. An extraordinarily gifted assassin, he deserves steady employment with plenty of work." Of the play, Atkinson said Percy dwelled too much on Heiss' home life, of which he added, "Mr. Karloff is too good an actor to waste on such domestic banality", written "with dreadful composure."

Howard Barnes of the *Herald-Tribune* said Karloff was persuasive and occasionally terrifying. "It is altogether the best characterization he has achieved since he renounced horror films." He remarked, "There is very little of the cumulative suspense which distinguished *Ladies in Retirement*." *The Sun*'s critic Ward Morehouse termed *The Shop at Sly Corner* "awkward and labored", but still thought it was well-acted and directed. John Chapman, reviewer in the *Daily News*, said, "I do hope that somebody opened several bottles of something at midnight for Karloff and his fellow players, for the play certainly was not their fault and they rated a stimulant after it was over--along with the audience."

As did *The Linden Tree*, *The Shop at Sly Corner* closed its doors after seven performances.

In July, it was announced by Charles C. Barry, Vice-President in Charge of Television at the ABC network, that Karloff had signed an exclusive, one-year contract to do a weekly series likely to begin in September. Under terms of the agreement, Karloff would do a radio show as well. The half-hour TV show would air live from New York, and feature original plays, adaptations of classics, and some stage and screen material. The working title of Karloff's first show of his own was *Conflict*.

When it premiered on Sept. 22, the new name was *Starring Boris Karloff*, with "Five Golden Guineas" as the kickoff episode. Karloff played a hangman for the Crown, who takes great satisfaction in his work, hearing the snap of the neck and seeing the dangling legs of his victims. For each execution, he is paid five golden guineas. His pregnant wife, played by Mildred Natwick, is appalled at her husband's line of work, and leaves him. Twenty years later, Karloff is given the duty of hanging a young man convicted of killing his sweetheart, whom Karloff learns is innocent. Not wanting to lose work, and refusing to divulge a letter that would free the condemned man, Karloff carries out the punishment. Afterward, his ex-wife returns, gives him payment, and reveals he has just hanged his own son. Consequently, he goes mad and strangles her, for which he is then hanged, and another executioner collects his guineas.

*Starring Boris Karloff*, said *Variety*, was "an excellent production" and "is an exciting newcomer to television." Director Alex Segal was commended for the show's mood and certain visual shots the critic said "were spine-tingling in their realism." The radio version was faulted by *Variety*, saying "story was slight and obvious in parts, and motivation was sketchy. Karloff's voice compels attention. His change of pace, his precise diction, and the English setting gave the broadcast interest."

Reaction to the radio and TV shows was just the reverse a few weeks later. About *Starring Boris Karloff*'s fourth installment, "Mad Illusion", *Variety* said, "the more imaginative sound medium permitted the illusion" of Karloff's escape from Devil's Island through shark-infested waters, and getting revenge on those who double-crossed him, whereas the TV version was written differently with the final explanation being that the story was just a bad dream. The star was not faulted though, as the review said "AM or TV, Karloff did a capital job."

Karloff was very comfortable with the new medium. He never used cue cards or TelePrompters, not only because he knew his lines perfectly, but, he said in 1958, that even if he did, "it wouldn't do me any good. If I took off my glasses, I couldn't see the cards". He added, "I've worked on shows with actors who use cue cards, and it's just plain hell. If you're playing a part, you ought to damn well know it. When these actors should be looking at the other persons in the scene, they're staring in the camera, reading their cards."

Mildred Natwick had met Karloff earlier, when she was appearing as Madame Arcati in *Blithe Spirit* for Maurice Evans during the war, and Evelyn Karloff introduced them. She saw them fairly often over the years, and told me about the time, several months before *Starring Boris Karloff*, she first worked with him on the *Suspense* TV series. During the live show, a scene called for them to look out a window, when Karloff suddenly grabbed her arm and moved her toward a set door. Not knowing what was going on, she continued with the scene, not breaking the rhythm. What had happened was that the quick-thinking Karloff noticed the camera at the window was disabled, so he went to the door where another camera was stationed and kept on acting.

*Starring Boris Karloff* was renamed *Mystery Playhouse Starring Boris Karloff* and cancelled by ABC after a run of just thirteen episodes. Still, it had whetted Karloff's taste for the small screen, with some of his best work yet to come.

# Haunting the Airwaves

**WITH THE ADVENT OF THE 1950S,** Karloff entered a period in his career when he would display his range as an actor perhaps more than ever before. He began the decade with a trip to Atlanta for another production of *On Borrowed Time,* directed by playwright Gerald Savory, a fellow Britisher.

Savory told me, "Whatever Karloff's stature was as an actor, he was certainly a most lovable man, liberal in his views, and firm in his friendships. It was in Atlanta that I first met him. I was directing a season at a theater-in-the-round on top of what was then the most noted hotel in the city. It was called Penthouse Theater. A different play was produced each week, and the star player, who had probably originated the particular part in another theater, would arrive on Sunday for a rehearsal with the resident company with the opening night on Monday.

"Boris had already played the part, with Atlanta supplying the other parts. What I mostly remember was our suppers after the show at a nearby eating joint. We talked and talked—Evie Karloff was there, too—until the waiters started stacking the chairs on the tables and sweeping up, upon which we put our feet on the table and went on talking. Of course, one of our abiding interests was our love (and in his case, knowledge) of cricket. I remember him loyally maintaining the actual play of the game was more than in baseball. Who is to say?

"As the years went by, we drifted apart. Boris was always busy, usually in America, and I was busy working in television here. [London] It was always a pleasure to hear his stories and his laugh. I would say he was a simple man in the best sense of the word, intelligent in the extreme, and, I imagine, willing to act his monster roles in order to give him security for what he thought was more important. His private life, laughter, comfort, and cricket."

Savory's production received enthusiastic response from the local critics. The *Atlanta Constitution* hailed it as "the greatest play of the current season" and added, "Many actors have performed before the eyes of thousands of theater regulars here during the past decade, but the tremendous ovation accorded Karloff will ring in his ears as a stirring tribute from a discriminating audience to a great trouper." Equally impressed was The *Atlanta Journal*. Noting that Karloff "made some 500 people forget he had ever been Frankenstein's monster", its critic said the star, and a ten-year-old Atlanta boy as Pud, "were so outstanding that the entire cast soared to new heights along with them." Playing the other of the two boys in the play, both locally cast, was Joseph Robinette, also a Georgia native. Of Karloff, he told me, "He was terrific."

The Penthouse Theatre was one of the first theaters-in-the-round in the United States, and an addition to the Atlanta theater community, having opened in 1949. During what Evelyn Karloff told me were "two very happy weeks" in the city, her husband was introduced to the Georgia House of Representatives. When asked by a reporter what he thought of Georgia politics, Karloff replied, "I think they've got very comfortable seats here."

On April 24, Karloff was back before the footlights in a New York revival of *Peter Pan* with Jean Arthur as the boy who wouldn't grow up, music and lyrics by Leonard Bernstein, and joint direction by John Burrell and Wendy Toye. As Captain Hook and Mr. Darling, Karloff had a grand time, entertaining adults as well as children. Writing for the *New York Times* after opening night, Brooks Atkinson said, "This is Mr. Karloff's day of triumph." Karloff's dual roles were described as "captivating" (the *New York Herald-Tribune*) and "wonderful" (the *Post*), while John Chapman in the *Daily News* remarked, "I'd like to see him in Gilbert and Sullivan." Much in the minority was the *Journal-American*'s Robert Garland, who said, "Mr. Karloff's Captain Hook is no more scary than Mr. Darling who is no more scary than Tinker Bell." The show was a hit and ran until the following January.

*Peter Pan* was a great joy for the cast and crew, as well as audiences, yet as Wendy Toye remembers, there were the usual adjustments and hurdles to get over. "When we first met for meetings and subsequent rehearsals, I was really worried that there would be the very stereotyped 'starry' with a capital S person. Far from it. He had spent a good deal of time in the theater early in his career and was a very dedicated actor and a super company member. You can imagine what it must have been like for him with a cast full of little boys knowing who he was. He treated them with such patience and good humor and we all adored him.

"Captain Hook has to sing, usually 'Avast Belay!". That song. Leonard Bernstein wrote the score and lyrics for our production brilliantly of course, and he was very involved in the whole show, and coached the folk who had any singing to do. I remember how nervous and insecure Boris was about it all, but he had a great untrained voice, and Lenny and all of us were delighted with it. It was a clever song about some of the pirates were tenors and others were basses, and Hook was the basest of all. Boris sang this with a great twinkle in his eye. His comedy was delicious.

"I think it's unusual in directors, but I always try and go to early costume fittings with the actors, because then one can see how they must use the costumes, and help them remember about them, so it's not such a shock when it comes to dress rehearsals. I went to an early one of Boris'. Elizabeth Montgomery, the designer from Motley's, was there and so was Mrs. Karloff. I was quite surprised and thought 'Oh, dear', because it's unusual for that to happen, and sometimes when it does it can be quite a problem. You know, a bit of interference here and there doesn't help.

"I learned that Evie looked after every aspect of Boris' career and life, and she was just marvelous. Always helpful, and if she had any suggestions about anything to do with the production, would discuss with me first. Boris and she and I became fast friends. They were a dear and wonderful couple. My life was enriched by knowing and working with them, and they had such a loving relationship and marriage. It was a real pleasure to be with them.

"He was a remarkable actor, and his Mr. Darling was just as excellent as his Captain Hook. It was a brilliant piece of casting with Jean as Peter, a great supporting cast, Leonard's music and lyrics, and the guiding hand of Peter Lawrence, the producer. I'll never forget the first night. The smart first nighters, who came to scoff at the fairy tale, finished by standing and applauding when Peter says, 'If you want to save

Tinker Bell's life, clap to show you believe in fairies.' The place went mad.

"It was a real thrill for me to see the first monster that I really cared for. As a young person, I had found him so sympathetic in all his monster films, he made such wonderful characters of them."

Among the actors comprising Captain Hook's motley crew was Nehemiah Persoff (Barbra Streisand's father in *Yentl*), who recalled what an impression Karloff made upon him. "I remember Mr. Karloff as being very serious and hard-working. During the time we were in *Peter Pan*, the American Federation of Television and Radio Artists was first being organized. One of our cast asked the cast to come to a meeting at Malin Studios after the show. I took off my make-up, and after visiting with some friends, found my way to the studios, and only one person sitting there.

"It was Boris. I said, jokingly, something like 'There isn't much of a turnout' and he very seriously said, 'No, there isn't.' Seeing he was not in a friendly mood, I didn't push the conversation, but about half an hour later, I suggested that possibly there was some mistake. He took a circular out of his pocket, checked it, and said no, there was no mistake. This was the time and place. I apologized for leaving him. He said he understood but would stay on as this was a very important matter and he wanted to give it his full attention. The following day, he expressed his disappointment to me. He said he could understand established, successful actors not showing up, but he could not understand the fear or lack of courage that young actors had about standing up for their rights.

"Soon after that, I went on a ten-week vacation to Israel, and he wrote to me there three or four times. When I returned to the show, I was ill, but came to the performance anyway. He approved of that. The following matinee, I came after the show had started, the only time in my life I ever came late to a show. Mr. Karloff was very stern about that and lectured me severely on the matter.

"He was a *good* man. I mean, a rare person indeed. I never met him after leaving *Peter* Pan, but I've always thought myself fortunate and a better person for having known him."

When the show was winding up, *The New York Times* reported, "*Peter Pan* will have grossed more than $1 million after it ends its local run after 321 shows on Jan. 27. It moves on to Boston to begin a coast-to-coast tour Feb. 5. It broke all records for all continuous performances of *Peter*. That included a forty-five year-old mark of 237 shows set in 1906 in the original American version with Maude Adams. A company of more than 100 people will make the road trip, which will involve transportation of involved flying equipment imported from England." Karloff did reprise Captain Hook and Mr. Darling for the national tour and the role of Peter was assumed by Veronica Lake and Joan McCracken. He again played Hook while riding a float in Macy's Thanksgiving Day parade in New York, and then in 1960 for a TV special called *The Secret World of Eddie Hodges*.

While still in New York for *Peter Pan*, Karloff found time to squeeze in broadcast appearances. Shortly before the play closed, he was Uriah Heep in a Christmas Eve production of "David Copperfield" for radio's *Theatre Guild on the Air*. Joining him were Cyril Ritchard, Flora Robson, and as the adult David, Richard Burton, just beginning his career in *The Lady's Not For Burning*. Also starting out was playwright Robert Anderson (*Tea and Sympathy, I Never Sang For My Father*), who wrote the adaptation. He told me, "I certainly remember 'David Copperfield'. The writer was present at all rehearsals. The practice was the writer wrote the script some months in advance and reworked it. First rehearsal, a reading, was on Tuesday, rewrite by Thursday for another rehearsal, and a last rehearsal all day Sunday for the Sunday night show, broadcast usually from the Belasco Theater.

"It was great experience working with the likes of that cast. Boris was a charmer. He was great as Uriah Heep, and whenever I saw him after, he would always greet me with a line from that show. I married Teresa Wright in 1959 and she was a great friend of Boris and Evie. We visited them several times in London and in their charming, quaint house in Bramshott. Wasn't it odd that a gentle man like that should have made his mark playing monsters?

"In those days, I was writing plays in the morning, radio and later TV in the afternoon, and teaching four nights a week. It was rigorous, but gave me a tremendous feeling of being involved in 'show business'. Whenever I talk about my early days, I talk about *Theatre Guild on the Air*. What a great chance for a young playwright to work with master works usually, to get a sense of shape and form and the essentials, to work with stars, and then to be put under the pressure of rehearsals with time limitations.

"I had some wonderful shows in addition to 'Copperfield'. 'Trilby' with Rex Harrison and Teresa, 'The Glass Menagerie' with Helen Hayes, Monty Clift, and Karl Malden, 'The Petrified Forest' with Bob Montgomery. It was on *Theatre Guild on the Air* that I met Deborah Kerr and that led to my asking her to do *Tea and Sympathy*."

*Variety* praised what it called Anderson's "skillful editing job" and particularly the actors, noting that Karloff's Uriah Heep "dripped with sinister hypocrisy". That same year, Karloff had another radio show of his own, this one for children, titled *Boris Karloff's Treasure Chest*, airing locally on WNEW in New York. As host, he displayed his gift for storytelling and reciting poetry, and spun records for an audience he appreciated and respected. Asked at the time about some protests concerning crime and horror programming on radio and television, Karloff had this response for the *Los Angeles Daily News*:

"I feel strongly against censorship of all kinds. Parents should be the judge of what their children see and hear in the home. Each child represents a different problem. What affects one won't make the slightest impression on another. Parents who have good taste and know their own children are fully capable of dealing with this matter.

"As a matter of fact, I doubt that, left to themselves, many children would go haywire over so-called horror entertainment. It seems to me that they have a pretty fair amount of common sense and are capable of arranging their own values."

In 1951, at the 15th American Exhibition of Educational Radio Programs, *Boris Karloff's Treasure Chest* was honored by Ohio State University's Institute for Education by Radio and Television. The show's station, WNEW, received the Institute's first award in the regional classification for a children's program.

Television was the medium Karloff worked in most often during the 50s, playing a wide assortment of characters that included King Arthur, Don Quixote, Rasputin, and the title role in Chekhov's *Uncle Vanya* opposite Eva Gabor ("he was a brilliant actor", she told me). He loved live television because it gave him a sense of being onstage, but with only one chance to get it right. As he put it, "If you make a muck of it, you make a muck of it." That literally came true when he starred in "Mutiny on the Nicolette", a *Studio One* drama directed by Franklin Schaffner, known for *Planet of the Apes* (1968), *Patton* (1970), and *The Boys From Brazil* (1978). Also cast were Anthony Ross, who had been one of the policemen in *Arsenic and Old Lace* with Karloff, and Ralph Nelson, later a director of such films as *Lilies of the Field* (1962). *Father Goose* (1964), and *Charly* (1968).

Nelson told me, "The melodramatic plot involved a jinxed freighter that was rechartered during World War II. In World War I, it had been involved in some evil incident and Boris had served as a member of the crew at that time. Anthony Ross played the captain and I was the first mate. The climax of the piece came when Mr. Karloff, in order to seek vengeance on the ship itself, aroused the crew to mutiny. This occurred during a storm at sea, with the ship pitching and rolling. Mr. Karloff and the crew were armed with grenades and handguns. At the moment when Mr. Karloff had the captain and first mate at bay on the deck, the ship's boom was supposed to fall and symbolically sweep him overboard, ending the mutiny. It was an ambitious program for live television.

"The art department did a magnificent job in painting the floor of the studio to resemble a ship's deck with rusting steel plates and bolts. Mr. Ross and I had a scene on the bridge when we were forewarned that the mutiny was beginning. Mr. Schaffner had told us there would be 'a little rain' in this scene. On the telecast, a special effects man stood next to the camera and shot a fire hose at us with full force. In order to yell the dialogue, we had to turn to each other and shout from the corners of our mouths, or else gargle.

"That scene concluded, it was my duty to go below decks to ascertain the mood of the crew. I saw immediately that the beautiful paint job on the floor had turned into a slippery quagmire with all the water. As I got to the set which represented the below decks, I just had time to warn the actors comprising the crew of the conditions on deck and to be careful that they did not skid during the action that followed.

"I preceded them to the deck and turned with my captain to face the snarling, mutinous crew. Instead of rushing us, as we had rehearsed, they turned into a bunch of careful actors, gingerly tiptoeing across the deck, concerned about the next job rather than this one. Mr. Karloff threw his grenades, but the special effects had been short-circuited by the rain, and nothing happened. When the boom fell, instead of swinging forward to knock him overboard, it dropped dead behind him and he stood awaiting its impact. The boom, of course, was a hollow carton. I had to destroy the symbolism by rushing to him and pushing him overboard.

"It was not one of *Studio One*'s superior achievements."

Moviegoers saw little of Karloff during this time, but the few pictures he made were hardly worth the effort. *The Strange Door*, based on a story by Robert Louis Stevenson, reunited him with Charles Laughton, almost twenty years after they met in *The Old Dark House*. Later, Laughton and agent Paul Gregory signed Karloff to play the Devil in the stage production of *Don Juan in Hell* directed by Laughton. They decided instead to use Vincent Price and had the stage manager tell Karloff he had been replaced.

*The Strange Door* had Laughton as a nobleman seeking revenge upon a young couple after his deceased sweetheart jilted him for his brother. It was a lame attempt to capture the flavor of earlier horror films. In a supporting role, Karloff contributed little to a picture one critic termed "more ludicrous than chilling." In the same vein a year later, and just as bad, was *The Black Castle*, which the presence of Karloff and Lon Chaney, Jr. could not help.

In January of 1952, Sidney Lumet directed Karloff in "Don Quixote" for the premiere of *CBS Television Workshop*, with Jimmy Savo as Sancho Pinza and Grace Kelly as Dulcinea. Television was still in the experimental phase and the show was a valiant failure. Producer Norris Houghton told me Karloff was capable of, in his words, "gentleness and wonderment" which came through in his portrayal, but of the show itself, Houghton added, "the less said, the better." This excerpt from Jack Gould's review in the *New York Times* reinforced Houghton's assessment:

"While Mr. Karloff was burdened with cumbersome armor and amateurish make-up, he played the central figure in a very somber and depressed key. Where elements of true inspiration and lofty purpose, coupled with perhaps even an opera bouffe appreciation of the ludicrous, were needed, Mr. Karloff's interpretation was drawn in terms of an errant Pagliacci.

"The production of Norris Houghton and the direction by Sidney Lumet were much too concerned with effect. The awkward use of a series of model windmills, all turning in precise synchronization, was never believable and only distracting. The sight of Mr. Karloff spread out on an arm of a larger windmill, which in contrast, never revolved a whit was just silly, not arty."

The write-up in *Variety* of the half-hour show had much the same tone. It said, in part, "Pace was static till it hurt, and the few possibilities on which they could have capitalized to project at least partially the flavor of the Cervantes classic were snafued or lost. End result, instead of carrying TV's drama techniques forward, pushed them back a couple of years." Karloff was more successful on the *I Spy* series in 1966, portraying a scientist with delusions that he is Don Quixote.

Martin Manulis, producer of many of TV's finer dramatic shows, several that showcased Karloff, summed up the actor's efforts to show viewers how versatile he truly was: "Many audiences, and many professionals, think that actors frequently reflect their own personalities in the parts they play. Karloff was a diametrically opposed case--dignified, warm, affectionate, witty. A true delight as a companion and friend.

"In the roles he played on *Climax!* and *Playhouse 90*, he revealed his sensitivity and his very special personal qualities as opposed to the horror side. However, we found that his *Frankenstein* personality had been so impressed on the audience that they often read into his characters a menace that wasn't there. This was dispelled as his character developed, and they realized they were watching Boris Karloff, a fine actor."

Karloff returned to England to star in *Colonel March of Scotland Yard*, a series produced by Hannah Weinstein for British television and later syndicated in the United States. The role of March, taken from stories by mystery writer John Dickson Carr and using the pseudonym Carter Dickson, fit Karloff perfectly. As the one-eyed, soft-spoken, and sharp-witted detective heading the Yard's Department of Queer Complaints, he was a treat to watch solving all sorts of unusual crimes. Three episodes were strung together and released as a feature film in England as *Colonel March Investigates*, but it was two years later in 1954 when the show reached America. In its usual style, *Variety* said the character had "socko video potential", while *TV Guide* remarked, "*Colonel March* should win Karloff almost as many fans as his grotesque movie roles."

Performers yet to be known who appeared on the show, made at Southhall Studios in Middlesex, were Arthur Hill, Christopher Lee, soon to become a horror star as Dracula for England's Hammer Films, John Schlesinger, director of *Darling* (1965), *Far From the Madding Crowd* (1967), and *Midnight Cowboy* (1969), and Dana Wynter, who was still in drama school. Anthony Newley, another supporting player, told me, "It was shot in a very small studio with only one soundstage. Probably a private house or commercial building that had been converted into a studio. I can feel quite clearly the closeness of the soundstage, so it was obviously very small."

While the show was running, its star opened the first exhibition of England's Crime Writers Association at the National Book Gallery in London. *The Times* reported, "Karloff said all of them, whether crime writers or crime readers, were partners in crime. What struck him as he looked around was the absurdity of the dictum that crime did not pay."

1955 would be an especially productive year for the actor. On CBS' *The Best of Broadway*, he redid *Arsenic and Old Lace*, and joining him again from the original cast were John Alexander and Bruce Gordon. Martin Manulis added Helen Hayes and Billie Burke as the Brewster sisters, Peter Lorre as Dr. Einstein, and Orson Bean as Mortimer. *Time* magazine commented, "Few TV revivals of Broadway plays have come off as entertainingly and inventively", while *Variety* called it "the best TV comedy of the year", and went on to say, "Karloff and Lorre made the perfect murderous pair, relishing every line and turning them out beautifully."

Of that program, Orson Bean told me, "Lorre was down in the dumps, and Boris was always saying, 'Cheer up, Peter.' The huge, crane-like apparatus on which a cameraman sits so he can swoop up into the air for an overhead shot is called 'the monster'. A floor manager yelled. 'Get that monster over here!' and Boris, turning in mock umbrage, said, 'I beg your pardon' to great laughter from the crew."

Although it was not in a play, as he would have liked, Karloff appeared onstage in England at the London Palladium for *Night of a 100 Stars*, a fund raiser for the Actors' Orphanage. The event featured a virtual who's who of mostly British performers. Among them were Richard Attenborough, Alec Guinness, Laurence Olivier, and Michael Redgrave, and Karloff did a sketch with Hermoine Gingold, who liked him a great deal. In the 60s, they planned to do a revue together which Karloff thought should be titled *The Monster and I*, as she related in her book *How to Grow Old Disgracefully*. She said, to the contrary, "never wanting to take second billing, I favored the title *I and the Monster*." Film commitments for both of them prevented the show from happening, yet in the States, they worked again that same year for ABC's *Elgin Hour* in "The Sting of Death", but in separate scenes.

In that program, Karloff played a retired detective named Mr. Mycroft, bearing a strong resemblance to Sherlock Holmes whose brother's name was Mycroft. Based on H.F. Heard's novel *A Taste for Honey*, which Karloff called "a triumph of horror", the show was directed by Daniel Petrie, known for *Eleanor and Franklin* (1974), *Sybil* (1976), and *Fort Apache: The Bronx* (1981)). In 1984, Petrie told me Karloff "was every bit adept as a light comedian as he was as a merchant of terror" and added, "I still miss him. It would be a more gentle world if Boris Karloff was still with us." The program received the Edgar Award from the Mystery Writers of America as the best mystery TV show of the year.

It was around this time that theatrical producer Kermit Bloomgarden, who had staged *Death of a Salesman*, began the groundwork for a Broadway version of *The Lark*, Lillian Hellman's adaptation of Jean Anouilh's *L'Alouette* about the struggle of Joan of Arc. It was one of seven plays by Hellman he would put on during his prolific career. In February, he wrote to Charles Laughton to see whether he'd be interested in directing it, but Laughton believed further work was needed on the translation, plus he didn't have the time to devote to it. In a letter to Anouilh written in July, Bloomgarden said he had also approached William Wyler.

He further wrote, "I just returned from the Coast where I went to see Wyler and Leslie Caron. Caron was interested in doing the play, but both Wyler and I felt that since we had never seen her on stage, we wanted her to read for us. This she was willing to do, and I must say she was very charming and warm when we met her. The studio, however, refused to permit her to read and while they were willing to give her permission to do the play, all they would release her for would be from January to June, so that with the limited amount of time they were willing to release her, and the fact they would not permit her to read, nor would she read without their consent, Wyler and I decided against it.

"As you know, my first choice when I read *L'Alouette* was Julie Harris and I'm very happy to say when we got together with her, we came to an agreement for her to do it with an unlimited amount of time, and expressing it in her own words 'will stay with the play as long as the play runs'. Both Wyler and I are very excited and happy about this and I hope you feel the same."

Harris, who first scored on Broadway in *The Member of the Wedding*, was no stranger to Anouilh, having appeared the year before in his play *Mademoiselle Colombe* with Eli Wallach. Bloomgarden had discussed the show with Audrey Hepburn as well. She expressed interest in playing the Maid of Orleans if it was pushed back another year. Jennifer Jones offered to audition for *The Lark*, yet her husband David O. Selznick wouldn't allow it.

With regrets, William Wyler withdrew due to his film work, and Joseph Anthony, director of Bloomgarden's production of *The Rainmaker*, stepped in. That spring, the London version of *The Lark* adapted by Christopher Fry opened. Brooks Atkinson, writing for *The New York Times*, found fault with it, saying the play's arguments were "tedious" and "undramatic". While Fry's version, Atkinson wrote, did not measure up to George Bernard Shaw's *Saint Joan*, he conceded that "as a whole, it is interesting."

To the cast, Bloomgarden added Theodore Bikel, Joseph Wiseman, and as Cauchon, the compassionate bishop trying to protect Joan from heresy, Boris Karloff. Karloff saw the London version, too, and had this to say in a letter to Bloomgarden:

"It was a very strange experience. After having read our version many times, it was like looking at a rather smudged carbon copy through a smoked glass, which is a very mixed metaphor! Our version is so much tighter and has so much more impact. With the possible exception of the Dauphin, I did not admire any of the playing, and some passages through sheer length became very dull. Fry has not indulged in his usual flights of verbal fancy and a curious tediousness supervenes. It's very sad, but perhaps a good omen for the play Miss Hellman has given us."

Rehearsals for *The Lark* began in October. Also joining the company was Karloff's friend Bruce Gordon, then doing television in New York, who visited the Karloffs' apartment at the famed Dakota building near Central Park. He told me, "Boris was shaving or something, and throws this script at me. He says, 'Read this. There's a good part in it for you.' So I sat there and read this thing, and I read and I read and I read. 'Where the hell is this? I can't find it.' In the middle of the second act, there's a part of Captain La Hire and a scene with Julie. One scene. "I said, 'You mean the part of La Hire?' He said, 'Yeah.' I said, 'Well, God, it's so *small*.' He said, "You, you horse's ass', that's always the way he talked to me, that's a *good* part. Try and get an audition for it.' I contacted an agent and I got a reading and the part. When Boris and Evie came back from Europe, I said, 'Hey, what do you think? I'm going to be in this with you.'"

According to Gordon, Joseph Anthony's directing style did not go over well with Lillian Hellman. William Ross, the show's production stage manager, agreed with Gordon's view. Ross told me, "Lillian was a very tough lady. She was there seventy to eighty percent of the time during rehearsal and voiced her objections very loudly. One day, we were in Boston after the performance, and Joe was addressing the cast and giving notes. I said, 'Lillian, can I see you a minute?' She came. I said, 'How'd you like to go for some Chinese food?' She said, 'That'd be wonderful, Bill. As soon as Joe's finished.' I said, 'Now.' She said, 'What do you mean?' I said, 'You're standing behind him, and every point he's making, you're shaking your head no. You're being very destructive.' She said, 'I'm not doing that.' I said, 'You absolutely are. Either stop it or come on out for Chinese food.' So she stopped it.

"One night, Joe was sitting in the last row with his secretary and dictating notes to her during the performance, whispering, and suddenly behind him, Lillian said, 'That's all wrong.' She was standing behind eavesdropping. He was right in many cases, I think, and proven right by the reception of the play, but it was a very difficult situation."

Ross added that from time to time, Hellman would pick on somebody and go after them. At one point, the target of her wrath was Joseph Wiseman, playing the inquisitor at Joan's trial. It was the role that Karloff, at first, very much wanted to play, according to Kermit Bloomgarden. Although Wiseman didn't speak until the second act, he was on stage with a big spotlight on him through the first act, during which he would move and gesture and point. When he spoke, he had a long speech addressed to members of the court. Hellman kept complaining that he wasn't getting the lines right. Finally, from the stage, a frustrated Wiseman retorted, "Now, stop it, Lillian. I know my words." Hellman shot back, "Yes, but do you know mine?" (William Ross said to me, "She was wrong.")

Hellman notwithstanding, *The Lark* came together after tryouts in Boston and New Haven. The New York premiere was slated for Nov. 17 at the Longacre Theater, where Julie Harris, being the lead, was assigned the star's dressing room. She would not accept it and insisted that it go to Karloff. William Ross said Karloff always came early, and in a cheerful mood as though he became happier when crossing the threshold to backstage. His dressing room became a meeting place where people felt free to drop in and say hello. If one entered at the right moment, Karloff could be found, clad in a robe, chinning himself with great effort on a bar he had put up. That was to loosen up his back on account of his arthritis.

Ever supportive of younger talent, Karloff always contributed to them, which Julie Harris can attest to. She told me, "It was *wonderful* working with Boris. He was a dream of a man. Kind, humorous, gentle, and very, very strong. I had trouble with my throat, a bad cold, and Boris gave me a corncob pipe stuffed with cotton where the tobacco would be. Cotton that had been soaked in oil of eucalyptus. I went puffing on this when not in rehearsal and it was good.

"He was a tireless worker, knew his lines backwards and forwards, was patient and giving to everyone. I thought he was a glorious actor, and wanted him to play King Lear, but he told me he had never played Shakespeare and now it was too late. I loved him as a man and an actor." The admiration was mutual from then on. Of his co-star, Karloff told *Time* magazine, "When Julie is at the height of her most emotional scene, she is always in complete control of herself, just as a fine pianist is always master of his music." She was one of many actresses Karloff admired, as well as Jean Arthur, Dorothy McGuire, Mildred Natwick, Teresa Wright, and Jane Wyatt.

Just days before *The Lark* opened, Christopher Plummer joined the show as a replacement in the role of Warwick, the earl who wants to proceed with Joan's eventual burning. On opening night, all but Harris and Karloff were distracted by nervousness. When the curtain came down, the audience stood, roaring its approval through eight curtain calls.

"Magnificent", "beautiful", "exciting", and "moving" were just a few of the adjectives applied by the critics to the show, and *Life* magazine simply called it "American theater at its finest."

For Karloff, the notices and the public's acceptance must have been gratifying, to be in a successful Broadway drama for the first time. He and Harris received two of the play's several Tony Award nominations. It was the only time in his career he was considered for a major acting award. His competition was made up of Ben Gazzara (*A Hatful of Rain*), Paul Muni (*Inherit the Wind*), Michael Redgrave (*Tiger at the Gates*), and Edward G. Robinson (*Middle of the Night*). At the award ceremonies on June 1, 1956, Harris won for Best Actress and the Best Actor prize went to Paul Muni.

*The Lark* enjoyed a run of 229 performances and closed in June. In an interview in 1974, Kermit Bloomgarden said it was "the best production I ever did. Magic in the theater." Karloff did not tour with the show, so Cauchon was assumed by Sam Jaffe. However, Karloff, Harris, and Bruce Gordon performed it on TV's *Hallmark Hall of Fame* the following year. Director George Schaefer, working with Karloff again several years after the ill-fated *The Linden Tree*, guided a cast as good as Joseph Anthony's. Assuming the roles played by Christopher Plummer and Joseph Wiseman were Denholm Elliott and Basil Rathbone, plus Eli Wallach and Jack Warden. Watching the program today and seeing Karloff and Rathbone act with such passion and conviction makes one wish they had been in a film of such depth. Screen rights to *The Lark* were, in fact, sold to Allied Artists at the time of its New York debut, but a film was never made.

During *The Lark*'s run, Karloff and Christopher Plummer worked in an outstanding drama for TV's *Alcoa Hour* titled "Even the Weariest River" a Western written in blank verse. Alvin Sapinsley's original teleplay was directed by Robert Mulligan, whose films included *To Kill A Mockingbird* (1962), *Inside Daisy Clover* (1965), *Summer of '42* (1971), and *The Man in the Moon* (1988). It dealt with an aging sheriff, played by Franchot Tone, of a dying town called Weary River, where a stagecoach robbery had taken place. A wounded stranger, played by Plummer, appears and the sheriff, forced to cope with the townspeople who want justice, jails him but knows he is innocent. Also part of the stark, desolate setting were the sheriff's daughter (Lee Grant) and the local doctor (Karloff) who related the tragic story, told in flashback.

Sapinsley told me, "The fact that I was able to write and get produced a television play in iambic pentameter, coupled with rhymed couplets at the conclusion of each scene, can be attributed to [producer] Herbert Brodkin's reluctant persuasion of NBC, who agreed to its presentation with equal reluctance. Fortunately for all, and mostly for me, it proved a resounding success, garnered extremely enthusiastic reviews in New York, and from prominent TV critics elsewhere in the country. On the basis of its success, I was able, in the same year, to write another blank verse play, this one for *Omnibus*: 'Lee at Gettysburg'.

"Boris was one of the two hardest-working actors I was associated with during the days of live television, hard-working in the sense that he rehearsed assiduously, studied his role and his lines unceasingly, made effort upon effort to sharpen, improve, and hone the part. During rehearsal breaks, while the others sat around the table drinking coffee, Boris would be off in a corner, working on his character. The other hardest-working actor of my acquaintance was Jackie Cooper.

"Boris was also modest. I was visiting him once in the apartment in London he had sublet for the summer. One of his duties was to tend the plants. The plants were languishing and Boris was concerned. He noted in the paper that day that Woolworth's was featuring a miracle plant food called 'Dried Blood'. He walked over there and turned around and walked back. He couldn't bring himself to step up to the counter and demand 'Dried Blood'. The plants perished."

Sapinsley was correct about the critics' response. Jack Gould, in his review for the *New York Times* said, "With Tone, Karloff, Plummer, and Grant contributing performances of quiet eloquence and intensity, 'Even the Weariest River' had much of the quality of a Sandburg work brought to life. In its philosophy, its expression, and its disciplined mood, the play was an hour of original stage artistry on television." He added, "Mr. Karloff had the most inspired and rewarding lines. He spoke them with compassion and beauty." Gould summed up, "It was one of the season's fine achievements." In the *New York Herald-Tribune*, John Crosby wrote, "It was all marvelously convincing, the blank verse spilling out of the mouths of the barroom idlers as readily as if they spoke the way all their lives. There were genuinely fine performances by all the four principals and a great job of direction by Robert Mulligan. Sapinsley wrote a stunningly unusual play."

*Variety*'s review said, "While this drama was rich in poetic qualities and an ethereal mood, its characters were hardly the types to be found in a frontier town on the Casper-Laramie stage line." Still, it had praise for Tone, Plummer, and Robert Mulligan, and, echoing Jack Gould's thoughts, said, "By far the best lines were handed Karloff, and he handled them in dignified, scholarly fashion that accented the grim, fatalistic mood of the piece."

Robert Mulligan told me, "Boris approached his work with a deep intelligence and a quiet strength. He was a gifted, serious, and subtle actor. Beyond his inherent personal dignity, there was a natural and easy kindness and generosity to everyone, and a surprising spontaneous and delightful sense of humor. In the hectic pace of live television, he found a way to remain calm and in control of his performance."

Maintaining his demeanor in the early years of television was a Karloff trademark. Appearing with Karloff and Eli Wallach on a *General Electric Theater* drama called "Mr. Blue Ocean", a Chinese fairy tale, was Susan Strasberg, She told me, "None of us were too thrilled about the rather primitive appliances to make us look Chinese. Mr. Karloff was lovely to me. He, I believe, played the man I was engaged to by my family, although I was in love with Tony Perkins -- such is life! During intermission, the director, who shall be nameless, came screaming backstage at all the actors, telling us it was too slow and to pick up the pace. Mr. Karloff just said, 'Carry on as normal.'"

Eli Wallach, who played Sakini in George Schaefer's London production of *Teahouse of the August Moon* told me, "As a specialist in film villains, I can well understand the surprise people got when they actually met him. Soft-spoken, witty, involved and interested in his work, Mr. Karloff was a delight. I knew him socially as well, and we talked often over tea in his flat in Knightsbridge. His characterizations always were multi-dimensional. You felt and sensed the inner workings of a real professional."

Television producer Norman Felton, whose shows included *Dr. Kildare* and *The Man From U.N.C.L.E.*, said there was one time when Karloff had doubts about the role he was given. He would work with Karloff four times, and of the first, he told me, "I cast him in the role of a businessman in a *Robert Montgomery Presents*, which I directed. When Mr. Karloff arrived in New York, he had not read the script. When he did so, he told me that perhaps I had made a mistake in casting, for he had not played such a part before. I told him I was aware that it would be different for him, but I felt it would also be challenging. He agreed and thanked me for the chance to do it. He was very good."

Another weekly show for Karloff was the hoped-for result of *The Veil*, a pilot he appeared in as host and frequent star. These half-hour stories of the unusual and unexplained phenomena were produced for Hal Roach, Jr. and directed primarily by Herbert L. Strock, who did several 1950s horror films including *I Was a Teenage Frankenstein*. Strock said, "These were for a potential series, but Roach was in financial trouble and blew the whole thing. I really loved Boris. He was the kindest and most considerate actor I ever worked with, and I have worked with hundreds. He always knew his lines and could be molded in and out of various characters with ease.

"I would tell him that I wouldn't need him until 10 a.m., yet he would be on the stage when I arrived in the morning, always ready to give of himself in any capacity. I would try and let him go home early, due to his age, stating that I would read his offstage lines for another actor's shots. He would tell me that he would prefer staying to give the other actor the original reading. The only other man I ever met with such a professionalism was Ed Wynn, whom I directed in an outstanding *Bonanza*." The programs were edited into TV-movies titled *Destination: Nightmare, Jack the Ripper,* and *The Veil,*

Karloff returned to the stage in March of 1957 when he and Evelyn went to Alaska for another production of *Arsenic and Old Lace*. Having done the show on Broadway, across the country, in the Central Pacific, and on radio and television, he was now doing it for a theater workshop at Anchorage Community College. In the process, he was the first performer of note to appear in the region.

As Frank Brink, director of both the workshop and the three-day run of *Arsenic*, explained to me, "Anchorage, and Alaska overall, was made up of people with a sense of adventure and the capacity to both survive and create an atmosphere they could not otherwise find in the next town." Therefore, with no centers of culture anywhere, the residents of Anchorage had to create their own. In the 50s, Brink pointed out, Anchorage had a majority of educated, professional people, many of whom would fly to "the lower forty-eight" to enjoy the theater and musical offerings of Seattle, Los Angeles, and Broadway.

Brink believed that the adventurous spirit of those people found what he called "a kindred spirit" in Boris Karloff. The engagement of *Arsenic and Old Lace* was a near sell-out and would prove to be "a tremendous experience" as Brink described it, for everyone involved. "Boris brought into his roles not only a combination of skills and insights, not accorded to every actor, but also a great measure of that indefinable human spirit for which there is no better word than love. Karloff could not hide the fact that he was, innately, an intelligent, car-ing, and forgiving human being. When Teresa Wright, who had never worked with a community theater before, and didn't intend to, was urged by Boris to accept the Alaskan invitation, she didn't hesitate. This was one small illustration of the trust Karloff inspired in everyone he knew.

"When he played in Alaska, he was not entirely surrounded by experienced performers. This might have been considered a disservice by anyone of lesser stature than Boris. Without hesitation, he offered his talent and experience to assist a few of our performers and make them feel at ease. I have a theory that, without his being aware of it, he projected a sense of solicitude and tenderness that went beyond ordinary courtesy. I believe that subconsciously this 'sense' crept gently into many of the roles he played, and certainly in *Frankenstein*.

"I am convinced that Evelyn Karloff remained a powerful influence on her husband and his career. She understood the nature of theater with its varied creative, emotional, and physical demands. In a very real sense, they were a team. Evie quietly smoothed the paths for Boris, and gently stole the hearts of all of us involved in the Karloff experience.

"Only once at the end of the run did she overtly betray any concern for her husband's welfare when, after a seemingly endless series of curtain calls, Boris walked out on stage, held his hands up to quiet the audience, and began to speak with them. Evie turned to me and said, 'Oh, Frank, he doesn't do that sort of thing! I'm worried.' She then listened, as I presumed to reassure her that the love Anchorage was trying to express would accept anything he did, even if he stood on his head.

"At that moment, he poured out a rare and unusual response to an appreciative audience who saw in him something more than great skill and talent. He revealed a sense of humanity and generosity that evidently went beyond mere courtesy when he said, 'This has been the most rewarding moment in my career.' I had the feeling that even Evie must have been surprised at such an extravagant response. Many of us would have been ashamed to admit we felt he was just being generous in his expression of appreciation for the Alaskan reaction to him and to Evie. Later, when he appeared on Louella Parsons' radio show, he again expressed that same enthusiasm about Alaska and its theater.

"After the cast party, Boris took me aside and said, 'I want to give you a gift and I don't want it to be something stupid or useless, so I want you to tell me what you would like.' After my stubborn protest and Boris' equally stubborn refusal to understand that he and Evie had already given us the greatest gift anyone could hope for—themselves—and that he and Evie would live in our hearts forever, Boris merely said, 'I shan't leave until you tell me.' Realizing he was adamant, I thought for a moment and suddenly blurted out, 'Your shoes!' I said, 'To have the shoes of the first great theater talent to walk on the Alaskan stage would be the most wonderful gift I can think of. But, if you can't part with them, I will understand!' With that, he said, 'I can't think why you would want these old shoes, but if you want them, they're yours!'

"On opening night, Boris invited me to his dressing room and asked a favor. 'Frank, would you have a small stool or ladder about eighteen inches tall?' I was puzzled, but I said, 'I'll get one.' The janitor's closet produced a stool. He placed it in the middle of the room, below the spot where a two-inch pipe crossed the room just before the ceiling. Then, before he stepped upon the stool, he solemnly announced, 'I'm going to hang myself.'

"Needless to say, I was startled. After he had his joke, he said, 'You needn't be alarmed. It's my arthritis. By hanging from that pipe, I can stop the irritation for a while.' I placed the stool under the pipe, he climbed upon it, then I removed it while he hung there, and replaced it when he was ready to come down and go to the stage. Many times Boris downplayed not only his physical problems, but problems created by the limited experience of some of the performers. The stool ritual went on each night and Boris insisted I tell no one. He did not wish the cast to be concerned with anything but the play itself." Before coming to Anchorage, Karloff told Brink, "Now, Frank, I want to do your show not mine. Whatever you decide, let me know. I will adapt. There's no sense in your forcing the others to do anything, except perhaps to learn their lines." The next day, March 11, Brink told his cast that Karloff would adapt, an announcement that brought forth applause and cheers.

In, his notes of March 13, Brink mentioned that he discussed with Karloff his arrival, needs, plans, and such. Karloff said to him, "Frank, please listen! You need not prepare any reception. I would prefer not. There will be plenty of time for that after you fit me into the play, for I want to give you the best performance I can." In parentheses, Brink wrote after that, "Is this man real?"

Just two hours after he and Evelyn arrived in Anchorage on March 16, rehearsals were underway. Karloff was quickly impressed with the city's theater movement, his fellow players, even the stagecraft. His first remark when he walked in the theater was, "What a perfect set."

Brink added, "I believe that Karloff's compassion and sense of decency subtly imbued the characters he created with qualities of being so seldom found in the distorted and sometimes ghoulish roles he often played. He seasoned the black and white roles with shades of gray.

"Evelyn was important, or better still, necessary to the middle and latter periods of Karloff's career. Her influence has been constant as an essential part of the decisions that affected the roles he accepted, as well as the attitude he carried to those roles. They, I truly believe, were genuine partners in every sense of the word. I believe this left a subtle stamp on the attitude he brought to the roles he played. I believe that Evie not only became an island of peace in her husband's life, but one whose output became important to the roles he accepted. Even though there were long periods when we did not communicate except at Christmas, we followed Boris' career with the firm conviction that a genuine and lasting love bound them together.

"I never felt it so strongly as I did when something prompted me to call London to make contact for a possible reunion. A nurse or someone tending Boris answered the phone and said, 'I'm sorry, but Mr. Karloff is ill and cannot talk with anyone.' At that moment, Evie interrupted and said, 'Oh, Frank, he's very sick, but I know he would want to talk with you.' At that point, I was devastated for I felt that she was saying he might not live. I was hardly ready to be cheerful, though I knew I must try. In talking with Boris, I found myself being led away from any sense of dejection with that same buoyant spirit that would have encouraged an inexperienced performer about to make his entrance on stage.

"It was this spirit, I believe, that motivated his entire life. Though his voice was weak, he immediately played down the seriousness of his illness, as he responded to my facetious attempt to hold him to his promise to play Gramps in *On Borrowed Time* which I still wanted to produce. Ironically, as we discussed the role, I had the feeling that he was already playing the final scene of that play. I know little of 'greatness', but I sincerely believe that Boris Karloff was endowed with the qualities that overused word implies. I feel he never fully realized the effect of his Frankenstein monster on the nascent film images of the unknown, the surrealistic quality of the nightmare made so horrible by Mary Shelley. Karloff's monster was unlike Shelley's demon-driven creation, who slaughtered out of hate and vengeance because of Frankenstein's abandonment or denial of him."

The audience reaction on closing night was electric. Brink wrote to me years afterward, "After seven curtain calls, only three of which we rehearsed, the stage manager came to me and said, 'Good Lord, what'll we do?' I said, 'Hell, I don't know. Just go through the single group then bring in Karloff again.' 'But we already did that' 'Well, do it again', I told him. And he did, and they still called for more, so I told John, 'Just push Boris on for the next call.' Boris went out there three more times and they continued to applaud. Boris came offstage and he looked sober as he lifted his arms in a hopeless shrug. I was at a total loss to know what to do and, while looking helplessly at Boris, I said, 'This has never happened before. I don't know what to do except ask if you'll go out one more time!'

Karloff did as told, and while speaking to the crowd, he praised his director whom he then called to join him. Brink recalled later, "So out I went not knowing what the hell to say. I was embarrassed. More applause. Boris turned to me, took my arm, and gently thrust me right towards center. I didn't know what to say. The audience applauded. Karloff applauded. I was scared out of my wits. I remember only that I said, 'Thank you. Thank you so very much. I'm not the one you should applaud. He's the one!' I turned to point to Karloff only to discover he had gone backstage, leaving me out there alone. I waved at the audience, left the stage, got on the intercom, and told Bob to dim the downstage lights and bring up some house lights. I yelled, 'Kill the curtain!' Not until then did the audience calm down. From the beginning of the applause to dimming up of the house lights, it was about thirty-three minutes."

Regarding Karloff, John Elliott, then a young Anchorage resident who was the show's stage manager, told me, "First and foremost, he treated me as a professional. I was doing the best I knew how, but he showed me how to work with a movie star/professional actor. He was teaching, yet not letting me know it, until I discovered it for myself years later.

"I remember his kindness to all around him, his incredible control over an audience, and his ability to recreate a scene exactly night after night. In the scene where he is about to drink the poisoned wine and Teddy charges loudly up the stairs, he would flip the glass over his shoulder into the corner, hitting an 18-inch square of carpet, so the glass would not break. He never missed and the glass never broke. I have that glass."

Further evidence of how much the Karloffs meant to the people of Anchorage was a letter from Don Gretzer, president of the theater workshop, to Actors' Equity representative Ed Russell in Hollywood. Written shortly after the run, it read in part, "Mr. Karloff most generously donated his percentage of the profits to the general funds of the Theatre Workshop. Mr. Karloff's generosity went so far as to assume the obligation of paying the agent's percentage without drawing from the percentage which was due him from the play production. We would like to have discussed this further with him in an effort to dissuade him from such further generosity and turn over to him at least the amount of the agent's commission. However, Mr. Karloff did not permit further mention of the subject. So much for the strictly business aspect of this letter.

"We would like you people to know of the great good which Mr. Karloff has done for the theater movement here in Anchorage. The wonderful personalities of Mr. and Mrs. Karloff, their understanding of people, and their wish to help us resulted not only in great admiration and respect for professional artists, but heightened community respect for local players which we may have had to strive for over a period of many years.

"It is difficult to say exactly how we feel about Mr. Karloff and his gracious wife. Superlatives can never tell the story of their effect upon our community and upon the future of, theater here. Statistically, *Arsenic and Old Lace* drew the largest crowd ever to attend any performance of any kind of show in the history of the territory. But statistics can never say as much about the Karloffs as the lump in our throats at their departure."

On April 7, from his home in London, Karloff wrote a letter expressing his gratitude to Brink. "Alaska is lucky to have you. You wondered how I could come to such a conclusion, so I will tell you. I learned that with every cast member you did far more than direct. You carefully and sympathetically taught the inexperienced. You cared more for their feelings than any director I have worked with." Referring to Teresa Wright, whom Brink directed in *The Dark at the Top of the*

*Stairs*, Karloff said, "When I talk with Terry, I will tell her she need have no fear of being embarrassed. She will be thrilled. As you indicated, you will be able to support her with professional quality talent right there in Anchorage."

In continued correspondence with Brink, Karloff often referred to "our theater" and said he would "return every time I am able." In addition to *On Borrowed Time*, Brink also considered as possible vehicles for Karloff *Goodbye, Mr. Chips*, *The Hunchback of Notre Dame*, and *Richard III*. None of them came to pass.

In a letter he wrote to Brink from London on Nov. 22, 1960, Karloff elaborated on their hoped-for production of *On Borrowed Time*, which clearly displayed his superior knowledge and understanding of stagecraft. At one point he referred to the version of the play published in New York in 1938. He wrote: "It is always nicer of course to be able to use the full settings of the New York version, but I realize what difficulty they may well present, and the unit stage can be made to work perfectly well in conjunction with the longer version. The only real advantage of the three sets lies in the fact that Granny can die decently in her own bed instead of in her rocking chair in the living room and that one has more room in the garden and the living room playing area. If the unit set is used, the curtain can be lowered at the end of each scene as indicated in the N.Y. version and, as required, the living room or the garden, as the case may be, can be dimmed out or brought up by lights." Karloff then explained in detail some rearrangement of scenes and a slight edit in the play. He went on to say, "The advantage of this is that poor old Granny does not have to sit dead and holding her breath while a rather rambunctious comedy scene is played under her nose in the garden. Also the closer her death is to the curtain, the more effective it is.

"As the living room only figures once in the second act, is it possible, in the unit set, to shove it back a bit before and after use so as to give more room in the garden, which gets pretty full in the second act with people and the fence? All of the above, of course, are only for your consideration but I thought if I laid them before you now it might save you some time and work.

"Now I have another suggestion. Why don't you play Brink? I'm not making a stupid pun! I think you would be wonderful in it and it would be marvelous to play with you, so think it over."

In 1957, Karloff, still making movies such as *Frankenstein 1970*, in which he played a modern-day descendant of the original Baron, and *Voodoo Island*, had a rare brush with William Shakespeare. For TV's prestigious *Omnibus* series, he narrated a series of sketches dramatizing the Bard's boyhood, to which New York drama critic Walter Kerr contributed. Kerr told me, "The program, in its original format, was written by Alfred Harbage, one of my favorite commentators on Shakespearean theater. It was much too long, however, and I was asked to do a fast cutting on it--with some re-arranging and some link-up writing--which I did.

"My work with *Omnibus* was largely advisory, with occasional scriptwriting and reworking of troubled scripts. It was also one hell of a lot of fun, with some of the nicest people I ever knew, particularly Bob Saudek and Mary Ahern. As a result, I was rarely on the floor during production, unless I was there to catch a Bert Lahr rehearsal for fun, or to just say hello to Chris Plummer and Irene Worth. Most of the people I met in the Saudek offices during pre-production conferences, and that's where I did meet Mr. Karloff.

"He was a wonderfully amenable, social, charming fellow, and from what I later heard, there had rarely been a more admired, and liked, man while the show was in work. He established an easy atmosphere for the crew and everyone else, and I heard nothing but good about him.

"Much earlier, in 1949, my wife and I had done a revue called *Touch and Go,* and we had brought one of the performers along to New York after the original production at Catholic University in Washington. Naturally, this performer was nervous as hell, never having been on Broadway before. And, along about the third or fourth performance, there was a knock on his dressing room door. He opened it to find Boris Karloff standing there, and Karloff simply said, 'If there are many more coming up with talents like yours, we older people had better look to our laurels.' It's the gist of it and shows something about his kindness."

Toward the end of the year, Karloff was seen to good effect in *The Deadly Game,* a thriller written for TV's *Suspicion* which could have put him back on Broadway. Playwright James Yaffe adapted for the series a novelette by Friedrich Durrenmatt (*The Visit*), involving an American businessman, played by Gary Merrill, who finds shelter in a

Swiss mansion from a blizzard. There, he encounters a judge, prosecutor, defense lawyer, and a state executioner, all of them retired. After dinner, the salesman is invited to join his hosts in a parlor game in which they hold mock trials. Accepting the offer, he finds himself being made the defendant and subjected to constant questioning. Merrill's character becomes both angry and afraid, for he is being put on trial for murder, having brought on a fatal heart attack suffered by his boss, whose job the businessman wanted.

In the end, Merrill is driven to commit suicide, and when his widow unexpectedly arrives, she agrees to stay for dinner, and perhaps a parlor game to ease her grief. *Time* magazine called the show "urbane and eerie", with kudos for Yaffe's script and the cast which, with Karloff as the judge, also featured Joseph Wiseman, Harry Townes, and Ian Wolfe. Yaffe later adapted *The Deadly Game* for the stage, and said, "When we were casting the play for Broadway production, we offered Karloff the same part he had played in the TV show, but he turned it down. Instead, he offered to play the somewhat meatier role of the prosecutor, which Wiseman played. Our director thought Karloff was wrong for that role (so did I) and that ended it." Yaffe's play did open in New York in 1960, starring Pat Hingle in the role of the businessman and closed after 39 performances.

Karloff worked on two fairly good pictures, filmed back to back in England, *The Haunted Strangler* and *Corridors of Blood*. In the former, he played a criminologist who believed that a man suspected to be a notorious strangler was wrongly executed. Upon discovery of a scalpel, the missing murder weapon, he reverts to earlier behavior as the strangler in a Jekyll and Hyde manner. In fact, he was the original killer and had suffered amnesia after escaping from an institution. *Variety* commented, "Karloff masters both characters and comes off well in each", but said *The Haunted Strangler* was "mild horror". *The New York Times* criticized the film's "flat direction" and, in addition, said it "has little more life than a chestful of old Victorian costumes".

*Corridors of Blood* was a better production, although its American release was pushed back until 1963. Karloff was a surgeon who develops an early form of anesthesia and becomes addicted to it. With echoes of *The Body Snatcher,* he is taken in by some lowlifes who plan to sell bodies to hospitals and get Karloff to sign phony death certificates by keeping him under the influence.

Playing one of the heavies was Christopher Lee, who had reached stardom by the time the film was released, but during its shooting was still unknown and not yet acquainted with Karloff offscreen. They became both friends and neighbors. *Corridors of Blood* started off well, said the review in *The New York Times*, but became "a plodding, shuddersome exercise in blood and pain."

In his autobiography *Tall, Dark, and Gruesome*, Lee said Karloff had an ongoing joke about himself being ready for the scrap heap. He quoted Karloff as saying, "I'm only a feeble old wreck, it'th plain to thee. What am I here for? Jutht to thweep up the odd jobth left behind." Karloff added, "All I'm fit for ith to thweep up the lawnth at night when the thet is deserted, and the playerth have all gone home." At the wrap party after the film was completed, the crew gave him a broom as a present, which delighted him, Lee wrote.

With few decent film scripts coming along, Karloff kept on directing his energies toward television primarily, as well as the occasional stage work and many recordings, of which he made more than two dozen. After *Corridors of Blood* was completed, he didn't make a film again until 1962.

Just as he had begun the decade by playing characters created by Cervantes and Chekhov, Karloff began to end it by essaying one from his favorite author, Joseph Conrad. He was cast as the enigmatic Kurtz in "Heart of Darkness" for *Playhouse 90*. Adapting Conrad's work was Stewart Stern, whose screenplays included *Rebel Without A Cause* (1955), *The Rack* (1956), and *Rachel, Rachel* (1968). In a letter to Fred Coe and Robert Goldman, the show's producers, Stern expressed, if asked, his casting choices for Marlow, the protagonist, and Maria, the woman he loves. His first suggestion was Paul Newman and Joanne Woodward, or, among the names he mentioned, possibly Anthony Perkins and Julie Harris. For the director, he asked for either Robert Mulligan or Arthur Penn, whom Stern thought could vitalize the human relationships in "Heart of Darkness".

Roddy MacDowall and Inga Swenson were cast in the leads and Ron Winston took the director's chair. Other characters were played by Richard Haydn, Oscar Homolka, Eartha Kitt, and Cathleen Nesbitt. Of Karloff, MacDowall told me, "He was a great gentleman. A man functioning in those years, despite crippling pain from arthritis, with enormous grace and bravery. He was a very elegant man and I enjoyed acting with him; he was simple and honest and direct in his work.

"I have always enjoyed him in films very much and really felt deeply privileged both to work with him and be around him; there was some special aura around Boris Karloff." MacDowall, an accomplished photographer, included a picture he took of Karloff offstage then in *Double Exposure*, his 1966 book of celebrity portraits.

Stern told me his adaptation was "a night journey of the soul", using all the symbols of Africa, which had to do with the healing of Marlow, a man who had repressed his dark side. His journey was into himself, where Marlow met his own horror, and in so doing, emerged as a more complete human being. He said, "I was tremendously thrilled and relieved to know that Mr. Karloff wanted to play Kurtz and was almost dumbstruck with awe and shyness at the first reading. We arrived at CBS at the same instant. His wife had dropped him off and the elevators were, for some reason, broken, so we walked up the steps together, he with the *Manchester Guardian* tucked under his arm, and looking extremely proper in his suit and tie.

"He was somewhat frail, somewhat stooped, and had a very gentle handshake, and there was an enormous sadness about that face when it turned to you. Great beauty. His eyes were deep and brown and looked at you directly. He had an enormous capacity for allowing you to feel received and was keenly interested in who you were and what you had to say.

"It was an amazing group of people that *Playhouse 90* had collected, and the director had certainly never done material of this kind that required the kind of style this did, and the psychological understanding, and he was simply lost. It drove the actors frantic because they had no guidance, and I remember Roddy MacDowall one Sunday, calling me in desperation because he didn't know really how to deal with one of the major soliloquies Marlow had. I found him in the studio working his head off, but it was a catch as catch can kind of production. Fred Coe finally took over and half-directed it himself, and I semi-directed, and everyone else was directing themselves.

"But for all of that, I'll never forget one afternoon, all the actors had left, as far as we knew, and Ron Winston and the art director and I—I think the cameraman too—were sitting around the conference table in the rehearsal room, trying to find some unity of approach. It was one of those agonizing moments for a writer when no one seems to have the proper vision, except in this case, the art director, who understood it completely. Two hours after we thought the rehearsal had ended, I happened to turn, and noticed Boris in the corner, sitting very quietly reading the newspaper.

"I went over to him and said, 'Mr. Karloff, are you waiting for someone?' He said, 'No, no, no, no.' I said, 'Well, why are you still here?' He said, 'Because I haven't been officially dismissed.' There was no rancor in it, no resentment. He was simply doing his part as a professional actor, and until he was given his dismissal, his place was on the set, and I'll never forget that."

During production, the only genuine disagreement was whether Karloff, as Kurtz, should don a wig and a beard. At great cost, they were made for Karloff, who summoned Stern to the makeup room. Stern arrived to find the actor seated and staring at himself in the mirror, so he asked if anything was wrong. In a depressed state, Karloff said yes, adding that he was aware of how much had been spent on the wig and beard, but thought it made him look like Michelangelo's Moses. He asked if that wasn't slightly different from what Stern intended Kurtz to be.

Stern recalled, "It was said with such wryness and sweetness, and it was just intolerable that he should be decked out in such a thing, so I went to Ron Winston and told him we simply couldn't do it, and he agreed. He saw at once it was not proper either to hide Mr. Karloff under all that, or for the character of Kurtz, so it was flung away and Boris was tremendously relieved."

Outside the studio, where there was more tension behind the camera than in front of it, the situation was much more relaxed. Inga Swenson told me, "I remember we used to have lunch together—Boris, Roddy, Richard Haydn—outdoors at a sort of lunch stand. There were tables with umbrellas, and it was nice to get out of the studio.

"Once there was a dog tethered to one of the cars in the parking lot nearby. Boris sat and looked at him for a while, and then said, 'I think I must go and talk to this fellow.' He walked his Boris Karloff walk over to the dog, which was one of those big, sweet breeds, maybe a yellow Lab or something and the dog rolled over with pure love, while Boris bent over and stroked and talked to him. He was so fond of animals." Despite the best intentions of a talented cast and screenwriter, "Heart of Darkness" was a failure. It was difficult to stage, with three cameras moving back and forth, and actors jumping behind them, donning new costumes, and jumping back in. That, as well as rewriting up to the moment of broadcast, and last-minute instructions to the actors resulted in what *Variety* called "a mental shambles", while the *New York Times* called it "a numbing exercise in dramatic mumbo-jumbo without merit or reason."

One of Karloff's TV credits that year was his narration of "The Legend of Sleepy Hollow" for the children's series *Shirley Temple's Storybook*, hosted by the former child star. Ordinarily, she would narrate, but since she acted in that episode, which was live, Karloff filled in. Director Paul Bogart told me, "We were staying in the same hotel. He lived upstairs in the Chateau Marmont and I was a floor or two below him. He was wonderful when I brought my kids up to see him. He knew they were shaking when they met him.

"I used to drive him to work every day. I had rented a convertible, and would drive with the top down, with him sitting in the passenger seat, and when you stopped at a traffic light with him, you really created a confusion. That was great fun."

Live programs airing from Los Angeles at that time would be shown in New York, then taped for playback later on the West Coast, with no editing. Between those times, a party was held at the Beverly Hills Hotel, where anyone who wanted to could see the program, as Bogart told Karloff.

"I said to him, 'Are you going to watch the show on the air?' He looked very puzzled and said, 'I don't understand what you mean.' So I explained that it had been taped, and he could sit down and watch himself doing what he had just done. He looked astonished, and said, 'Oh, *no*, dear boy. That's rather like a dog returning to his own vomit.' Which I thought was a very colorful way of expressing it."

Karloff's reaction to seeing his own work was fairly common. While making movies, he would never watch the rushes of the day's shooting. He preferred to wait a while to see the final product and watch it from a more critical perspective.

That same year, Karloff was excellent in a strong *Studio One* drama, "The Shadow of a Genius", directed by Ralph Nelson, with whom he had acted several years before on the same series. His role was that of a Nobel Prize-winning scientist who somewhat dismisses receiving the honor and subsequent publicity. His wife was played by, in a rare television appearance, theater veteran Eva LeGallienne. Nelson told me, "It was refreshing for him to occasionally play something like 'Shadow of a Genius' in which he played a man of high intelligence. He was a gentle, quiet, and unassuming man; rather given to the portrait of the English country gentleman, dressed in tweeds. His relationships with the cast and crew and myself were always correct and proper and warm.

"There were script problems as we began rehearsals. Normally, a director does not involve the actors in the resolution of these problems. However, Mr. Karloff was a man of rare intelligence and knowledge about the theatre, and he was very helpful in making sound suggestions." *Variety* said, "LeGallienne and Karloff turned in highly effective performances to make 'Shadow of A Genius' an emotion-packed hour of dramatics, one of the best of 'Studio One' since the series moved to the Coast."

The Karloffs made a change in their lifestyle in 1959 by moving permanently to England. They continued to travel wherever Karloff's work took him, but it was in his homeland that he lived out his last decade, having left it to become an actor a half-century before.

# Photos

The young William Henry Pratt.

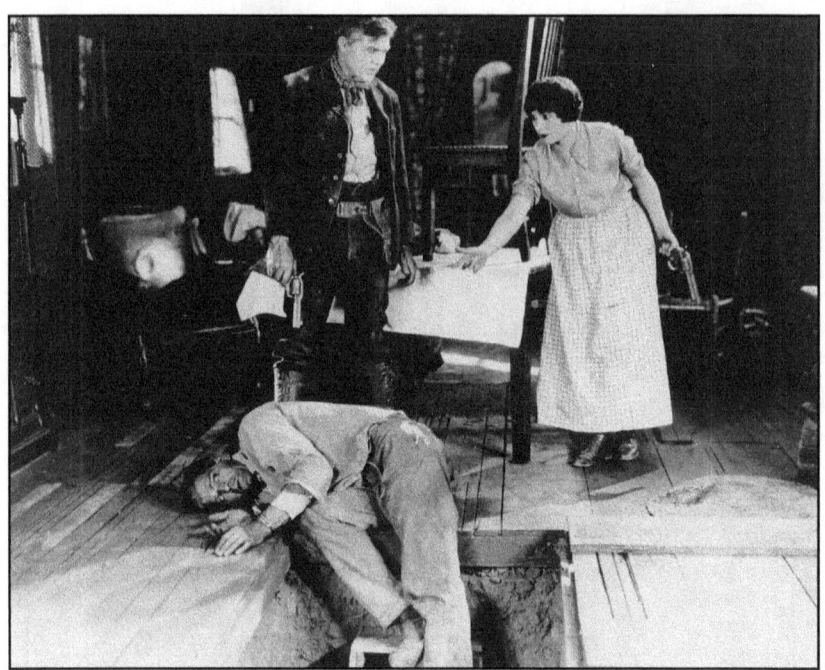
*The Prairie Wife* (1925)

*Parisian Nights* (1925)

*Lady Robin Hood* (1925)

*The Bells* (1926)

*Valencia* (1926)

*The Love Mart* (1927)

*The Criminal Code* (1931)

*Frankenstein* (1931) with Colin Clive.

James Whale, the director of *Frankenstein*.

Karloff and his wife Dorothy at leisure.

*The Old Dark House* (1932) with Gloria Stuart and Lillian Bond.

*The Mask of Fu Manchu* (1932) with Myrna Loy.

With Bela Lugosi in *The Black Cat* (1934), their first film together.

*The House of Rothschild* (1934) with George Arliss.

*The Bride of Frankenstein* (1935) with Ernest Thesiger.

*The Man Who Lived Again* (1936) with Frank Cellier.

Mercedes McCambridge and Karloff on radio's *Lights Out* in 1938.

With his daughter Sara Jane, born in 1938.

Boris and Dorothy Karloff.

Checking the script while filming *Tower of London* (1939).

*The Man They Couldn't Hang* (1939) with Lorna Gray.

Karloff enjoying himself with C. Aubrey Smith.

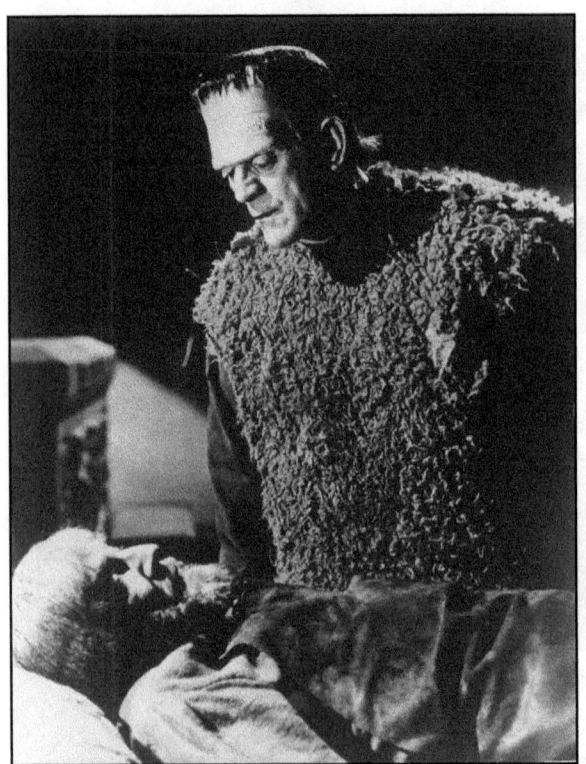

*Son of Frankenstein* (1939) with Bela Lugosi.

With child actor Larry Simms during production of *The Man with Nine Lives* (1940).

His Broadway debut in *Arsenic and Old Lace* (1941) with Jean Adair and Josephine Hull.

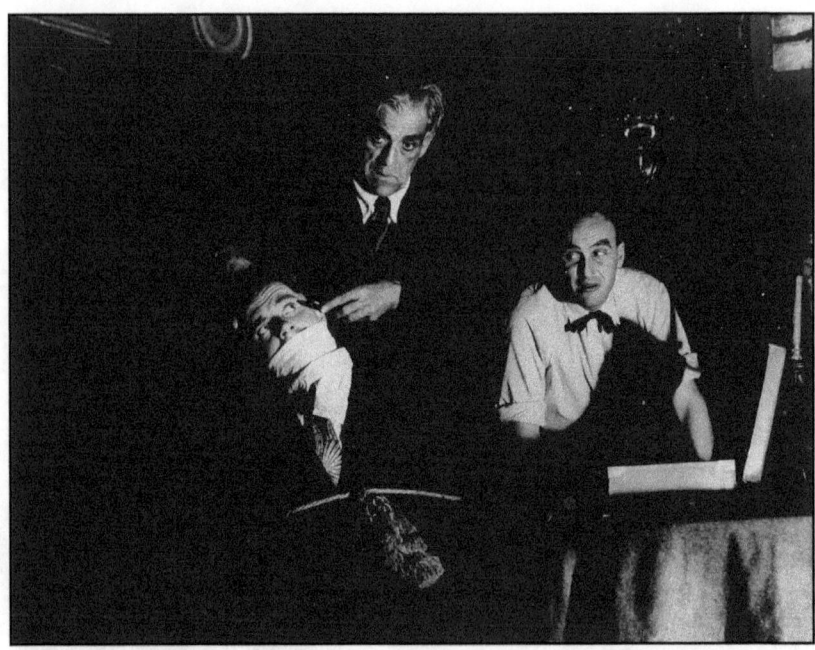

In character for an Army production of *Arsenic and Old Lace* with Werner Klemperer as Dr, Einstein.

Director George Schaefer and Karloff in Hawaii during World War II.

*The Body Snatcher* (1945) with Henry Daniell.

Karloff showing his lighter side while filming *Bedlam* (1946).

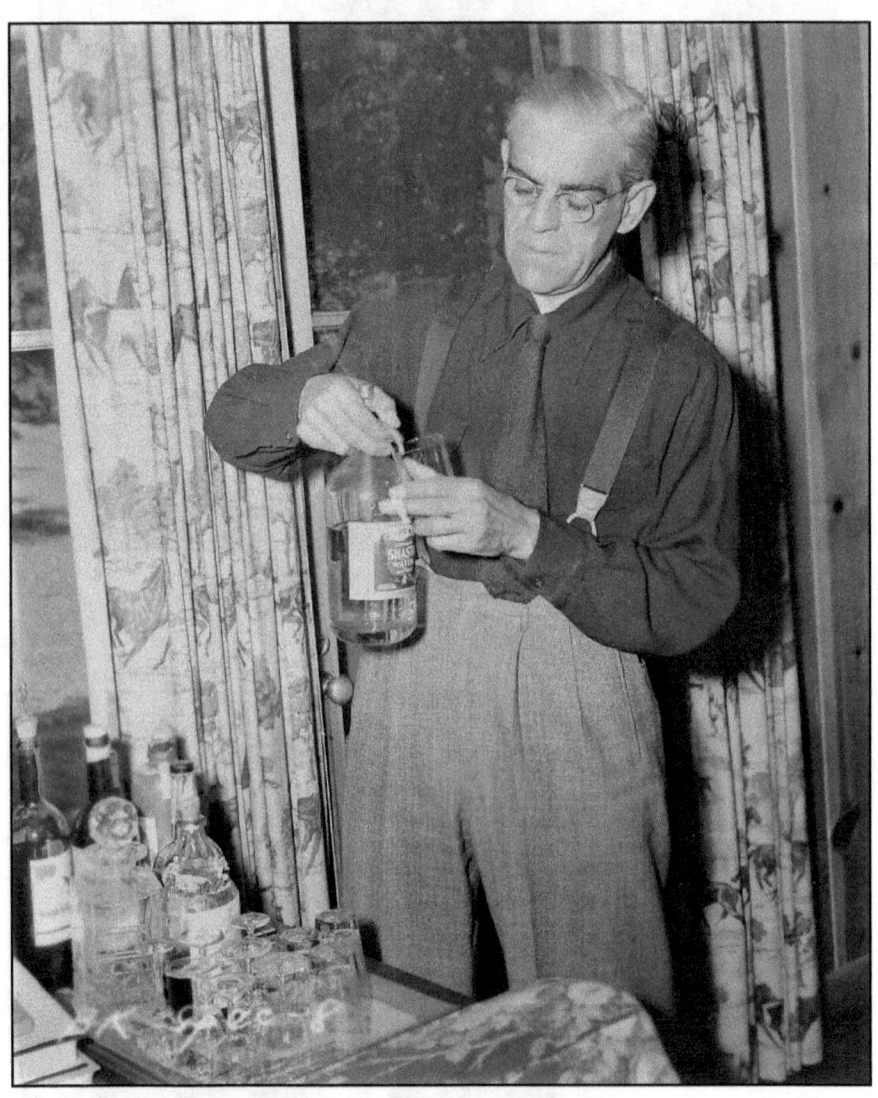
At home.

In the short-lived *The Linden Tree* on Broadway in 1948.

*The Shop at Sly Corner* (1949) with Ethel Griffies on Broadway.

Photos • 101

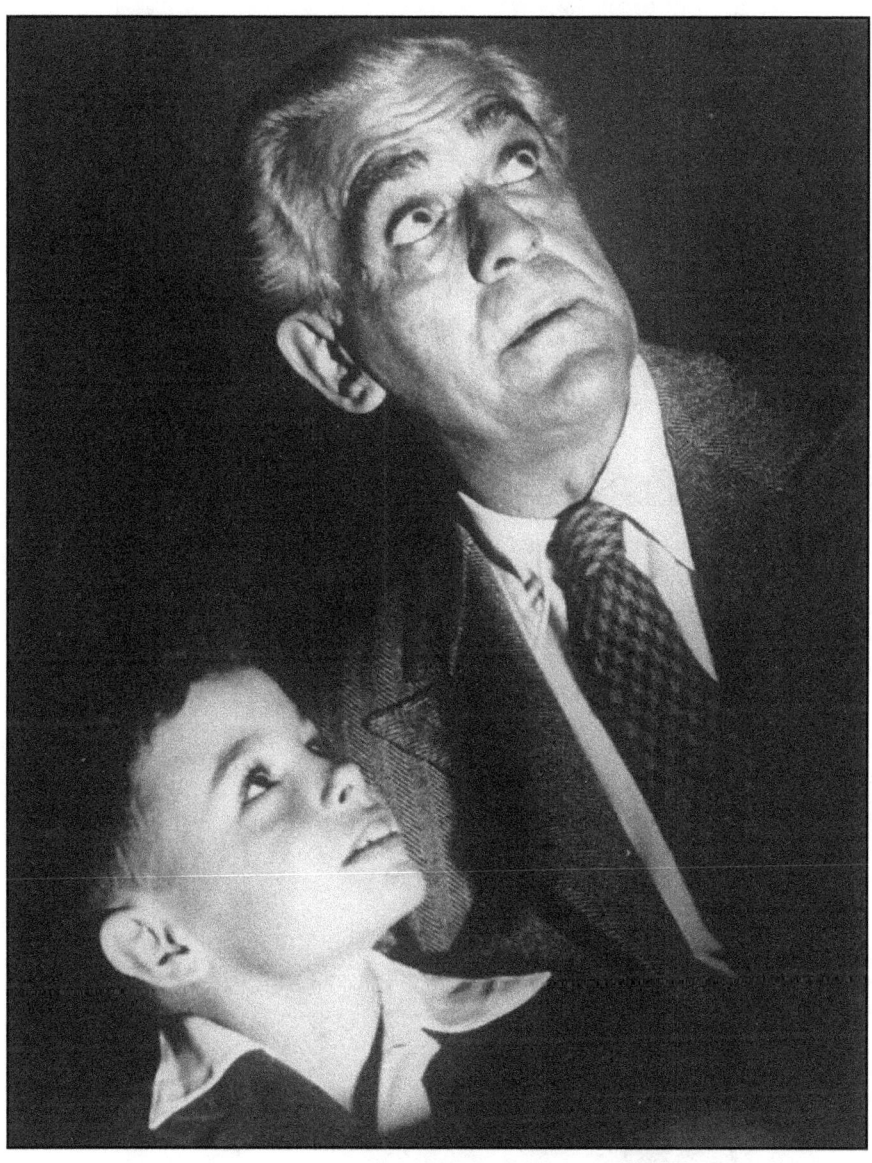

A promotional shot for *On Borrowed Time* (1950) in Atlanta.

The set for *On Borrowed Time* at Atlanta's Penthouse Theatre.

As Captain Hook in Broadway's *Peter Pan* (1950) with David Kurlan.

With his fellow cast in 1951 for radio's *Stars on Parade*.
On the far left is actor Ross Martin.

At London's Heathrow Airport in 1953 with his wife Evelyn.

In the title role as *Colonel March of Scotland Yard*, a British TV series.

As Mr. Mycroft in "The Sting of Death" for TV's *Elgin Hour* (1955).

Rehearsing with Hermoine Gingold for *Night of a 100 Stars*, a fundraiser in London.

Karloff and Susan Strasberg when they were appearing on television in 1955.

Karloff and Susan Strasberg in "Mr. Blue Ocean" on *General Electric Theatre*.

With Julie Harris in the Broadway success *The Lark* (1955). Both received Tony Award nominations.

With director George Schaefer while they were filming the TV version of *The Lark* (1957).

The Karloffs in Anchorage, Alaska in 1957 with Frank Brink, who directed him in a local production of *Arsenic and Old Lace*.

In "The Shadow of a Genius" for TV's *Studio One* (1958) with Skip Homeier and Eva LeGallienne.

With Betty White in 1958 when he appeared on her TV show.

*The Haunted Strangler* (1958).

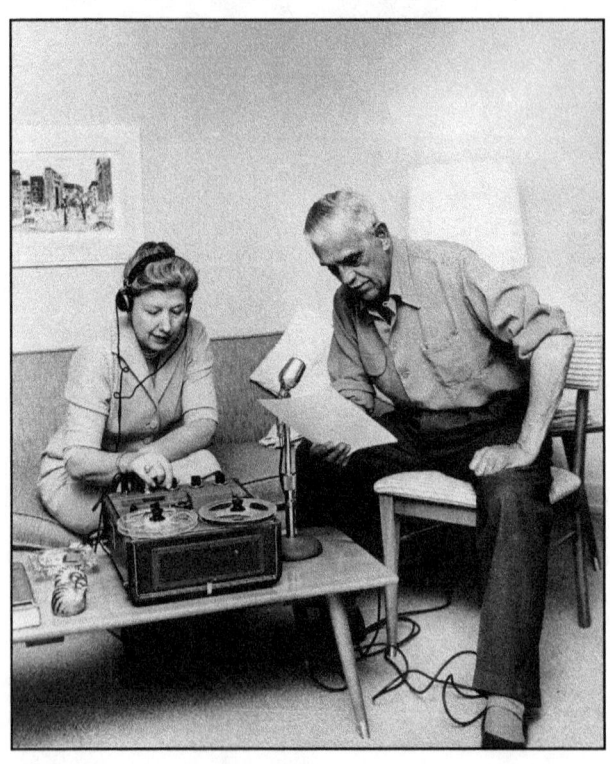

A recording session with Evelyn.

The Karloffs in Puerto Rico with Gypsy Rose Lee and festival director Barry Yellen at the opening night party for the San Juan Drama Festival (1960).

With Patricia Medina in "The Premature Burial" on *Thriller* in 1961.

An offscreen portrait from 1961.

"Arsenic and Old Lace" (1962) on *Hallmark Hall of Fame*.
L-R: Mildred Natwick, George Voskovec, Dorothy Stickney,
Karloff, Tony Randall, and Tom Bosley.

With Peter Lorre while promoting *The Raven* (1963).

*The Terror* (1963) with Jack Nicholson.

*Black Sabbath* (1964).

Karloff in drag with Bernard Fox on *The Girl from U.N.C.L.E.* (1966).

Bill Cosby, Karloff, and Robert Culp in *I Spy* (1967).

*The Sorcerers* (1967) with Catherine Lacey.

Director Peter Bogdanovich and Karloff filming *Targets* (1968).

The Karloffs on the set of *Targets*.

Karloff and producer Tony Tenser while making *The Crimson Cult* (1970).

With Gene Barry on *The Name of the Game* (1968). Karloff's final work on film.

# The Last Decade

**IN 1959,** TV producer Hubbell Robinson was scouting around for a new series to air on NBC, the network of which he had once been president. When he left that position, NBC settled his contract by giving him two hours of prime time to fill. One would be *87th Precinct*, based on the Ed McBain novels. Robinson's concept for the other was, as he put it, "the *Studio One* of mystery". He wanted the series, known as *Thriller*, to be an anthology, with different casts and stories each week that would draw upon the works of writers such as Edgar Allan Poe and Cornell Woolrich. To help bring this about, Robinson recruited Fletcher Markle, an alumnus of *Studio One*, as executive producer, and writers Maxwell Shane and James Cavanagh, the latter as story editor. The host was Boris Karloff, who agreed to the project wholeheartedly, under the terms that he could perform in the series, as well. Robinson told me, "When I first discussed the series with David Levy, then vice president in charge of programming for NBC, Boris was my recommendation, with which he was in total agreement. To the best of my recollection, no one else was ever considered." Karloff later told an interviewer for *TV Guide*, "I'm quite delighted with the whole thing."

Once *Thriller* went on the air in September of 1960, those involved could not seem to reach a consensus on the type of story material the show required. As Fletcher Markle informed me, "We put together a wonderful pilot, directed by Arthur Hiller, pre-*Love Story*, who also directed at least two more of the early shows, which sold the series in a matter of days. I wrote the intros for Boris initially, and planned the back-projection patterns, but once we were into production on a series basis, a bizarre conflict developed between the then-head of the studio and myself. They had to do with quality versus quantity, an ancient TV battleground, and in this instance I was happy to lay down my lance."

At first, reaction to *Thriller* was mixed. The first installment, "The Twisted Image", written by James Cavanagh, was, said the *Los Angeles Times*, "slightly out of focus, but there was still enough flesh-crawling qualities to keep one fascinated", while *Variety* said "Cavanagh seemed more anxious to make his script a heart-stopper than an engrossing, plausible play. He succeeded in neither."

What the creative personnel couldn't agree on was whether *Thriller* would be a horror or suspense program, or a combination of both. Within weeks of the premiere, reports appeared in *Variety* saying that Allstate, one of the sponsors, found some of the content objectionable, especially scenes of an axe murder and a strangulation. The company, said the trade paper, had believed *Thriller* would rank with such series as *Alfred Hitchcock Presents* and *The Twilight Zone*.

By October, *Thriller* focused primarily on horror stories. According to Robinson, "the reason we dropped our original policy on story material was simply we could not get enough of it to satisfy our weekly requirements." Douglas Benton, who soon became associate producer, told me, "After they ran the first six shows, NBC called Universal and said they were going to cancel because they were getting the same story week after week, and they weren't pleased with production values. Lew Wasserman, who even then was chief executive officer at MCA, sat down and looked at all six hours in one running. The next morning, he had the show taken away from Fletcher Markle and assigned it to William Frye, who for many years was producer of the filmed segments of the *General Electric Theater*."

Before Frye assumed Markle's duties, some criticism of the show fell on its host. A *TV Guide* article a few months later said "some people" believed Karloff was a poor host and seemed ill-suited for the job, as opposed to Alfred Hitchcock who hosted his own show. This reaction appears to have been unjustified. William Frye told me, "Boris was always considered a first-rate host and, when after two years the series was discontinued, we received thousands of letters asking why, and praising Boris." Hubbell Robinson concurred: "The network thought Mr. Karloff was an ideal and excellent host". He added (responding to the article's statement that "most impartial observers agree Karloff is not ideally suited for the role"), "I never heard anybody make any remark of that sort whatsoever. He enjoyed it and I would say he was one of the show's great strengths."

Frye was a personal friend of the Karloffs, and once he took over, *Thriller* improved. Noted mystery and fantasy writers Charles Beaumont, Robert Bloch, and Cornell Woolrich contributed scripts, and among the directors were Paul Henreid, Ida Lupino, and Ray Milland. Douglas Benton remembered, "I was amazed at how much energy Karloff had. He had a tremendous sense of humor and was very happy that Bill had been put on the show and we already had begun to work out a new format. He was very enthusiastic about this. He watched the show on the air and we got criticism. Some. Not as much as you'd think, because he seemed to like everything we did, and was very desirous of doing as many of the stories as he could himself.

"He particularly liked doing the little introductions. They were little playlets in themselves roughly, I suppose, copied after the Hitchcock introductions. I always thought ours were better produced. Hitchcock's might have been a bit cleverer."

A frequent writer for *Thriller* was Donald Sanford, brought on for a rewrite when Frye came aboard. Sanford often adapted stories from *Ellery Queen's Mystery Magazine* and *Weird Tales,* and told me, "Frye was a fabulous guy because he liked his writers to come into the first cast reading of a script, which is unusual in this business. Generally, they want to get rid of the writer as soon as they can. The director doesn't want the writer there, but Frye insisted writers be there, and he would not allow the directors to change one damn line unless he approved of it. I had a chance to work with Boris because I was at the readings of the scripts I wrote for him.

"Boris would come in letter perfect. He gave his reading with exactly the reading he would give in front of the cameras. Without looking at the script. He could read a double-jointed or triple-jointed line with no problems at all. By that I mean a complex sentence that has a lot of information in it. A lot of actors can't do that. They don't know how to read it, and particularly in Boris' openings, where he had to set up the premise, you had to squeeze in as much information as you could in a very few lines.

"When I write dialogue for a normal actor, I don't do that. I don't give them a compound sentence, because dialogue direction, I came out of radio originally, is dreadful, and the actors just don't learn how to read lines. Give 'em a lot of information in a line and you don't get it. It doesn't come out unless you have a very good actor. Boris was a consummate expert."

Karloff would appear in five episodes, the first being "The Prediction" about a nightclub mentalist who finds he can actually predict the future. Douglas Benton said to me, "I'll never forget one night on the back lot at Universal. John Brahm, really an expert in the horror genre, was directing Mr. Karloff. The scene was for him to be killed, he fell in the gutter, and this great wash of dirty water swept over him. As a matter of fact, it swept through him. He was lying on an incline with his head down, and the water ran up his pants leg, through his clothes, and came out his collar. So Mr. Brahm instructed Mr. Karloff where he wanted to fall, and said, 'Then we'll put in the double and run the water.' Boris looked at John, offended, and said, 'Oh, no, I wouldn't allow anybody else to do that. That water was meant for me.'

"And, by golly, he laid down and they made three takes, and every time he was drenched. I think that was the time I said, 'Jesus, Boris, you're at a time in your life and on a plateau in this business that you don't have to do that sort of thing.' 'Have to?', he says. 'I want to.' Then he went into his speech about how marvelous it was to make a good living doing what you enjoyed so much.

"I think, all in all, the shows that John Brahm made were probably the best, although every once in a while, Ida Lupino would make a beauty. John might make a great one and then a bad one. Ida, I don't think she really took it seriously, although she did take her directing seriously. She was a great favorite of Boris', as both used to tell slightly off-color English stories with a great deal of relish. He really would laugh when he was amused, and she was one of the best storytellers I ever heard in my life." Lupino directed Karloff and Phyllis Thaxter in "The Last of the Sommervilles" for the series, and Miss Thaxter told me she was "a great director."

One of Benton's memories of Karloff away from the studio was the actor's bartending skill. He said, "He made the most potent martini out of Bombay gin that anyone ever concocted. Several occasions I'd gotten flat-out roaring drunk, sitting there watching him matching me drink for drink, and never even getting a glow. He was amazing."

After its shaky beginning, *Thriller* drew enough viewers to last a full season, and was picked up for another. Making guest appearances were some of Karloff's co-stars from his films such as John Carradine and Henry Daniell. It was on the series that Karloff met and became friends with Robert Bloch, who wrote several episodes, in addition to the novel *Psycho*, among his many books, short stories, and film and TV scripts. Bloch told me, "He was a fine and intelligent actor—and never, except in *The Lark*—did he really get much opportunity to demonstrate his capability for serious drama. He told me this was his best role.

"What he probably would have liked was to have starred in a play for London's West End, but, he told me ruefully, he was too old for such a grind. He and Evie visited us, and we were at the flat and the summer cottage in England. And we still miss him!" Evelyn Karloff confirmed to me that her husband was offered a run in London of *Arsenic and Old Lace*, but was too far along in years to handle it. She added, "Especially all that jumping in and out of the window seat!"

Another of Karloff's acting assignments on *Thriller* was in "The Premature Burial", based on the Poe story. Douglas Heyes, whose other directorial credits included some of the best-remembered shows of *The Twilight Zone*, recalled the impression Karloff made upon him: "One thing I noticed, having been brought up to think of him as the Monster or in some hideous make-up, was that he was a strikingly handsome man, even at the age he'd attained when I was with him. He had style, elegance, and wonderful soulful eyes, which illuminated all his characters and set them apart from the over-gruesome ghouls you see today.

"I had a sequence in which his character had to climb a flight of stairs to a balcony, and I was going up with him on a crane. We had some truly incpt guys working the crane, and though Boris did his part of the scene perfectly every time, the camera kept blowing the shot due to technical difficulties, a euphemism for screwing up. Boris' legs were killing him, but he went up and down that long staircase again and again, never once complaining or blaming anyone until, at last, we got it right. His greatest lamentation was to murmur on occasion with a gentle sigh, 'My, my, this business does eat into your day!'"

*Thriller* perhaps unevitably, was compared with *Alfred Hitchcock Presents*. Not only were the formats alike, but they were both on NBC, and at one time, aired on the same night, back to back. After its second year, *Thriller* was considered very successful, but the network had run out its commitment to Hubbell Robinson and canceled it. There may have been more to it than that. *Thriller* was the first hour-long series of that type and *Alfred Hitchcock Presents* was a half-hour. When he chose to expand his show, *Thriller* was no longer available.

Douglas Benton told me, "Here at the studio, we felt that some politics was involved. Hitchcock was a very, very close friend of Lew Wasserman, the head man. He wanted to go to an hour and couldn't as long as Boris was holding forth in another hour show.

"The ratings on *Thriller*, although they'd be marvelous today, averaged about a twenty-eight, twenty-nine share, and that was marginal in those days. If you didn't have a 30 share, chances are you wouldn't be renewed, and the fact that we were marginal, and Hitch wanted to go to an hour, I think, were factors in the cancellation." Evelyn Karloff told me decades later, "I have no doubt Hitch was involved."

In the time since, *Thriller* has been in and out of syndication, and enjoyed something of a rebirth, to the pleasure of horror fans then and now. Among that legion is author Stephen King, who appreciated the show for a number of reasons. One of them being its frequent source material of mystery and pulp magazines. In *Danse Macabre* (1981), his entertaining overview of horror in popular culture, King termed *Thriller* "probably the best horror series ever put on TV."

Between work on *Thriller*, Karloff, at seventy-two, continued to work on the stage. In January of 1960, he went to Puerto Rico to do *Arsenic and Old Lace* at the San Juan Drama Festival. Festival director Barry Yellen told me, "Boris and Evie were wonderful friends! Boris was one of the nicest people I have ever met. He never had a nasty word to say about anyone. Their apartment building in New York, the Dakota, was the perfect building for Boris to live in. The Gothic architecture fitted him perfectly. It was interesting to walk on the street with him. Children would stop and point at him and say, "There's Frankenstein'. He did other things, but that was the thing that always stood out in people's minds. He wasn't happy about that, but he never complained. He was proud of the story readings he did for children.

"Their favorite restaurant in New York was a tiny, unpretentious, mom and pop operation across from the old Madison Square Garden. We enjoyed many excellent dinners there with them. Pop was a former chef at '21' and he did the cooking. Mom was the waitress. If they had a fight, the restaurant closed early."

Boris returned to the festival a year later to star in *On Borrowed Time*. Yellen told me, "It was opening night and Tom Helmore had just arrived to begin rehearsals of *Witness for the Prosecution*, in which he co-starred with Farley Granger. I invited him to the party, and when he arrived I took him over and introduced him to Boris and Evie. She looked at me and said, 'I already know him. He's my ex-husband!' For me, a twenty-five year-old, that was a very embarrassing moment."

Two months later, Karloff was at the Wharf Theater and Opera House in Monterey, Calif, for what would be his last stage appearance. It was again in *On Borrowed Time*, and opening night on March 17, 1961 was met with warm audience reaction. In its review, the *Monterey Peninsula Herald* said, "Boris Karloff proved beyond a doubt that the fearsome monsters with which he has so long been associated have indeed been purely masquerades. As Gramps, he came clearly in focus with every lovable trait of a little boy's cherished companion. His militant forthrightness, his stubbornness, even his colorful profanities were endearing. He created an unforgettable personage last night with never a suggestion of 'acting.'" The entire cast and production of the week-long run received equal praise.

As *Thriller* was winding down its last season, Karloff played Jonathan Brewster one final time in *Arsenic and Old Lace* on *Hallmark Hall of Fame* for his friend George Schaefer. Playing the Brewster sisters were Karloff's friends Mildred Natwick and Dorothy Stickney, in addition to Tony Randall as Mortimer and Tom Bosley as Teddy. Of the three TV versions Karloff did, Schaefer's was the least appreciated by critics, though the Associated Press called it "very funny, quite mad, and a real treat", and while it is entertaining, Schaefer was not entirely pleased with it. He did point out to me, "Boris was magnificent". Years later, he wrote that he wished he had filmed it instead before a live audience.

Tom Bosley told me, "Boris was one of the kindest and gentlest persons I have ever known. We spent about three weeks together, and since he lived across the street from me in New York, I would drive him and Tony to rehearsal each day at the studio in Brooklyn.

"He was an extremely literate person who never spent too much time telling of his career, as so many senior actors have a tendency to do. He loved life and was extremely charitable, as I learned later that he made donations to various charities all the time."

Tony Randall told me how Karloff was, in his words, "very clearheaded about things, saw things as they were. For instance, someone said how brave of Truman to drop the atomic bomb, and Boris said, 'The Japanese were ready to sue for peace before that.'"

Worth noting that same year (1962) was the October 26 episode of TV's *Route 66*, as it gave Karloff the opportunity to appear once more, if fleetingly, as the Frankenstein monster. "Lizard's Leg and Owlet's Wing", was written by Stirling Silliphant, a frequent contributor to the series and who won an Academy Award for adapting *In the Heat of the Night* (1967). The episode featured Karloff, Lon Chaney Jr., and Peter Lorre, as themselves, meeting to decide whether to produce a series of horror films, if such films still had the power to scare people. Shot at a motel near Chicago's O'Hare Airport, the underwritten show did not require its guest stars to do very much. It took just forty-five minutes to make Karloff up as the Monster by using mostly prefabricated appliances. George Maharis, one of the show's two leads, told me, "Peter was very vocal and could swear up a storm, Boris was very English and proper, and Lon was quiet."

Karloff never referred to *Route 66* as one of his appearances as the Monster, wisely thinking of only the Universal pictures. His reasons for going to the Windy City were twofold. He also went to see Tom Helmore who was onstage there in the road company of *Mary, Mary*. As he told the *Los Angeles Times*, "This way I had an opportunity to visit with him and get paid for it, too."

With the demise of *Thriller*, Karloff returned to the movies after a four-year hiatus. By this time, American-International Pictures had launched a successful series of Edgar Allan Poe adaptations, many of which starred Vincent Price. These flashy, Technicolor pictures were directed mostly by Roger Corman, who was given the combined talents of Price, Karloff, and Peter Lorre, and decided for a change of pace to make a flat-out comedy inspired by Poe's *The Raven*. Given that the source material was simply a poem, screenwriter Richard Matheson devised a story in which Price and Lorre played 16th-century magicians pitted against Karloff, a rival magician.

With all three stars playing tongue-in-cheek and having a ball, *The Raven* was highlighted by its visual effects and broad to dry humor. In a supporting part as Lorre's son was a young Jack Nicholson, one of many who started out working for Corman, prior to reaching success in the late Sixties and early Seventies. Among those under Corman's tutelage were actors Bruce Dern and Ed Nelson and directors Francis Ford Coppola, Jonathan Demme, Martin Scorsese, and Robert Towne.

Although Corman was not a director who worked much with actors, *The Raven* was a pleasure for both its stars and for audiences, who made it a box-office hit in 1963. One thing the leads had in common was the the same agent, Arthur Kennard, who had represented Price at first. Kennard told me, "When I acquired Vincent, he said to me, 'You should have Boris Karloff.' Here I am, just a fledgling agent at the time. I agreed with him. With that, he called and told Boris that he had this hotshot agent, and that when Boris comes to the United States next time, he should meet with me. Boris agreed, and during the interim, much talk back and forth between Vincent and Boris.

"We met with Boris. He said, 'Vincent tells me you're a hotshot, Arthur' and I agreed. Then both of them got hold of Peter. We met in the Beverly Hills Health Club because that's where Peter was taking a sauna. That was quite a picture to see Vincent and Boris and myself and Peter in a sheet. And that's how I got Peter. That whole part of my life was infected with humor. The dialogue between these people was rapier wit and great enjoyment."

Of Karloff, Kennard went on to say, "He had the driest humor of anybody I've ever met. So did Peter. One night, we were all sitting around, and a reporter said, 'How was it when the Nazis came into Vienna, Peter?' Peter was doing theater in Vienna just before the war, and he said, 'Well, when Hitler, God rest his soul, came into the thing, etc.'. He just threw out the 'God rest his soul', nobody heard it until a minute went by, and then everybody broke out laughing."

Corman, for the most part, let his cast do as they pleased, so when Karloff, a carefully prepared and by-the-script performer, had to deal with Lorre's light-hearted, improvisational approach, Price acted as a buffer between them. Price said later that the three of them conceived jokes and bits of business which they added to the film. The reviews of *The Raven* were somewhat mixed, between those which said it was a silly waste of talent, and others that termed it sheer escapist fun. *The New York Times*' Bosley Crowther wrote it off as "comic-book nonsense" and "strictly a picture for the kiddies and the bird-brained, quoth the critic". *Variety*, on the other hand, labeled it "a cornpop of considerable comedic dimensions" and said the cast "played straight for greater comedy value, sparked by sometimes ridiculous lines and situations."

American-International Pictures was founded by Samuel Z. Arkoff and James H. Nicholson. When they released *The Raven* in February of 1963, Arthur Kennard discovered the sly humor and wickedness his clients displayed could take form in a manner he didn't expect. He told me, "When we worked for Sam Arkoff and AIP, they came up with an idea to have a personal appearance tour of Boris and Peter. It was the RKO movie houses in and around New York. We flew to New York--Boris, Peter, and myself--and stayed at the Hampshire House. The office sent me along with them to keep things in order, and I knew how difficult it was for Boris to get on and off the bus and walk into the theater. It was the dead of winter.

"When we got to the Hampshire House, there was a young lady, Rica Moore by name, who I was pursuing. Eventually married her. We were touring around Brooklyn and so on, and there was a blizzard one day, and I feigned illness. I said to Boris, 'My throat is killing me.' and said to Peter, 'Oh, I can't go the rest of the day.' The snow was piling up and they both looked at me and smiled and said, 'Well, why don't you go back to the hotel?' That was the whole thing, because I had arranged to meet with Rica at the hotel at 5:00. 1 left the bus, and twenty-three of New York's finest that were assigned to get us in and out of the theaters, because we were mobbed by fans all the time. They'd grab your hand and rip the cufflinks off your shirt.

"I met with the young lady at the hotel, all strictly above board. She and I were sitting in the living room of this gorgeous suite, balcony and everything. We were in front of the fireplace, having a drink. The door burst open, and in came twenty-three cops and Boris and Peter. They knew I had a date. I never told them, but they figured it out. I could hear Boris and Peter shoveling all the police into the bedrooms, so I could get Rica out of the place to avoid any embarrassment. We were fully clothed and all that, but it looked bad because her galoshes were sitting in the vestibule when they came in. Fur top galoshes, very feminine. Something I wouldn't wear.

"When Rica left, Boris became the judge, the jury was the policemen, Peter was the prosecuting attorney, and they sat me in the middle of this big living room, surrounded by these policemen, and started to interrogate me. Boris would sit at the head in another chair and rap on the arm and say, 'You're out of order, you're out of order.' We had a kangaroo court and I'll always remember that as one of the highest memories of my life. All ad-lib, all fun. We spent a couple of hours doing the courtroom business, and took a recess when Boris rapped and said, 'We will recess for one hour.' At which point, they called down to the kitchen, had room service send up trays and trays at $80 a tray to feed the policemen. The blizzard had gotten so bad everybody couldn't leave, so you woke up in the morning with uniforms and guns and billy clubs strewn all over and police sleeping everywhere."

Having completed *The Raven*, Roger Corman had the grand, palatial sets, as well as Karloff, at his disposal, so he and screenwriters Leo Gordon and Jack Hill concocted a new picture titled *The Terror*. Karloff was used for two days of shooting opposite Jack Nicholson as a Napoleonic soldier drawn to Karloff's castle by a woman, played by Sandra Knight, who turns out to be Karloff's dead wife. Offscreen, Knight and Nicholson were married. Further explanation of the story would be futile. Over a period of months, the rest of the film was completed by four other people. The production ran out of money for union crews, and being a member of the Directors Guild, Corman couldn't direct non-union people. He asked four others, including his associate producer Francis Ford Coppola and assistant director Monte Hellman, who were non-union, if they wanted to direct for a day or two, and they did. Nicholson himself directed the last scene of the movie.

While *The Terror* in its finished form made almost no sense and Nicholson showed little sign of the actor he became, it proved to become another box-office winner. In addition, it gave Karloff a good deal of screen time and the opportunity to carry off lines such as "You think I'm mad, don't you?" Just a few years later, it factored into the final milestone of Karloff's career.

While Karloff enjoyed making *The Raven*, Roger Corman was not high on his list of favorite directors. According to Arthur Kennard, "Roger called one day and wanted Boris for a movie, and I explained to him it would have to be in a wheelchair. I looked at the script, and if you blinked, he wouldn't be in the movie. I called Roger back and said, 'You're going to offer him $50,000, $25,000', it was a nothing amount, 'to have Boris in the picture.' Simply because he wanted to put Boris above the title in whatever that film was.

"I said, 'You're cheating the audience. The part, you can phone it in.' I told this to Boris. He said, 'That would be naughty of Roger to do that.' I said, 'Boris, I think we should not do this picture.' He said, 'I absolutely agree, Arthur.' And we didn't do it, because Boris' scruples and, forgive me, my own scruples wouldn't allow Roger to cheat the audiences who would go to the picture, expecting to see Boris Karloff, and him make no more than a cameo role. I told that to Roger. I'll never forget Boris' comment. He said, 'Roger would rather steal a picture than make one.'"

As on radio and for occasional narration assignments, Karloff continued to use his mellifluous voice to its fullest by doing spoken word recordings. Most of them were produced and released by Caedmon Records, which had begun using numerous luminaries from show business and literature in 1952. From both sides of the Atlantic came performers the likes of Noel Coward, John Gielgud, Rex Harrison, Katharine Hepburn, Laurence Olivier, and Jessica Tandy, as well as William Faulkner, Edna St. Vincent Millay, Carl Sandburg, Gertrude Stein, and Tennessee Williams.

With a few exceptions, Karloff read works for children. Barbara Holdridge, co-founder and later president of Caedmon, told me, "It was his agent who first suggested him for our recording of *Mother Goose*, for which we had already chosen Celeste Holm and Cyril Ritchard. Dubious that the monster of film renown could not only read *Mother Goose*, but sing, we were crass enough to ask that he audition for us. He did so with not the least trace of irritation. On the contrary, he was totally obliging and charming, and so very good that we were convinced that he would be just what the production needed.

"And he was. We never had a better time than at those recording sessions. Celeste was hilariously adept with lascivious innuendoes and plays on words that were later cut out of the edited tape, and Boris was not only appreciative of her quips, but reciprocated with his own quiet humor, as Cyril did, too. I visited Boris' apartment several times, and was impressed by the love of antiques, and particularly of old, polished wood, that was shared by Boris and Evie. When I asked her about this, she confirmed that Boris was very partial to fine wood furnishings." Karloff's other releases included *Aesop's Fables*, *Cymbeline*, and *The Reluctant Dragon*. It was after hearing Karloff's recording of *The Jungle Book* that animated cartoon veteran Chuck Jones sought to have him narrate Dr. Seuss' *How the Grinch Stole Christmas* for CBS in 1966.

For some reason, the network resisted the choice of Karloff, but Jones was adamant and prevailed. The show became an annual broadcast and made Karloff known to millions of children at an early age, who otherwise might not have until they were older. It is Sara Karloff's favorite work of her father's, and she also favors his work in *Peter Pan*, *The Lark*, *The Raven* (Roger Corman's version), and *Targets*. Jones' persistence paid off in another way. The soundtrack album from *How the Grinch Stole Christmas* earned Karloff a Grammy Award for the year's best children's recording.

During the 60s, the Karloffs, already having an apartment in the Kensington section of London, bought a cottage called "Roundabout" in the village of Bramshott, East Hampshire. It got its name from the fact that three roads intersected, forming a triangle, and the cottage was located there. "Roundabout" was the last place the Karloffs lived in, and after his death, Evelyn continued living there, and at the London apartment, until her death in 1993.

Kristin Helmore told me, "I don't think we ever saw Boris at 'Roundabout', although I might have because I was in school in England in those days. Somebody was having tea in the garden with them, and a hearse went by on the road. When you were sitting in the garden, you could just see the tops of cars. It was clear that it was a funeral procession going by. There was a church just up the lane, so they were on their way to the church. The hearse goes by, and Boris kind of waves his hand and says, 'Won't be a minute!'"

While Miss Helmore was a student, still in her teens, she often visited the Karloffs, and when she did, "Boris would slip me a ten-pound note or something. Stuff like that, so he was very sweet and generous." She recalled Evelyn's great sense of style and decorating. In both residences, she said there was a lot of honey-colored wood. In her words, "It's something to remember because I noticed this all the time. People of that generation who were born in the Edwardian period or just when the Victorian style was ending. They rejected Victorian things. In furnishings and in decoration and style, people like Boris and Evie and my parents looked ahead. They liked modern things. Today, we look back and we love chintz and dark wood and antiques, and they didn't. That was not their style, because they actually remembered their childhood in Edwardian and Victorian houses in England, which they didn't like." Her father Tom Helmore, she said, wanted sunny, bright California-style colors and, in the London apartment, Evelyn had rusty, natural, autumn-like hues.

At one time, wishing to mark a special occasion, the Helmores gave a gift to the Karloffs. They had a small china piggy bank made, with the pig formed to look like Frankenstein's monster, complete with bolts in the neck. It was, they felt, a cute way of teasing Boris that the Frankenstein persona was the Karloffs' piggy bank. It.didn't get the response they expected. Said their daughter: "They were kind of disappointed it didn't get the hilarity that they hoped. My mother said when they saw Boris' reaction to the joke, even though he was his usual charming self, she could tell it was a sensitive issue with him. She never realized before the extent to which he did not like having it all depend on the Monster."

Following the success of *The Raven*, Karloff, Peter Lorre, and Vincent Price appeared in another horror spoof, *The Comedy of Terrors*, with the addition of Basil Rathbone. Directed by Jacques Tourneur, who had shown years before in *Cat People* and *I Walked with a Zombie* his flair for fantastic subject matter, the film was a broad farce, again written by Richard Matheson. His script had Price and Lorre as a pair of undertakers, whose business is slow, so they decide to drum up some business on their own. In the process, they are set upon by their landlord, played by Rathbone, who wants the back rent they owe. Price and Lorre try to murder him more than once, but Rathbone won't stay dead. Karloff played Price's senile father-in-law and was very funny, particularly when giving the eulogy at a funeral for a man he knows nothing about.

At first, Karloff was to play the landlord and Rathbone the father-in-law, Richard Matheson told me. Due to Karloff's physical condition, and scenes requiring a lot of exertion, he and Rathbone switched roles. The four had a grand time making the film, which was shot in less than three weeks, and had a director who really worked with actors. It had its flaws and was not without some labored attempts at humor. Referring to a poorly made coffin, Price remarks, "Nobody would be caught dead in that thing." And, Joyce Jameson, as Price's shrewish wife, was a little much at times.

Yet, Price and Lorre worked well together, and Rathbone about stole the show. Richard Matheson told me Rathbone "had more energy than any of them." *The Comedy of Terrors* was more fun for the people in it than for the critics. In the *New York Times*' eye, it was "a musty, rusty bag of tricks" and *Variety* said, "The raw material for a jovial spoof of chillers was there, but the comic restraint and perception necessary to capitalize on those natural resources is conspicuously ' missing." The critic summed it up in four words: "Poof goes the spoof."

Matheson wrote a third picture for American-International, *Sweethearts and Horrors*, that was to again showcase Karloff, Lorre, Price, and Rathbone, plus Tallulah Bankhead, portraying the Sweethearts, a family of show business people attending the reading of their father's will. It was never made. Within five years, all but Price had died.

Karloff, without ever trying to do so, almost instinctively had an influence on his co-workers, be it a writer or director or fellow actor, some of whom were personal admirers of his. One of them was Chita Rivera. With the Broadway hits *West Side Story and Bye Bye Birdie* to her credit then, and later *Chicago* and *Kiss of the Spider Woman*, she appeared with him in 1965 on *The Entertainers*, a short-lived variety show with Carol Burnett, Bob Newhart, Caterina Valente, Dom DeLuise, and Ruth Buzzi. She remembered him vividly.

"He is an artist. Seriously an artist. He was so handsome and all of that white hair. And his eyes. Nobody had eyes like Boris Karloff. The slightest tilt of his head, he understood the slightest physical movement. Without a word being said, he says a million words. He got up to move, and I saw the Monster. Physically, there is nothing like him. He made a great impression on me physically and as an artist.

"He is definitely a defined soul, one that reaches millions and millions of people. Some of us don't. He certainly does. I wish I could have said face to face that he was one of the most extraordinary people I've ever met. I don't know what I said to him that day because I was just so amazed. He was smart enough to do a television show as himself, smart enough to a Lou Costello movie and joke about it, and still be as powerful as he was and frightening as he was and as sensitive as the Monster as he was. He knew what drama was. Whatever the word horror means, but he made it artistic. He totally understood fear and gentleness."

Due to the American-International pictures, as well as such TV series as *The Addams Family* and *The Munsters*, the horror field was enjoying a resurgence in popular culture, thus Karloff was always in demand, as a new generation of fans embraced him and his contemporaries. At 76, he made the cover of *Look* magazine, spotlighted as "The Old Master Monster". Again, the suitability of horror as a source of pleasure, especially for young people, was raised in the press. Interviewed in England by *The Times*, Karloff addressed the subject in, as always, a thoughtful manner:

"Horror suggests physical repulsion, disgust, and that seems to me a worthless, pointless reaction for any work of entertainment to aim at; it's so easy it isn't worth doing. An eye, say, plopping all bloody into a glass dish may provoke a gasp of revulsion when it is first seen on the screen, but this is an entirely physical thing, and something one can get used to, no doubt with a certain coarsening of one's responses in the process. The second or third time something like that happens in a film, the surprise and excitement is gone, and then you come back to the old, inevitable question. What is there to support it in the way of plot and characterization, to give it some point other than providing an immediate physical shock? In other words, what is there to appeal to the spectator's imagination?" Those words are as apropos today as they were then.

Karloff's first appearance as an actual monster in quite a while was in Mario Bava's *Black Sabbath*, also released in 1964. The Italian-made trilogy of horror tales, each of them introduced by Karloff on-camera, was an effective, low-key film without any lurid attempts at shocking audiences. In the best and most haunting story, "The Wurdalak", based on a tale by Leo Tolstoy, Karloff eerily portrayed the patriarch of a family in Eastern Europe, awaiting his return from a journey to kill a wurdalak, a form of vampire. He arrives, bearing the wurdalak's severed head, but had become one himself.

One of the remaining pictures he did for a major studio was MGM's *The Venetian Affair*, starring Robert Vaughn, popular then for his TV series *The Man from U.N.C.L.E.* from the same studio. It was another entry in the glut of cinematic spy stories of the time and based on a popular novel. In a sluggish, unsuspenseful film, Karloff as a scientist was a key factor in the plot and had one of the better roles. Another supporting player was Edward Asner, who told me he had no personal contact with Karloff, although he did say "he was fascinating to look at and to watch."

Karloff's looks were even more distinctive when he played a woman in "The Mother Muffin Affair", an episode of *The Girl from U.N.C.L.E.*, a spinoff that lasted only one season and starred Stefanie

Powers. Both shows were produced by Norman Felton who told me, "My last adventure with Mr. Karloff came about when I thought it would be marvelous fun to cast him as a woman. He was in London at the time, and had gone, as usual, to see the cricket matches at Lord's. He was told about the role, and later he told me that he said to his agent, 'For Felton? He wants me to play a role in drag? Of course I will.'"

That episode is one of the show's more memorable. Arthur Kennard said to him, "Boris, you're going to play a woman." To which, Karloff said, with humor, "Well, I won't fool anybody" and once in make-up, he quipped, "I look like a two-dollar whore."

Despite his ailments, Karloff never lost the desire to keep on working, no matter what. He was now almost 80 and a grandfather of Sara's two sons, Michael and David. Retirement was apparently never a consideration. Teresa Wright told me, "The last time I saw him, my former husband Bob Anderson and I were in London, and we went by to see them at the apartment, and he was having lots of trouble with emphysema. He had to have oxygen nearby, and was in a wheelchair, but he had a job coming up. Whether they'd written it especially for him or not, he was to do it in a wheelchair. He was as excited as a kid. He was just so excited about it and saying, 'Isn't this marvelous? That I can, at my age, go do this and they can let me do it in a wheelchair?' He had great enthusiasm, really."

Continuing to go wherever there was a gig, Karloff went to Spain for a couple of them. One was an episode of the series *I Spy*, shot in Madrid, with Robert Culp and Bill Cosby. Playing a nuclear scientist with delusions of being Don Quixote, Karloff gave an eloquent and touching performance, capturing the essence of the wandering knight of La Mancha. Years later, when I asked Culp what stood out to him about that experience, he said it was, as he put it, "the courage" it took Boris to play the role despite his age, health, and physical limitations.

He needn't have bothered for *Blind Man's Bluff*, another rehash of the *House of Wax* plot of murder victims being used to make wax figures, with Karloff as a blind sculptor who, with a visiting writer (Jean-Pierre Aumont), uncovers a conspiracy by his wife, played by Viveca Lindfors, and her lover. Karloff substituted for Claude Rains, the first choice for the role, who was not well and died that year (1967). The film, a dubbed disaster, hit American screens in 1971 and was renamed *Cauldron of Blood*.

One of Karloff's more interesting films during this stage in his life was *The Sorcerers*, filmed in London by a promising new director named Michael Reeves, still in his early twenties. Karloff played a retired hypnotist who developed a mind control device, which he and his wife use to experience the physical sensations felt by their test subject. (A variation on this theme was later used in 1983's *Brainstorm*.) Co-producing the picture was Patrick Curtis, a former child actor who, at the time, was married to Raquel Welch and produced some of her work.

*The Sorcerers* was another low-budget release, as Curtis told me: "I bought my wife a Rolls-Royce convertible. We went over to do *One Million Years B.C.* and stayed for a long time. For Christmas, I bought her this Rolls, and that was our camera car, and I would pick up Mr. Karloff every morning and take him to the studio. Once he was ensconced and they were working, many times we took the trunk lid off the car and the cameraman would sit in front. Or, we'd put the top down and he'd fix himself in the back seat and we did all the chase scenes.

"That was badly paid, but I owned the only convertible in the company, so I did it. Then I had to rush back and sometimes put the top up and the trunk lid back on and take him home." Karloff was not the only horror star Curtis crossed paths with. His father, D.A. Curtis, had been a director at Republic and Universal. Growing up in Hollywood, he met Karloff many times, and was a childhood friend of Bela Lugosi, Jr. Years later when he and Raquel arrived in London for *The Sorcerers*, their agent asked what they wanted to do. The couple replied they wanted to meet Christopher Lee, whose Dracula pictures they enjoyed so much. The agent, Dennis Salinger, also represented Lee, so he invited them to his house for dinner. Curtis remembered, "Christopher and Mrs. Lee were there, with another fellow with sandy hair and glasses. I didn't catch his name, didn't care. Christopher's had a fabulous life, so I was just enthralled. This other guy was trying to get a word in edgewise. He kept trying to get into the conversation, but he didn't say ten words. Nobody paid any attention to him.

"It was Michael Caine. *Ipcress File* opened two weeks after that and we just didn't know who he was. Even if I had, I don't think I would have given a damn. I was in my element, having dinner with Christopher Lee, so we became fast friends."

Karloff looked visibly unwell in *The Sorcerers*, but still dominated the screen. Due to his age and infirmity, the producers were unable to insure him. He was equally matched by Catherine Lacey as his wife, whose willpower over their subject becomes stronger than his, and forces the young man, played by Ian Ogilvy, to commit crimes. At the end, Karloff wills him into wrecking his car, and from the ensuing explosion, all three of them die. Ogilvy told me this about a scene he had with Karloff.

"We were sitting behind the door waiting to go on and waiting for a cue to say 'Action' and it didn't come and it didn't come and it didn't come. Boris turned to me and said, 'By the time they say 'action', I shall probably be dead.' He was like that. He made jokes about his age and his infirmity.

"The sound man said to Mike Reeves, 'Every time Mr. Karloff moves, I'm picking up a squeak and I don't know where it's coming from. Could you ask him? I'm too embarrassed.' Mike said, 'Boris, every time you move, we're picking up a little noise.' Boris just howled with laughter. He rolled up his trousers leg. He had this steel brace, and he just asked for some bicycle oil to oil his leg. It was a Frankensteinian moment that the Monster had fabricated. He was lovely. He'd do anything Mike asked him to do as long as he was physically able to do it."

Of Catherine Lacey, Ogilvy said, "She was a highly professional old lady. She hated her role. It was beneath her, really, in a way, and she did her job beautifully, I thought. To her, it was just another little movie."

Michael Reeves, whom Patrick Curtis told me was "terribly talented", went on to direct Vincent Price in *Witchfinder General*. It would prove to be his last work. In 1969, just two days after Karloff's death, Reeves himself died from a drug overdose. He was twenty-five years old.

Karloff stayed busy with the TV appearances, recordings, and voiceovers, but thanks to Roger Corman, he was able to make one outstanding film that stood above anything he had done in a long time. Peter Bogdanovich, a former writer for *Esquire* and author of a number of books on directors, had worked as assistant director, second-unit director, and screenwriter on Corman's *The Wild Angels* and wanted to make a film of his own. He would become known just a few years later with his breakout film *The Last Picture Show* and go on to subsequent works as *What's Up, Doc?*, *Paper Moon*, and *Mask*.

Corman, realizing that Karloff still owed him a few days' work, said that Bogdanovich could make whatever kind of movie he pleased, but stipulated that there had to be a part for Karloff, a certain amount of footage from *The Terror* would have to be included somehow, and the production cost was not to exceed $125,000. Karloff was also used so Corman could avoid a lawsuit by the actor regarding the profits from *The Terror*. Thus, Corman promised to pay Karloff $15,000 for no more than two days' work on a new picture which turned out to be *Targets*.

Bogdanovich said later that Corman told him, "I want you to shoot for two days with Karloff. You can shoot twenty minutes in two days. I want you to take twenty minutes out of *The Terror*. Then get another bunch of actors and shoot for about ten days for about another forty minutes, and you've got an eighty-minute Karloff picture I can release." Given all that, Bogdanovich and his wife at the time, production designer Polly Platt, future producer of such films as *Pretty Baby*, *Broadcast News* and *The War of the Roses*, wrote a screenplay that he thought would utilize two kinds of horror, the cinematic type personified by Karloff and the violence in current American society.

The plot involved two men, one of them an aging star of horror films who wants to call it quits, and the other an apparently normal, clean-cut young man who one day snaps and goes on a killing spree. Their stories were intertwined at the climax, when the killer, played by Tim O'Kelly, wreaks havoc at a drive-in theater where Byron Orlok, the actor, is attending the premiere of his latest film *The Terror*. That type of senseless, random violence the script dramatized had taken place most prominently in 1966 at the University of Texas in Austin, where twenty-three year-old Charles Whitman fired at people below from a campus tower. He claimed the lives of thirteen people and wounded thirty-one others before he was shot and killed by authorities.

An early idea of Bogdanovich's was to have Karloff play an actor who secretly wishes he was Cary Grant, so he puts on a mask making him look handsome. He then goes into grocery stores where he strangles people behind the frozen food sections. Bogdanovich aptly remarked, "That didn't work out, thank heaven."

With the completed script, Bogdanovich went to Arthur Kennard and laid out what he wanted to do. Kennard passed the information on and Karloff said, "Well, let's meet with the young man." They did, and

Karloff had faith in the project to the point where he worked five days, instead of the required two. Bogdanovich cast himself in the role of Sammy Michaels, a director trying to persuade Orlok into doing one more picture before going back to England and retiring. Orlok refers to himself as "an anachronism" whose old-style movie horror, in his mind, is passé. Initially, Karloff, modest man that he was, had reservations about some of his dialogue. He said to Bogdanovich, "Peter, since I am playing a character who's not far away from what I really am, couldn't we tone down some of these awful things I say about myself?" Bogdanovich, just twenty-eight at the time, replied, "No. The audience will like it if you put yourself down." Karloff agreed and supported his director throughout the shoot.

As his assistant, Bogdanovich chose his friend Daniel Selznick, son of David O. Selznick. Both men had been journalists in New York before moving to California. Selznick told me, "I was hired on and there was sort of a critical moment in the casting when the role of the young director had to be cast. Peter said, 'Well, look it's down to two people, but I'm going to let you decide who should play this role. I'm going to audition for you and Polly, and then Henry Jaglom, who's a friend of ours.' I knew Henry from New York. I think he was more of a Strasberg student than a Stella Adler student. I attended both Stella Adler and Strasberg. Henry came and auditioned for us and gave a very funny, original interpretation of the role. I thought Peter was a little flat, frankly. I said, 'Well, my choice would be Henry.' And he said, 'Wrong choice. I've decided I should play it.' I said, 'How are you going to direct yourself?' He said, 'You're going to direct me. That's the bonus. You get to direct me in my scenes.' Sure enough, from a performance point of view, I got to direct Peter, and otherwise he was directing the movie. In the end, he felt I'd been so involved in the pre-production, production, and post-production that when it came time for the credits, he gave me the title of assistant producer."

No actual reason was given in *Targets* for the behavior of killer Bobby Thompson, the product of a strait-laced, antiseptic home environment, but that made the film more powerful. At a turbulent time in American history, there was no purpose in trying to explain it, though many have tried ever since.

Where Bogdanovich truly succeeded was in giving Karloff a role he played brilliantly. In a straight dramatic film, without any macabre settings or detailed make-up, Karloff could not have gone out more gracefully. Nearing almost fifty years on the screen, with the subtle underplaying that served him for so long, Karloff made *Targets* an apt and moving self-portrait. While it wasn't his last film, it served as fitting a swan song as were *The Shootist* (1976) for John Wayne and *On Golden Pond* (1981) for Henry Fonda, two other stars with an indelible cinematic image.

*Targets*, which Bogdanovich has referred to as his "Hitchcock picture", is notable in other aspects. Other than Karloff, the main cast had no other then-prominent actors or actresses, which perhaps made the characters even more believable, and there was no film score at all. The cinematographer was Laszlo Kovacs, who shortly thereafter shot *Easy Rider* and *Five Easy Pieces* (both 1969) and several other Bogdanovich works.

Karloff had a wonderful moment in the film when Orlok prepares for his drive-in appearance, and a disc jockey scheduled to interview him reads off several hackneyed questions he's prepared. Orlok tells Michaels, "Sammy, this is dull." Instead, Orlok suggests he tell the audience a story and then relates the tale of Death having an appointment in Samarra. (Karloff recorded this on his first *Tales of the Frightened* album.) Bogdanovich wanted the scene done without any editing, so though it was past midnight and everyone was tired, Karloff did it in a single take, with the camera moving into close-up as he spoke. Bogdanovich told me it is one of his favorite moments in the film.

Regarding Karloff, Daniel Selznick told me, "I thought Boris' performance was really excellent and very thoughtful, and you really felt, as we did on the production side, you got to know the man watching the film. I thought he was going to take offense at the fact that Peter was sort of making some subtle digs at the kind of movies he starred in. He had a sense of humor about them himself. He thought it was kind of wonderful that Peter was saying that violence is endemic in all of us, but there are many kinds of violence.

"He was exactly pointed in the direction Peter wanted him to be in. When he'd done one take perfectly, he'd say, 'Now do you want another take?' and Peter said, 'Well, maybe one for safety, but really that was so good, I don't need another one.' His graciousness and generosity, considering the fact he was working very hard during those five days. I mean, Roger Corman was getting his money's worth."

*Targets* was finished in twenty-five days. With its release imminent, both Sen. Robert Kennedy and Dr. Martin Luther King, Jr. were assassinated that year. No studio wanted to release the film. Some thought it should be shown to capitalize on the violence and others wanted to shelve it entirely. Paramount picked it up, but a foreword about gun control was inserted, and the question "Why gun control?" was used in the print advertising.

The reviews were mixed. Bogdanovich's directorial debut, the *New York Times* said, was an "admirably spun and gripping little movie" that "scores an unnerving bulls-eye" and *Variety* said "Bogdanovich has made a film of much suspense and implicit violence". The *New York Daily News*' Wanda Hale commented, "'Boris Karloff plays the part of Byron Orlok beautifully" and added, "Bogdanovich gets E for effort." Writing for *New York* magazine, Judith Crist hailed *Targets* as "a hard-hitting melodrama" and added, "the casting is excellent."

On the down side, *Newsweek* said, "The workmanship is sloppy, the dramatic potential is unfulfilled, and the violence is painfully repetitive." One of the highlights, it added, was Karloff whose "presence takes charge of the film." *Time* referred to Karloff "stoically suffering though a prolonged cameo appearance" and said the film "eventually falls victim to artistic overkill". Particularly unkind to the entire film were *The New Republic* and *The New Yorker*. The former said, "Bogdanovich just cooked up some clever ideas out of the backer's prerequisites and filmed them smoothly with little regard for credibilty or conclusion." The latter remarked, "The picture has a clumsy, diagrammatic plot (wanly acted and fidgety to sit through)" and further criticized it by saying, "How intellectually chaotic to make a gun control parable that is so empty of any sense of the people in it that the only response left to an audience is to recline with a bag of popcorn and lust after a manly score of assassinations." Of the violence, it was fairly tame and non-graphic as compared to *Bonnie and Clyde* (1967) or *The Wild Bunch* (1969).

*Targets* was not released in England until 1969, after Karloff's death, no doubt giving his character's feelings about the mark he has left on the movies and ending his career added resonance. Despite fourteen minutes cut out by the British arm of Paramount and being stuck as the lower half of double features, the film did receive kind treatment from at least the critics there. Said *The Manchester Guardian*: "The more you think about *Targets*, the more it grows." *The Illustrated*

*London News* called it "the most important and surprising film of the week" and, referring to Bogdanovich, was correct in saying "more will obviously be heard of him". One of the truest summations was from *The Times*: "A distinguished directorial debut and a movingly appropriate farewell to a great star."

During this twilight of his career, and on a purely social basis, Karloff met another man noted for his contributions to the fantastic, with whom he shared a sense of magic and wonderment that manifested in their work. It was the gifted writer Ray Bradbury, whose vast input included such classics as *Fahrenheit 451*, *The Martian Chronicles*, and *Something Wicked This Way Comes*. I asked Bradbury what he took with him. With the simplicity of language that was part of his style, he wrote: "It was exceptionally brief, but in its briefness was warmth. He knew my work, I knew his. There was a mutual love, which pleased me, of course. After all, I had known his face since I was ten, and he scared the hell out of me with *Frankenstein*. Then after that, *The Mummy*, which I saw four or five times when I was twelve, and a radio actor, and got free tickets to see my favorite films, in Tucson, Arizona.

"Good memories, summoned up by my one encounter. There's nothing to add. We shook hands, chatted a few minutes, and he was gone. A nice man, I hear. A nice man, I saw."

The lure of work was too strong for Karloff to resist, so he went to Middlesex, England to make *The Crimson Altar*, with Christopher Lee. A middling horror film about modern-day witchcraft, it went through much rewriting, and was not worth Karloff showing up and shooting some of his scenes at night in freezing rain. His part was not villainous, and about the only interesting one, even including the work of Lee and Barbara Steele, with such horror films to her credit then as *Black Sunday* and *The Pit and the Pendulum*. Retitled *The Crimson Cult* for America, and in England, *Curse of the Crimson Altar*, it wasn't released until 1970, and inaccurately advertised as "His final evil role". There were a few more he made afterward yet to be shown at the time it came out.

It was dismissed by *Variety* as "a totally unabashed rehash of a formula that Karloff has been identified with through the years" and, writing for the *New York Times*, critic Roger Greenspun observed, "Karloff acts with a quiet lucidity of such great beauty that it is a refreshment merely to hear him speak old claptrap. Nothing else in *The Crimson Cult* comes close to him."

In the time between his first work with Karloff in *Corridors of Blood* and then making this film, Christopher Lee had shared with him some of the same roles—the Frankenstein monster, Fu Manchu, the Mummy, and Rasputin. Of his friend and one-time neighbor, Lee told me, "He was one of the most versatile actors I have ever known, and certainly one of the warmest human beings. I feel very strongly that only rarely was he able to fulfill his immense potential."

In its issue of March 29, 1968, *Variety* announced that Karloff would arrive in Los Angeles to start work on four films produced by Filmica Azteca, a Mexican studio, with financial backing from Columbia Pictures. Producer Luis Enrique Vergara had intended that Karloff go to Mexico to make them, but the actor's emphysema was so advanced that he was now functioning with only half of one lung and required use of an oxygen tank. An added factor was the higher altitude in Mexico, necessitating he remain in Hollywood. Three of the films were co-written by Jack Hill, who shared the writing of *The Terror*, and, with Vergara and Juan Ibanez, jointly directed each of them. All were made back-to-back using largely American crews and Mexican actors. Titled *The Fear Chamber*, *House of Evil*, *The Incredible Invasion*, and *Isle of the Snake People*, Columbia was to distribute them theatrically with eventual sale to television. When the domestic shooting ended with Karloff working for five weeks, the Mexican crew members completed the rest south of the border.

All four were dubbed and wretchedly made, and Karloff's screen time was relatively short which may have been a blessing. He didn't think much of them and they were barely distributed after he died. With the future development of home video, they were released under a variety of titles.

His remaining assignments were making the cover of *Life* magazine to mark the 150th anniversary of *Frankenstein*'s publication, a couple of commercials, and three more television shows. One of the latter was with Vincent Price on *The Red Skelton Show* in their last work together (doing a sketch with Skelton and a musical number), followed by similar duties on *The Jonathan Winters Show*, where he did a solo version of the song "It Was a Very Good Year", a hit at the time for Frank Sinatra. Winters told me, "I found Mr. Karloff to be delightful. I have long been a fan of his and that is why I wanted him on the show. As a matter of fact, I do a horror house routine in which I use his voice.

He was very sweet to work with. He was confined to a wheelchair, and it was only when he was forced to stand on his feet that he did. He is certainly missed by millions of fans and fellow actors everywhere."

*The Name of the Game*, at the time it premiered on NBC, was heralded as television's first motion-picture series, meaning more production time was allowed for each ninety-minute show by alternating three lead actors. Every episode was filmed like a TV-movie, with up to three weeks' shooting time allotted. It was in one of that first season's shows which aired Nov. 29 that Boris Karloff last worked in front of a camera, and, coming full circle, at Universal where he became a star. He was joined by series lead Gene Barry, and an all-star cast in "The White Birch", that included Jean-Pierre Aumont, Richard Jaeckel, and Roddy MacDowall. Playing a Czech writer who wanted his book smuggled out of the country, Karloff contributed what he could to the character. Director Lamont Johnson shared these memories with me:

"He was an obvious choice for 'The White Birch' role, but we were kept in suspense until virtually the day of shooting his first scene, because of his many health problems. When word came his car was coming through the Universal gates, I felt a signal of excitement and relief all around the set, only to be shocked into silence when he was wheeled through the stage door, looking pitifully emaciated and breathing with loud and disturbing symptoms of his emphysema.

"Then his nurse brought him to me directly, and he promptly dissipated the anxiety. As he shook my hand, he said in a loud, firm, and witty voice, 'What you see before you is not encouraging, I'm sure, but what there is entirely at your service, sir.'

"He was never so much as a single beat behind in anything related to his role. A complete and heartening joy to all. His reminiscences of Peter Lorre were particularly delightful. The work and the community of his fellow actors seemed to feed his energy and elan vital. He left more dynamically than he came to us, and always charming, humorous, and strongly concentrated on his character and the telling of the story we had at hand."

Roddy MacDowall and Karloff, working together again ten years after their *Playhouse 90* version of "Heart of Darkness", had little contact this time. MacDowall told me, "We didn't talk very much together during that show, as it was evident that he was very frail, and it seemed that it would be a burden to him."

Back in February, Karloff had been briefly hospitalized in London for treatment of bronchitis. A year later, on Feb. 2, 1969, his hour upon the stage was heard no more when, at eighty-one, he died at King Edward VII Hospital in Midhurst, England, from heart and lung disease. It was prominent in many newspapers and the broadcast media.

In the Covent Garden section of London, is St. Paul's Church, consecrated in 1638 which has a long-lasting connection with the arts, especially the theater. Its architect Inigo Jones was a theatrical designer. It is there that Boris Karloff joined the many performers commemorated at the church, where a small funeral was held following his cremation. The walls are adorned with many plaques honoring British luminaries such as Charlie Chaplin, Vivien Leigh, Sybil Thorndike, Laurence Harvey, and Robert Shaw. Bearing his name and the dates 1887-1969 is Karloff's, which quotes Andrew Marvell's "Upon Cromwell's Return to England".

Less than two weeks after Karloff's death, *Variety* reported that Tigon Pictures was negotiating the lease of a site on which it planned to build a small theater devoted entirely to showing horror films and named The Karloff Cinema. Tony Tenser, executive producer of *The Crimson Cult* and co-producer of *The Sorcerers*, had written the actor for permission to honor him this way, and asked him to open it when the time came. Karloff's response was, "Permission gladly granted providing somewhere in the cinema you find room for my bones." Tenser received the letter a couple of weeks before Feb. 2. The project did not materialize.

In California, Karloff is remembered not with one, but two stars on the Hollywood Walk of Fame, one for his film work, the other for hosting *Thriller*. In the summer of 1969, Evelyn Karloff donated five thousand dollars to the Motion Picture and Television Relief Fund in his honor. The memory of Boris Karloff has remained green through the decades and the generations. A Karloff tribute by the Academy of Motion Picture Arts and Sciences was held in 1988, attended by a number of his co-workers and friends. As the evening's host, George Schaefer remarked that students at UCLA, where he was then chairman of the Department of Theater, Film, and Television, often didn't know the names of performers such as Robert Donat, Alfred Lunt, or Paul Muni, but at the mention of Boris Karloff, "they're delighted and seem to know exactly what you're talking about."

Evelyn Karloff continued living at the cottage in Bramshott and the apartment in London, and travelled frequently until her death in 1993 at 89. Sara Karloff lives in Rancho Mirage, Calif. and runs Karloff Enterprises, which sells and distributes merchandise bearing her father's name and image. On September 30, 1997, after a long and vigorous campaign by Sara, Bela Lugosi, Jr., and Ron Chaney, grandson of Lon Jr., the United States Postal Service released a set of Classic Movie Monster stamps. Pictured were Karloff as both Frankenstein's Monster and the Mummy, Bela Lugosi as Dracula, Lon Chaney as The Phantom of the Opera, and Lon Jr. as the Wolf Man. Appropriately, the unveiling ceremony was held at Universal Studios.

Fan interest in horror films and the people involved with them has not waned. In fact, it is probably more popular now than ever before, thanks to such innovations as home video, the growth of cable television, and the Internet. Conventions devoted to them have been and still are held around the world. A Karloff retrospective at the American Museum of the Moving Image in October of 1997 was the largest attended event at the museum up until that time, and fans had to be turned away. *Frankenstein* and *The Bride of Frankenstein* are among the films added to The National Film Registry, based on their aesthetic, historical, or cultural importance. The Registry was established at the Library of Congress in 1988 to help preserve America's movie heritage. Acts such as these certainly would have pleased Karloff to know his appeal and his work have not withered with age. People still recognize the name, no matter what aspect of his career they know it from. And, because film retains an image, he will always be with us.

While Boris Karloff is largely remembered for the images emitted from the light of a film projector, his everlasting impression on the world is the intensity of the light that came from within. This is perhaps his greatest legacy.

# Credits

## FILM

*The Lightning Raider* (1919) Director: George B. Seitz. Script: Charles Goddard and John B. Clymer. Released by Pathe Pictures. 15-chapter serial. Cast: Pearl White, Warner Oland, Henry G. Sell, Boris Karloff.

*The Masked Raider* (1919) Director: Aubrey M. Kennedy. Released by Arrow Pictures. 15-chapter serial. Cast: Harry Myers, Ruth Stonehouse, Paul Panzer, Boris Karloff.

*His Majesty, the American* (1919) Director: Joseph Henabety. Producer: Douglas Fairbanks. Script: Joseph Henabery and Elton Banks. Based on a story by Elton Banks (Fairbanks). Photography: Victor Fleming and Glen MacWilliams. Released by United Artists. Cast: Douglas Fairbanks, Marjorie Daw, Lillian Langdon, Frank Campeau, Sam Southern, Jay Dwiggins, Albert McQuarrle, Boris Karloff.

*The Prince and Betty* (1919) Director: Robert Thornby. Producer: Jesse D. Hampton. Based on the novel by P.G. Wodehouse. Released by Pathe Film Exchange. Cast: William Desmond, Gary Thurman, Anita Kay, George Swann, Walter Peng, Wilton Taylor, William Levaull, Frank Lanning, Boris Karloff.

*The Deadlier Sex* (1920) Director: Robert Thornby. Script: Fred Myton. Based on a story by Bayard Veiler. Released by Pathe Pictures. Cast:

Blanche Sweet, Winter Hall, Roy Laidlaw, Russell Simpson, Boris Karloff.

*The Courage of Marge O'Doone* (1920) Director: David Smith. Script: Robert North Bradbury. Based on the novel by James Oliver Curtwood. Released by Vitagraph Pictures. Cast: Pauline Stark, Niles Welch, George Stanley, Jack Curtis, William Dryer, Boris Karloff, Billie Benedict, James O'Neill.

*The Last of the Mohicans* (1920) Directors: Maurice Tourneur and Clarence Brown. Producer: Maurice Tourneur. Script: Robert A. Dillon. Based on the novel by James Fenimore Cooper. Photography: Philip R. Dubois and Charles Van Anger. Released by Associated Producers. Cast: Wallace Beery, Barbara Bedford, Albert Roscoe, Lillian Hall, Henry Woodward, James Gordon, George Hackathorne, Nelson McDowell, Harry Lorraine, Theodore Lorch, Jack McDonald, Sydney Dean, Boris Karloff.

*The Hope Diamond Mystery* (1921) Director: Stuart Payton. Script: Charles Goddard and John B. Clymer. Based on a story by May Yohe. Released by Kosmik Films. 15-chapter serial. Cast: Grace Darmond, William Marion, Harry Carter, George Cheseboro, Boris Karloff, Carmen Phillips, May Yohe, Frank Seka, Harry Archer, William Buckley.

*Cheated Hearts* (1921) Director: Hobart Henley. Script: Wallace Clifton. Based on the novel *Barry Gordon* by William Farquar Payson. Photography: Virgil Miller. Released by Universal Pictures. Cast: Herbert Rawlinson, Warner Baxter, Marjorie Daw, Doris Pawn, Winter Hall, Josef Swickard, Murdock MacQuarrie, Anna Lehr, Boris Karloff.

*The Cave Girl* (1921) Director: Joseph J. Franz. Script: William A. Parker. Based on the play by Guy Bolton and George Middleton. Photography: Victor Milner. Released by First National Pictures. Cast: Teddie Gerard, Charles Meredith, Wilton Taylor, Eleanor Hancock, Lillian Tucker, Frank Coleman, Boris Karloff, Jake Abrahams, John Beck.

*The Man From Downing Street* (1922) Director: Edward Jose. Producer: A.E. Smith. Script: Bradley J. Smollen. Based on a story by Clyde Westover, Lottie Horner, and Florine Williams. Photography: Ernest Smith. Released by Vitagraph Pictures. Cast: Earle Williams, Betty Ross Clarke, Boris Karloff, Charles Phillips, Kathryn Adams, Herbert Prior, Henry Burrows, Eugenia Gilbert, James Butler, George Stanley.

*The Infidel* (1922) Director: James A. Young. Producer: B.P. Schulberg. Script: James A. Young. Based on a story by Charles A. Logue. Photography: Joseph Brotherton. Released by First National Pictures. Cast: Katherine MacDonald, Robert Ellis, Joseph Dowling, Boris Karloff, Melbourne McDowell, Oleta Otis, Charles Smiley, Loyala O'Connor, Barbara Tennant, Charles Force.

*The Altar Stairs* (1922) Director: Lambert Hillyer. Script: Doris Schroeder and George Hively. Based on a story by G.B. Lancaster. Photography: Dwight Warren. Released by Universal Pictures. Cast: Frank Mayo, Dagmar Godowsky, Louise Lorraine, Harry Devere, Hugh Thompson, Boris Karloff, Nick De Ruiz, Lawrence Hughes, J.J. Lanoe.

*Omar the Tentmaker* (1923) Director: James A. Young. Producer: Richard Walton Tully. Script: Richard Walton Tully, based on his play *Omar Khayam the Tentmaker*. Photography: George Benoit. Released by First National Pictures. Cast: Guy Bates Post, Virginia Brown Faire, Nigel De Brulier, Noah Beery, Rose Dione, Patsy Ruth Miller, Douglas Gerard, Boris Karloff, Maurice B. Flynn, Edward M. Kimball, Walter Long, Evelyn Selbie, John Gribner.

*The Woman Conquers* (1923) Director: Tom Forman. Producer: B.P. Schulberg. Based on a story by Violet Clark. Photography: Joseph Brotherton. Released by First National Pictures. Cast: Katherine MacDonald, Bryant Washburn, Mitchell Lewis, June Elvidge, Clarissa Selwynne, Boris Karloff, Francis McDonald.

*The Gentleman From America* (1923) Director: Edward Sedgwick. Producer: Carl Laemmle. Script: George Hull. Based on a story by Raymond L. Schrock. Photography: Virgil Miller. Released by Universal

Pictures. Cast: Hoot Gibson, Tom O'Brien, Louise Lorraine, Carmen Phillips, Frank Leigh, Jack Crane, Bob McKenzie, Albert Prisco, Rosa Rosanova, Boris Karloff.

*The Prisoner* (1923) Director: Jack Conway. Script: Edward T. Lowe, Jr. Based on the novel *Castle Craneycrow* by George Barr McCutcheon. Photography: Benjamin Reynolds. Released by Universal Pictures. Cast: Herbert Rawlinson, Eileen Percy, George Cowl, June Elvidge, Lincoln Stedman, Gertrude Short, Bertram Grassby, Mario Carillo, Hayford Hobbs, Lillian Langdon, Bert Sprotte, Boris Karloff.

*Riders of the Plains* (1924) Director: Jacques Jaccard. Released by Arrow Pictures. 15-chapter serial. Cast: Jack Perrin, Marilyn Mills, Ruth Royce, Boris Karloff.

*The Hellion* (1924) Director: Bruce Mitchell. Producer: Anthony J. Xydias. Script: Bruce Mitchell. Released by Sunset Pictures. Cast: J.B. Warner, Marin Sais, William Lester, Alline Goodwin, Boris Karloff.

*Dynamite Dan* (1924) Director: Bruce Mitchell. Producer: Anthony J. Xydias. Script: Bruce Mitchell. Photography: Bert Longenecker. Cast: Kenneth McDonald, Diana Alden, Boris Karloff, Frank Rice, Harry Woods, Jack Waltemeyer, Jack Richardson, Eddie Harris, Emily Gerdes.

*Perils of the Wind* (1925) Director: Francis Ford. Released by Universal Pictures. 15-chapter serial. Cast: Joe Bonomo, Margaret Quimby, Jack Mower, Boris Karloff.

*Forbidden Cargo* (1925) Director: Thomas Buckingham. Script and story: Frederick Kennedy Myton. Photography: Silvano Balboni. Released by FBO. Cast: Evelyn Brent, Robert Ellis, Boris Karloff.

*The Prairie Wife* (1925) Director: Hugo Ballin. Assistant Director: James Chapin. Script: Hugo Ballin. Based on a story by Arthur Stringer. Photography: James Diamond. Editors: Katherine Hilliker and H.H. Caldwell. Released by MGM. Cast: Dorothy Devore, Herbert

Rawlinson, Gibson Gowland, Leslie Stuart, Frances Prim, Boris Karloff, Erich von Ritzau, Rupert Franklin.

*Parisian Nights* (1925) Director: Alfred Santell. Assistant Directors: Robert Florey and Roland Asher. Script: Fred Myton and C. Doty Hobart. Based on a story by Emil Forst. Photography: Ernest Haller. Released by FBO. Cast: Elaine Hammerstein, Gaston Glass, Lou Tellegren, William J. Kelly, Boris Karloff, Renee Adoree.

*Never the Twain Shall Meet* (1925) Director: Maurice Tourneur. Producer: William Randolph Hearst. Script: Eugene Mullin. Based on a novel by Peter B. Kyne. Photography: Ira H. Morgan and J.B. Shackleford. Art Director: Joseph Urban. Editor: Donn Hayes. Released by MGM. Cast: Anita Stewart, Bert Lytell, Huntley Gordon, Justine Johnstone, George Siegmann, Lionel Belmore, William Norris, Emily Fitzroy, Princess Marie de Bourbon, Florence Turner, Boris Karloff.

*Lady Robin Hood* (1925) Director: Ralph Ince. Assistant Director: Pandro S. Berman Script: Fred Myton. Based on a story by Clifford Howard and Burke Jenkins. Photography: Silvano Balboni. Released by FBO. Cast: Evelyn Brent, Robert Ellis, Boris Karloff, William Humphrey, Darcy Corrigan, Robert Cauterio.

*The Greater Glory* (1926) Director: Curt Rehfeld. Producer: June Mathis. Based on the novel *Viennese Medley* by Edith O'Shaughnessy. Photography: John Boyle and Arthur Martinelli. Art Director: E.J. Shulter. Editor: George McGuire. Released by First National Pictures. Cast: Conway Tearle, Anna Q. Nilsson, May Allison, Ian Keith, Lucy Beaumont, Jean Hersholt, Nigel De Brulier, Bridgetta Clark, John Sainpolis, Marcia Manon, Boris Karloff.

*Her Honor, The Governor* (1926) (Alternate title: *The Second Mrs. Fenway*) Director: Chet Withey. Producer: Joseph P. Kennedy. Script: Doris Anderson. Based on a story by Hyatt Daab and Weed Dickinson. Photography: Andre Balatier. Cast: Pauline Frederick, Carroll Nye, Thomas Sanschi, Greta Von Rue, Stanton Heck, Boris Karloff, Jack Richardson, Kathleen Kirkham, Charles McHugh, William Worthington.

*The Bells* (1926) Director: James A. Young. Producer: I.E. Chadwick. Script: James A. Young. Based on the play *Le Juif Polonais* by Emile Erckmann and Alexandre Chatrian. Photography: William O'Connell. Released by Chadwick Pictures. Cast: Lionel Barrymore, Gustaf von Seyffertitz, Edward Phillips, Lola Todd, Boris Karloff, Fred Warren, Otto Lederer, Lorimer Johnson.

*The Golden Web* (1926) Director: Walter Lang. Producer: Renaud Hoffman. Script: James Bell Smith. Based on a novel by E. Phillips Oppenheim. Photography by Gotham Pictures. Cast: Lillian Rich, Huntley Gordon, Jay Hunt, Boris Karloff, Lawford Davidson, Nora Hayden, Syd Crossley, Joe Moore.

*The Eagle of the Sea* (1926) Director: Frank Lloyd. Producers: Adolph Zukor and Jesse L. Lasky. Associate Producer: B. P. Schulberg. Script: Julian Josephson. Based on the novel *Captain Sazarac* by Charles Tenney Jackson. Photography: Nobert Brodine. Released by Paramount Pictures. Cast: Ricardo Cortez, Florence Vidor, Sam De Grasse, Andre Beranger, Mitchell Lewis, Guy Oliver, George Irving, Irvin Renard, James Marcus, Charles E. Anderson, Boris Karloff.

*Flames* (1926) Director and Producer: Lewis H. Moonmaw. Script and story: Alfred A. Colm. Photography: Herbert Brownelli and King Gray. Editor: Frank Lawrence. Released by Associate Exhibitors, Inc. Cast: Eugene O'Brien, Virginia Valli, Jean Hersholt, Bryant Washburn, George Nichols, Boris Karloff, Cissy Fitzgerald.

*Old Ironsides* (1926) (Alternate title: *Sons of the Sea*) Director: James Cruze. Assistant Director: Harold Schwartz. Producers: Adolph Zukor and Jesse L. Lasky. Script: Dorothy Arzner, Walter Woods, and Harry Carr. Based on the novel by Laurence Stallings. Photography: Alfred Gilks and Charles Boyle. Music: Hugo Riesenfeld. Cast: Esther Ralston, Wallace Beery, George Bancroft, Charles Farrell, Johnny Walker, George Godfrey, Guy Oliver, Eddie Fetherston, Boris Karloff, Effie Ellsler, William Conklin, Fred Kohler, Charles Hill Mailes, Nick De Ruiz, Mitchell Lewis.

*Flaming Fury* (1926) Director: James Hogan. Producer: Joseph P. Kennedy. Script: Ewart Adamson. Photography: Joe Walker. Released by FBO. Cast: Charles Delaney, Betty May, Boris Karloff, Eddie Chandler.

*The Man in the Saddle* (1926) Directors: Lynn Reynolds and Clifford S. Smith. Script and story: Charles A. Logue. Released by Universal Pictures. Cast: Hoot Gibson, Virginia Brown Faire, Fay Wray, Charles Hill Mailes, Clark Comstock, Boris Karloff.

*The Nickel Hopper* (1926) Director: Hal Yates. Producer: Hal Roach. Released by Pathe Film Exchange. Cast: Mabel Normand, Michael Visaroff, Margaret Seddon, Theodore von Eltz, James Finlayson, Oliver Hardy, Boris Karloff.

*Valencia* (1926) (Alternate title: *The Love Song*) Director and Producer: Dmitri Buchowetzki. Script: Alice D.G. Miller. Based on a story by Dmitri Buchowetzki and Alice D.G. Miller. Photography: Percy Hilburn. Editor: Hugh Wynn. Art Director: Cedric Gibbons. Released by MGM. Cast: Mae Murray, Lloyd Hughes, Roy D'Arcy, Max Barwyn, Michael Vavitch, Michael Visaroff, Boris Karloff.

*Tarzan and the Golden Lion* (1927) Director: J.P. McGowan. Producer: Joseph P. Kennedy. Script: William F. Wing. Based on the novel by Edgar Rice Burroughs. Photography: Joseph Walker. Released by FBO. Cast: James Pierce, Dorothy Dunbar, Edna Murphy, Frederic Peters, Harold Goodwin, Liu Yu-Ching, D'Arcy Corrigan, Boris Karloff, Robert Bolder.

*Let It Rain* (1927) Director: Edward Francis Cline. Producer: Douglas MacLean. Script and story: Wade Boteler, George J. Crone, and Earle Snell. Photography: Jack MacKentie. Released by Paramount Pictures. Cast: Douglas MacLean, Shirley Mason, Wade Boteler, James Bradbury, Jr., Lincoln Stedman, Lee Shumway, Edwin Sturgis, Boris Karloff, James Mason.

*The Meddlin' Stranger* (1927) Director: Richard Thorpe. Producer: Lester F. Scott, Jr. Script and story: Christopher B. Booth. Photography: Ray Ries. Released by Pathe Film Exchange. Cast: Wally Wales, Nola

Luxford, James Marcus, Boris Karloff, Charles K. French, Mabel Van Buren.

*The Princess From Hoboken* (1927) Director: Allan Dale. Producer: John M. Stahl. Screenplay and story: Sonya Levieni. Photography: Joseph Dubray and Robert Martin. Editor: James McKay. Art Director: Edwin B. Willis. Released by Tiffany Pictures. Cast: Edmund Burns, Blanche Mehaffey, Ethel Clayton: Lou Tellegen, Julie (Babe) London, Will R. Walling, Charles McHugh, Aggie Herring, Charles Crockett, Robert Homans, Harry Bailey, Sidney D'Albrook, Boris Karloff.

*Soft Cushions* (1927) Director: Edward Francis Cline. Producer: Douglas Maclean. Script: Wade Boteler and Frederic Chapin. Based on a story by George Randolph Chester. Photography: Jack MacKenzie. Art Director: Ben Carre. Released by Paramount Pictures. Cast: Douglas MacLean, Sue Carol, Richard Carle, Russell Powell, Frank Leigh, Wade Boteler, Nigel DeBrulier, Albert Prisco, Boris Karloff, Albert Gran, Fred Kelsey, Harry Jones.

*Two Arabian Knights* (1927) Director: Lewis Milestone. Assistant Director: Nate Watt. Producer: Howard Hughes. Supervised by John W. Considine, Jr. Script: James O'Donohue and Wallace Smith. Based on a story by Donald McGibney. Adapted by Wallace Smith and Cyril Gardner. Photography: Tony Gaudio and Joseph August. Art Director: William Cameron Menzies. Released by Caddo/Howard Hughes Pictures. Cast: William Boyd, Mary Astor, Louis Wolheim, Michael Vavitch, Ian Keith, De Witt Jennings, Michael Visaroff, Boris Karloff.

*The Love Mart* (1927) Director: George Fitzmaurice. Producer: Richard A. Rowland. Script: Benjamin Glazer. Based on the novel *The Code of Victor Jailot* by Edward Childs Carpenter. Photography: Lee Garmes. Editor: Stuart Heisler. Released by First National Pictures. Cast: Billie Dove, Gilbert Roland, Noah Beery, Raymond Turner, Armand Kaliz, Emil Chautard, Boris Karloff, Mattie Peters.

*The Black Ace* (1928) Director: Leo D. Mahoney. Script and story: Ford I. Beebee. Photography: Edward A. Kull. Editor: Joseph Kane. Leo Maloney Productions. Released by Pathe Exchange. Cast: Don Coleman, Jeanette Loff, Billy Butts, J.P. McGowan, Noble Johnson, William Steele, Ben Corbett, Edward Jones, Boris Karloff.

*Sharp Shooters* (1928) Director: J.G. Blystone. Script: Marion Orth. Titles: Malcolm Stuart Boylan. Story: Randall H. Faye. Photography: Charles Clarke. Assistant Director: Jasper Blystone. Presented by William Fox. Released by Fox Film Coporation: Cast: George O.'Brien, Lois Moran, Noah Young, Tom Dugan, William Demarest, Gwen Lee, Josef Swickard, Boris Karloff.

*Vanishing Rider* (1928) Director: Ray Taylor. Released by Universal Pictures. 10-chapter serial. Cast: William Desmond, Ethylene Clair, Bud Osborne, Nelson McDowell, Boris Karloff.

*Vultures of the Sea* (1928) Director: Richard Thorpe. Producer: Nat Levine. Released by Mascot Pictures. 10-chapter serial. Cast: Johnnie Walker, Shirley Mason, Tom Sanschi, Boris Karloff, John Carpenter, George Magrill, Joe Bennett, Arthur Dewey, Frank Hagney.

*Burning the Wind* (1928) Directors: Henry MacRae and Herbert Blache. Script by Raymond Script: Raymond Schrock, George Plympton, and George Morgan. Based on the novel *A Daughter of the Dons* by William MacLeod Raine. Photography: Harry Neuman and Ray Ramsey. Editors: Maurice Pivar and Thomas Malloy. Released by Universal Pictures Cast: Hoot Gibson, Virginia Brown Faire, Cesare Gravina, Robert Homans, George Grandee, Boris Karloff, Pee Wee Holmes.

*The Little Wild Girl* (1928) Director: Frank Mattison.. Script: Cecil Burtis Hill. Based on a story by Putnam Hoover. Photography: Charles Cronjager. Editor: Minnie Steppler. Cast: Lila Lee, Cullen Landis, Frank Merrill, Sheldon Lewis, Boris Karloff, Jimmy Aubrey, Bud Shaw.

*The Fatal Warning* (1929) Director: Richard Thorpe. Producer: Nat Levine. Released by Mascot Pictures. 10-chapter serial. Cast: Helene Costello, Ralph Graves, Tom Lingham, Phillips Smalley, Lloyd Whitlock, George Periolat, Boris Karloff, Syd Crossley, Martha Mattox, Symona Boniface.

*The Devil's Chaplain* (1929) Director: Duke Worne. Producer: Trem Carr. Script: Arthur Hoerl. Based on the novel by George Bronson Howard. Photography: Hap Depew. Editor: J.S. Harrington. Released by Rayart-Richmond Pictures. Cast: Cornelius O'Keefe, Virginia Brown Faire, Josef Swickard, Boris Karloff, Wheeler Oakman, George McIntosh, Leland Carr.

*The Phantom of the North* (1929) Director: Harry Webb. Script: George Hull and Carl Krusada. Based on a story by Flora E. Douglas. Photography: Arthur Reeves and William Thornley. Editor: Frank Bain. Released by Biltmore Productions--All Star Pictures. Cast: Edith Roberts, Donald Keith, Kathleen Kay, Boris Karloff, Joe Bonomo, Josef Swickard.

*Two Sisters* (1929) Director: Scott Pembroke. Producer: Trem Carr. Script: Arthur Hoerl. Based on a novel by Virginia Terhune Vandewater. Photography: Hap Depew. Released by Rayart Pictures. Cast: Viola Dana, Rex Lease, Claire DeBrey, Irving Bacon, Boris Karloff, Tom Lingham, Tom Curran, Adalyn Asbury.

*Anne Against the World* (1929) Director: Duke Worne. Script: Arthur Hoerl. Based on a story by Victor Thorne. Photography: Hap Depew. Editor: J.S. Harrington. Released by Rayart Pictures. Cast: Shirley Mason, Jack Mower, James Bradbury, Jr., Isabelle Keith, Tom Curran, Henry Roquemore, Boris Karloff, Billy Franey, Belle Stoddard.

## SOUND FILMS

*Behind That Curtain* (1929) Director: Irving Cummings. Producer: William Fox. Script: Sonya Levien and Clarke Silvernail. Based on the story by Earl Derr Biggers. Assistant Director: Charles Woolstenhume. Photography: Conrad Wells, Dave Ragin, and Vincent Farrar. Editor: Alfred De Gaetano. Released by Fox Pictures. Cast: Warner Baxter, Lois Moran, Gilbert Emery, Claude King, Philip Strange, Boris Karloff, Jamiel Hassan, Peter Gawthorne, John Rogers, Montague Shaw, Frank Finch-Smiles, Mercedes de Velasco, E.L. Park.

*King of the Kongo* (1929) Director: Richard Thorpe. Producer: Nat Levine. Released by Mascot Pictures (silent and sound versions). 10-chapter serial. Cast: Jacqueline Logan, Walter Miller, Richard Tucker, Boris Karloff, Larry Sheers, Harry Todd, Richard Neil, Lafe McKee, J.P. Leckray, William Burt, Gordon Russell, Robert Frazer, Ruth Davis.

*The Unholy Night* (1929) Director: Lionel Barrymore. Script: Edwin Justus Mayer. Based on a story by Ben Hecht. Adaptation: Dorothy Farnum. Photography: Ira Morgan. Editor: Grant Whytock. Released by MGM. Cast: Ernest Torrence, Roland Young, Dorothy Sebastian, Natalie Moorhead, Claude Fleming. John Miljan, Richard Tucker, John Loder, Philip Strange, Polly Moran, Boris Karloff, Sidney Jarvis, Clarence Geldert.

*The Bad One* (1930) Director: George Fitzmaurice. Producer: Joseph M. Schenck. Script: Carey Wilson. Based on a story by John Farrow. Dialogue: Howard Emmett Rogers. Assistant Director: Walter Mayo. Photography: Karl Struss. Editor: Donn Hayes. Art Director: William Cameron Menzies. Music: Hugo Riesenfeld. Released by United Artists. Cast: Dolores Del Rio, Edmund Lowe, Don Alvarado, Blanche Frederici, Adrienne D'Ambricourt, Ullrich Haupt, Mitchell Lewis, Ralph Lewis, Charles McNaughton, Yola D'Avril, John Sainpolis, Henry Kolker, George Fawcett, Tom Dugan, Boris Karloff.

*The Sea Bat* (1930) Director: Wesley Ruggles. Script: Bess Mereduth and John Howard Lawson. Based on a story by Dorothy Yost. Photography: Ira Morgan. Editors: Harry Reynolds and Jerry Thomas. Art Director: Cedric Gibbons. Released by MGM. Cast: Raquel Torres, Charles Bickford, Nils Asther, George M. Marion, John Millian, Boris Karloff, Gibson Gowland., Edmund Breese, Mathilde Comont, Mack Swain.

*The Utah Kid* (1930) Director: Richard Thorpe. Script and story: Frank Howard Clark. Photography: Arthur Reed. Editor: Billy Bolen. Cast: Rex Lease, Dorothy Sebastian, Tom Santschi, Mary Carr, Walter Miller, Lafe McKee, Boris Karloff, Bud Osborne.

*Mothers Cry* (1930) Director: Hobart Henley. Producer: Robert North. Script: Lenore J. Coffee. Based on the novel by Helen Grace Carlisle. Photography: Gilbert Warrenton. Editor: Frank Hare. Released by First National Pictures. Cast: Dorothy Peterson, Helen Chandler, David Manners, Sidney Blackmer, Edward Woods, Evalyn Knapp, Jean Bary, Pat O'Malley, Claire McDowell, Charles Hill Mailes, Reginald Pasch, Boris Karloff, Marvin Jones, Meredyth Burel.

*King of the Wild* (1931) Directors: Richard Thorpe and B. Reeves Eason. Producer: Nat Levine. Script and Story: Wyndham Gittes and Ford Beebee. Photography: Benjamin Kline and Edward Kull. Released by Mascot Pictures. 12-chapter serial. Cast: Walter Miller, Nora Lane, Dorothy Cristy, Tom Santschi, Boris Karloff, Arthur McLaglen, Carroll Nye, Victor Potel, Martha Lalade, Mischa Auer.

*The Criminal Code* (1931) Director: Howard Hawks. Producer: Harry Cohn. Script: Fred Niblo, Jr. and Seton I. Miller. Based on the play by Martin Flavin. Photography: James Wong Howe. Released by Columbia Pictures. Cast: Walter Huston, Philips Holmes, Constance Cummings, Mary Doran, DeWitt Jennings, John Sheehan, Boris Karloff, Otto Hoffman, Clark Marshall, Arthur Hoyt, Ethel Wales, Nicholas Soussanin, Paul Porcasi, James Guilfoyle, Lee Phelps.

*The Last Parade* (1931) Director: Erle C. Kenton. Script and Dialogue: Dorothy Howell. Based on a story by Casey Robinson. Photography: Teddy Tetzlaff. Released by Columbia Pictures. Cast: Jack Holt, Tom Moore, Constance Cummings, Gaylord Pendleton, Robert Ellis, Earle D. Bunn, Vivi, Jess De Vorska, Ed Le Saint, Edmund Breese, Clarence Muse, Boris Karloff.

*Dirigible* (1931) Director: Frank Capra. Script: Jo Swerling and Dorothy Howell. Based on a story by Lt. Cmdr. Frank W. ("Spig") Wead. Dialogue: Jo Swerling. Photography: Joe Wilbur and Elmer Dyer. Released by Columbia Pictures. Cast: Jack Holt, Ralph Graves, Fay Wray, Hobart Bosworth, Roscoe Karns, Harold Goodwin, Clarence Muse, Emmett Corrigan, Al Roscoe, Selmer Jackson, Boris Karloff.

*Young Donovan's Kid* (1931) Director: Fred Niblo. Producer: Louis Sarecky. Script: J. Walter Ruben. Based on the novel *Big Brother* by Rex Beach. Photography: Edward Cronjager. Released by RKO-Radio Pictures. Cast: Richard Dix, Jackie Cooper, Marion Shilling, Frank Sheridan, Boris Karloff, Dick Rush, Fred Kelsey, Richard Alexander, Harry Tenbrook, Wilfred Lucas, Phil Sleeman, Charles Sullivan.

*Cracked Nuts* (1931) Director: Edward Francis Cline. Producer: Douglas MacLean. Script: Ralph Spence. Story: Douglas MacLean and Al Boasberg. Dialogue: Ralph Spence and Al Boasberg. Photography: Nicholas Musuraca. Released by RKO-Radio Pictures. Cast: Bert Wheeler, Robert Woolsey, Edna May Oliver, Dorothy Lee, Leni Stengel, Stanley Fields, Boris Karloff, Harvey Clark, Ben Turpin, Frank Thornton, Frank Lackteen, Wilfred Lucas.

*Smart Money* (1931) Director: Alfred E. Green. Screenplay and dialogue: Kubec Glasmon, John Bright, Lucien Hubbard, and Joseph Jackson. Based on the story *The Idol* by Lucien Hubbard and Joseph Jackson. Photography: Robert Kurle. Music: Leo F. Forbstein. Make-up: Perc Westmore. Released by Warner Brothers. Cast: Edward G. Robinson, James Cagney, Evalyn Knapp, Noel Francis, Morgan Wallace, Paul Porcasi, Maurice Black, Margaret Livingston, Boris Karloff, Billy House, Polly Walters, Ben Taggart, Gladys Lloyd.

*The Public Defender* (1931) Director: J. Walter Ruben. Producer: Louis Sarecky. Script: Bernard Schubert. Based on the novel *The Splendid Crime* by George Goodchild. Photography: Edward Cronjager. Editor: Archie Marshek. Released by RKO-Radio Pictures. Cast: Richard Dix, Shirley Grey, Edmund Breese, Boris Karloff, Paul Hurst, Purnell Pratt, Alan Roscoe, Ruth Weston, Nela Walker, Frank Sheridan, William Halligan, Carl Gerrard.

*Pardon Us* (1931) (French version) Director: James Parrott. Producer: Hal Roach. Screenplay and dialogue: H.M. Walker. Photography: Jack Stevens. Editor: Richard Currier. Released by MGM. Cast: Stan Laurel, Oliver Hardy, June Marlowe, James Finlayson, Boris Karloff, Charlie Hall, Sam Lufkin, Silas D. Wilcox, George Miller, Wilfred Lucas.

*Five Star Final* (1931) Director: Mervyn LeRoy. Screenplay: Byron Morgan. Based on the play *Late Night Final* by Louis Weitzenkorn. Adaptation: Robert Lord. Photography: Sol Polito. Music: Leo Forbstein. Released by Warner Brothers--First National Pictures. Cast: Edward G. Robinson, Marian Marsh, H.B. Warner, Anthony Bushell, George E. Stone, Frances Starr, Ona Munson, Boris Karloff, Robert Elliott, Aline McMahon, Purnell Pratt, David Torrene, Oscar Apfel, Harold Waldridge, Gladys Lloyd, Polly Walters.

*I Like Your Nerve* (1931) Director: William McGann. Script: Houston Branch. Based on a story by Roland Pertwee. Dialogue: Roland Pertwee and Houston Branch. Photography: Ernest Haller. Editor: Peter Fritsch, Cast: Douglas Fairbanks, Jr., Loretta Young, Edmund Breon, Henry Kolker, Claude Allister, Ivan Simpson, Paul Porcasi, Boris Karloff, Henry Bunston.

*Graft* (1931) Director: Christy Cabanne. Producer: Carl Laemmle, Jr. Script and story: Barry Barringer. Photography: Jerome Ash. Editor: Maurice Pivar. Released by Universal Pictures. Cast: Regis Toomey, Sue Carol, Dorothy Revier, Boris Karloff, William Davidson, Richard Tucker, William Robertson, Harold Goodwin, George Irving, Carmelita Geraghty.

*The Guilty Generation* (1931) Director: Rowland V. Lee. Producer: Harry Cohn. Script: Jack Cunningham. Based on the play by Jo Milward and J. Kirby Hawkes. Photography: Byron Haskin. Released by Columbia Pictures. Cast: Leo Carrillo, Constance Cummings, Robert Young, Boris Karloff, Leslie Fenton, Jimmy Wilcox, Elliott Roth, Phil Tead, Frederick Howard, Eddie Boland, W.J. O'Brien, Ruth Warren.

*The Mad Genius* (1931) Director: Michael Curtiz . Script: J. Grubb Alexander and Harvey Thew. Based on the play *The Idol* by Martin Brown. Photography: Barney McGill. Editor: Ralph Dawson. Art Director: Anton Grot. Choreography: Adolph Bolm. Released by Warner Brothers--First National Pictures. Cast: John Barrymore, Marian Marsh, Donald Cook, Charles Butterworth, Luis Alberni, Carmel Myers, Andre Luguet, Frankie Darro, Boris Karloff, Mae Madison.

*The Yellow Ticket* (1931) Director: Raoul Walsh. Script: Jules Furthman and Guy Bolton. Based on the play by Michael Morton. Photography: James Wong Howe. Editor: Jack Murray. Released by Fox Pictures. Cast: Elissa Landi, Lionel Barrymore, Laurence Olivier, Walter Byron, Sarah Padden, Arnold Korff, Mischa Auer, Rita LaRoy, Boris Karloff, Edwin Maxwell, Alex Malesh.

*Frankenstein* (1931) Director: James Whale. Producer: Carl Laemmle, Jr. Associate Producer: E.M. Asher. Script: Garrett Fort, Francis Edwards Faragoh, John Russell, and Robert Florey. Based on the novel by Mary Wollstonecraft Shelley and the play by Peggy Webling. Adaptation: John L. Balderston. Scenario edited by Richard Schayer. Photography: Arthur Edeson. Special Electrical Effects: Kenneth Strickfaden. Make-up: Jack P. Pierce. Art Director: Charles D. Hall. Musical Theme: David Broekman. Special Effects: John P. Fulton. Editor: Clarence Kolster. Released by Universal Pictures. Cast: Colin Clive, Mae Clarke, Joh Boles, Edward Van Sloan, Boris Karloff, Frederick Kerr, Dwight Frye, Lionel Belmore, Marilyn Harris, Michael Mark, Arletta Duncan, Pauline Moore, Francis Ford.

*Tonight or Never* (1931) Director: Mervyn LeRoy. Producer: Samuel Goldwyn. Script: Ernest Vajda. Based on the play by Lili Hatvany. Adaptation: Frederick Hatton and Fanny Hatton. Photography: Gregg Toland. Editor: Grant Whytock. Art Director: Willy Pogany. Music: Alfred Newman. Costumes: Chanel. Released by United Artists. Cast: Gloria Swanson, Melvyn Douglas, Ferdinand Gottschalk, Robert Grieg, Greta Meyer, Warburton Gamble, Alison Skipworth, Boris Karloff.

*Behind the Mask* (1932) Director: John Frances Dillon. Producer: Harry Cohn. Screenplay and dialogue: Jo Swerling. Adapted from the story *In the Secret Service* by Jo Swerling. Photography: Ted Tetzlaff. Continuity: Dorothy Howell. Editor: Otis Garrett. Released by Columbia Pictures. Cast: Jack Holt, Constance Cummings, Boris Karloff, Claude King, Bertha Mann, Edward Van Sloan, Willard Robertson, Tommy Jackson.

*Alias the Doctor* (1932) Director: Michael Curtiz. Script: Houston Branch. Based on the play by Imre Foeldes. Dialogue: Charles Kenyon. Photography: Barney McGill. Editor: William Holmes. Art Director

Anton Grot. Technical Advisor: Dr. Henry Morton. Released by Warner Brothers--First National Pictures. Cast: Richard Barthelmess, Marian Marsh, Lucille La Verne, Norman Foster, Adrienne Dore, Oscar Apfel, John St. Polis, Wallis Clark, Claire Dodd, George Rosener, Boris Karloff, Nigel De Brulier, Reginald Barlow, Arnold Lucy, Harold Westridge, Robert Farfan.

*Business and Pleasure* (1932) Director: David Butler. Producer: Al Rockett. Script and dialogue: Gene Towne and William Copselman. Based on the novel *The Plutocrat* by Booth Tarkington and the play by Arthur Goodrich. Photography: Ernest Palmer. Released by Fox Pictures. Cast: Will Rogers, Jetta Goudal, Joel McCrea, Dorothy Peterson, Peggy Ross, Cyril Ring, Jed Prouty, Oscar Apfel, Vernon Dent, Boris Karloff.

*Scarface* (1932) Director: Howard Hawks. Producer: Howard Hughes. Script: Seton I. Miller, John Lee Mahin, W.R. Burnett, and Fred Palsey. Based on the novel by Armitage Trail. Adaptation: Ben Hecht. Photography: Lee Garmes and L.W. O'Connell. Editor: Edward Curtiss. Assistant Director: Richard Rosson. Music: Adolph Tandler and Gus Arnheim. Production Designer: Harry Oliver. Released by United Artists. Cast: Paul Muni, Ann Dvorak, Karen Morley, Osgood Perkins, Boris Karloff, George Raft, Vince Barnett, C. Henry Gordon, Inez Palange, Edwin Maxwell, Tully Marshall, Harry J. Vejar, Bert Starkey, Henry Armetta, Maurice Black.

*The Cohens and Kellys in Hollywood* (1932) Director: John Frances Dillon. Producer: Carl Laemmle, Jr. Script and story: Howard J. Green. Based on characters created by Aaron Hoffman. Dialogue: James Mulhouser. Photography: Jerome Ash. Editor: Harry Webb. Released by Universal Pictures. Cast: George Sidney, Charlie Murray, June Clyde, Norman Foster, Emma Dunn, Esther Howard, Eileen Percy. Edwin Maxwell, Dorothy Christy, Luis Alberni, John Roche. As themselves: Lew Ayres, Harry Barris, Sidney Fox, Boris Karloff, Tom Mix, Genevieve Tobin.

*The Miracle Man* (1932) Director: Norman Z. McLeod. Screenplay: Waldermar Young. Based on a story by Frank L. Packard and the play by George M. Cohan and Robert H. Davis. Dialogue: Walderma Young and Samuel Hoffenstein. Photography: David Abel. Art Director: Hans Drier. Released by Paramount Pictures. Cast: Sylvia Sidney, Chester Morris, Robert Coogan, John Wray, Ned Sparks, Hobart Bosworth, Lloyd Hughes, Virginia Bruce, Boris Karloff, Irving Pichel, Frank Larien, Florine McKinney, Lew Kelly, Jackie Searle.

*Night World* (1932) Director: Hobart Henley. Producer: Carl Laemmle, Jr. Script: Richard Schayer. Based on a story by P.J. Wolfson and Allen Rivkin. Photography: Merritt Gerstad. Editor: Maurice Pivar. Music: Alfred Newman. Musical Director: Hal Grayson. Choreographer: Busby Berkeley. Released by Universal Pictures. Cast: Lew Ayres, Mae Clarke, Boris Karloff, Dorothy Revier, Russell Hopton, Bert Roach, Dorothy Peterson, Paisley Noon, Hedda Hopper, Clarence Muse, George Raft, Robert Emmett O'Connor, Florence Lake, Huntley Gordon.

*The Old Dark House* (1932) Director: James Whale. Producer: Carl Laemmle, Jr. Script and Adaptation: Benn W. Levy. Additional Dialogue: R.C. Sheriff. Based on the novel *Benighted* by J.B. Priestley. Photography: Arthur Edeson. Editor: Clarence Kolster. Art Director: Charles D. Hall. Make-up: Jack Pierce. Special Effects: John P. Fulton. Released by Universal Pictures. Cast: Boris Karloff, Melvyn Douglas, Charles Laughton, Gloria Stuart, Raymond Massey, Lillian Bond, Ernest Thesiger, Eva Moore, Brember Wills, John/Elspeth Dudgeon.

*The Mask of Fu Manchu* (1932) Directors: Charles Brabin and Charles Vidor. Producer: Irving Thalberg. Script: Irene Kuhn, Edgar Allan Woolf, and John Willard. Based on the novel by Sax Rohmer. Photography: Tony Gaudio. Editor: Ben Lewis. Art Director: Cedric Gibbons. Make-up: Cecil Holland. Costumes: Adrian. Special Effects: Kenneth Strickfaden. Released by MGM. Cast: Boris Karloff, Lewis Stone, Karen Morley, Charles Starrett, Myrna Loy, Jean Hersholt, Lawrence Grant, David Torrence, Herbert Bunston, Gertrude Michael, Ferdinand Gottschalk, C. Montague Shaw.

*The Mummy* (1932) Director: Karl Freund. Producer: Carl Laemmle, Jr. Script: John D. Balderston. Based on a story by Nina Wilcox Putnam and Richard Schayer. Photography: Charles Stumar. Editor: Milton

Carruth. Art Director: Willy Pogany. Make-up: Jack Pierce. Special Effects: John P. Fulton. Released by Universal Pictures. Cast: Boris Karloff, Zita Johann, David Manners, Edward Van Sloan, Arthur Byron, Bramwell Fletcher, Noble Johnson, Leonard Mudie, Katherine Byron, Eddie Kane, Tony Marlow, Arnold Gray, James Crane, Henry Victor.

*The Ghoul* (1933) Director: T. Hayes Hunter. Producer: Michael Balcon. Script: Leonard Hines, Roland Pertwee, and John Hastings Turner. Adaptation: Rupert Downing. Based on a novel by Frank King. Photography: Gunther Krampf. Editor: Ian Dalrymple. Art Director: Alfred Junge. Music: Louis Levy. Make-up: Heinrich Heitfeld. Released by Gaumont-British Pictures. Cast: Boris Karloff, Cedric Hardwicke, Ernest Thesiger, Dorothy Hyson, Anthony Bushnell, Kathleen Harrison, Ralph Richardson, Harold Huth, D.A. Clarke-Smith, Jack Raine.

*The Lost Patrol* (1934) Director: John Ford. Producer: Cliff Reid. Executive Producer: Merian C. Cooper. Screenplay: Dudley Nichols. Adaptation: Garrett Fort. Based on the novel *Patrol* by Philip MacDonald. Photography: Harold Wenstrom. Editor: Paul Weatherwax. Art Directors: Van Nest Polglase and Sidney Ullman. Music: Max Steiner. Released by RKO-Radio Pictures. Cast: Victor McLaglen, Boris Karloff, Wallace Ford, Reginald Denny, J.M. Kerrigan, Billy Bevan, Alan Hale, Brandon Hurst, Douglas Walton, Sammy Stein, Howard Wilson, Neville Clark, Paul Hanson, Francis Ford.

*The House of Rothschild* (1934) Director: Alfred Werker. Producer: Darryl F. Zanuck. Script: Nunnally Johnson. Based on the play by George Humbert Westley. Photography: Peverell Marley. Editors: Alan McNeil and Barbara McLean. Music: Alfred Newman. Released by United Artists. Cast: George Arliss, Boris Karloff, Loretta Young, Robert Young, C. Aubrey Smith, Arthur Byron, Helen Westley, Reginald Owen, Florence Arliss, Alan Mowbray, Noel Madison, Ivan Simpson, Holmes Herbert, Paul Harvey, Georges Renavent, Murray Kinnell, Oscar Apfel, Lumsden Hare, Leo McCabe, Gilbert Emery, Ethel Griffies.

*The Black Cat* (1934) Director: Edgar G. Ulmer. Producer: Carl Laemmle, Jr. Script: Peter Ruric. Story: Edgar G. Ulmer and Peter Ruric. Suggested by the story by Edgar Allan Poe. Photography: John

J. Mescall. Editor: Raymond Curtis. Art Director: Charles D. Hall. Special Effects: John P. Fulton. Make-up: Jack Pierce. Music: Heinz Roemheld. Released by Universal Pictures. Cast: Boris Karloff, Bela Lugosi, David Manners, Jacqueline Wells, Lucille Lund, Egon Brecher, Harry Cording, Henry Armetta, Albert Conti, Anna Duncan, Herman Bing, Andre Cheron, Luis Alberni.

*Gift of Gab* (1934) Director: Karl Freund. Producer: Carl Laemmle, Jr. Script: Rian James. Adaptation: Lou Breslow. Based on a story by Jerry Wald and Philip G. Epstein. Photography: George Robinson and Harold Wenstrom. Editor: Raymond Curtis. Music: Edward Ward. Released by Universal Pictures. Cast: Edmund Lowe, Gloria Stuart, Ruth Etting, Phil Baker, Ethel Waters, Alice White, Victor Moore, Hugh O'Connell, Helen Vinson, Gene Austin, Thomas Hanlon, Henry Armetta, Andy Devine, Marion Byron, Sterling Holloway, Edwin Maxwell, Leighton Noble, James Flavin, Billy Barty, Richard Elliott, Florence Enright, Warner Richmond, Sidney Skolsky, Dennis O'Keefe, Dave O'Brien, Boris Karloff, Bela Lugosi, Alexander Woolcott, Paul Lukas, Chester Morris, Roger Pryor, Douglass Montgomery, Binnie Barnes, Douglas Fowley, June Knight.

*The Bride of Frankenstein* (1935) Director: James Whale. Producer: Carl Laemmle, Jr. Script: William Hurlburt. Adaptation: John L. Balderston and William Hurlburt. Based on the novel *Frankenstein* by Mary Wollstonecraft Shelley. Photography: John J. Mescall. Editor: Ted Kent. Special Effects: John P. Fulton. Special Electrical Properties: Kenneth Strickfaden. Art Director: Charles D. Hall. Musical Score: Franz Waxman. Make-up: Jack Pierce. Released by Universal Pictures. Cast: Boris Karloff, Colin Clive, Valerie Hobson, Ernest Thesiger, Elsa Lanchester, O.P. Heggie, Una O'Connor, Gavin Gordon, Douglas Walton, E.E. Clive, Lucien Prival, Dwight Frye, Reginald Barlow, Mary Gordon, Anne Darling, Ted Billings, Gunnis Davis, John Carradine.

*The Black Room* (1935) Director: Roy William Neill. Producer: Robert North. Script: Henry Myers and Arthur Strawn. Based on a story by Arthur Strawn. Photography: Al Siegler. Editor: Richard Cahoon. Art Director: Stephen Gooson. Musical Director: Louis Silvers. Costumes: Murray Mayer. Released by Columbia Pictures. Cast: Boris Karloff,

Marian Marsh, Robert Allen, Thurston Hall, Katherine DeMille, John Buckler, Henry Kolker, Colin Tapley, Torbin Meyer, Egon Brecher, John Bleifer, Frederick Vogeding, Edward Van Sloan, Alan Mowbray.

*The Raven* (1935) Director: Louis Friedlander (Lew Landers). Producer: David Diamond. Script: David Boehrn. Suggested by *The Raven* and *The Pit and the Pendulum* by Edgar Allan Poe. Photography: Charles Stumar. Editor: Alfred Akst. Art Director: Albert S. D'Agostino. Musical Director: Gilbert Harland. Choreography: Theodore Kosloff. Make-up: Jack P. Pierce. Released by Universal Pictures. Cast: Boris Karloff, Bela Lugosi, Irene Ware, Lester Matthews, Samuel S. Hinds, Inez Courtney, Ian Wolfe, Spencer Charters, Maidel Turner, Arthur Hoyt.

*The Invisible Ray* (1936) Director: Lambert Hillyer. Producer: Edmond Grainger. Script: John Colton. Based on a story by Howard Higgin and Douglas Hodges. Photography: George Robinson. Editor: Bernard Burton. Special Effects: John P. Fulton. Art Director: Albert S. D'Agostino. Music: Franz Waxman. Make-up: Jack P. Pierce. Released by Universal Pictures. Cast: Boris Karloff, Bela Lugosi, Frances Drake, Frank Lawton, Walter Kingsford, Beulah Bondi, Violet Kemble Cooper, Nydia Westman, Georges Renavent, Frank Weicher, Paul Wegel, Adele St. Maur.

*The Walking Dead* (1936) Director: Michael Curtiz. Producer: Lou Edelman. Script: Ewart Adamson, Peter Milne, Robert Andrews, and Lillie Hayward. Based on a story by Ewart Adamson and Joseph Fields. Photography: Hal Mohr. Editor: Thomas Pratt. Art Director: Hugh Reticker. Dialogue Director: Irving Rapper. Costumes: Cary Odell and Orry Kelly. Make-up: Perc Westmore. Released by Warner Brothers Pictures. Cast: Boris Karloff, Ricardo Cortez, Warren Hull, Robert Strange, Joseph King, Edmund Gwenn, Marguerite Churchill, Barton MacLane, Henry O'Neill, Paul Harvey, Joseph Sawyer, Eddie Acuff, Ruth Robinson, Addison Richards, Kenneth Harlan.

*The Man Who Lived Again* (1936) (British title: *The Man Who Changed His Mind*. Also called *Dr. Maniac* and *The Brain Snatcher*.) Director: Robert Stevenson. Producer: Michael Balcon. Script: L. DuGarde

Peach and Sidney Gilliat. Based on a story by John L. Balderston. Photography: Jack Cox. Editors: R.E. Dearing and Alfred Roome. Art Director: Alex Vetchinsky. Make-up: Roy Ashton. Released by Gaumont-British Pictures. Cast: Boris Karloff, Anna Lee, John Loder, Frank Cellier, Donald Calthrop, Cecil Parker, Lyn Harding, Clive Morton, D.J. Williams, Brian Pawley.

*Juggernaut* (1936) (Re-released as *The Demon Doctor*) Director: Henry Edwards. Producer: Julius Hagen. Script: Cyril Campion and H. Fowler Mear. Adaptation and dialogue: Heinrich Fraenkel. Based on a novel by Alice Campbell. Photography: Sidney Blythe and William Luff. Editor: Michael Chorlton. Art Director: James Carter. Music: W.L. Trytel. Released by Grand National Pictures. Cast: Boris Karloff, Joan Wyndham, Arthur Margetson, Mona Goya, Anthony Ireland, Morton Selten, Nina Boucicault, Gibb McLaughlin, J.H. Roberts, Victor Rietti.

*Charlie Chan at the Opera* (1937) Director: H. Bruce Humberstone. Producer: John Stone. Screenplay: W. Scott Darling and Charles Belden. Based on a story by Bess Meredyth and on characters created by Earl Derr Biggers. Photography: Lucien Andriot. Editor: Alex Troffoy. Opera *Carnival* by Oscar Levant. Libretto: William Kernell. Orchestrations: Charles Maxwell. Musical Director: Samuel Kaylin. Costumes: Herschel. Art Directors: Duncan Cramer and Lewis Creber. Released by 20th Century Fox. Cast: Warner Oland, Boris Karloff, Keye Luke, Charlotte Henry, Thomas Beck, Margaret Irving, Gregory Gaye, Frank Conroy, Guy Usher, William Demarest, Maurice Cass.

*Night Key* (1937) Director: Lloyd Corrigan. Producer: Robert Presnell. Script: Tristam Tupper and John C. Moffitt. Based on a story by William Pierce. Photography: George Robinson. Editor: Otis Garrett. Art Director: Jack Otterson. Special Effects: John P. Fulton. Musical Director: Lou Forbes. Make-up: Jack P. Pierce. Released by Universal Pictures. Cast: Boris Karloff, Jean Rogers, Warren Hull, Hobart Cavanaugh, Samuel S. Hinds, Alan Baxter, David Oliver, Edwin Maxwell, Ward Bond.

*West of Shanghai* (1937) Director: John Farrow. Producer: Bryan Foy. Script: Crane Wilbur. Based on the play *The Bad Man* by Peter Emerson Browne. Photography: L. William O'Connell. Editor: Frank Dewar.

Costumes: Howard Soup. Make-up: Perc Westmore. Released by Warner Brothers--First National Pictures. Cast: Boris Karloff, Beverly Roberts, Ricardo Cortez, Gordon Oliver, Sheila Bromley, Vladimir Sokoloff, Gordon Hart, Richard Loo, Douglas Wood, Chester Gan, Luke Chan, Selmer Jackson, James B. Leong.

*The Invisible Menace* (1937) Director: John Farrow. Producer: Bryan Foy. Screenplay: Crane Wilbur. Based on a play by Ralph Spencer Zink. Dialogue Director: Harry Seymour. Photography: L. William O'Connell. Editor: Harold McLernon. Released by Warner Brothers Pictures. Cast: Boris Karloff, Regis Toomey, Marie Wilson, Eddie Craven, Cy Kendall, Frank Faylen, Harland Tucker, John Ridgely, Henry Kolker, Charles Trowbridge, William Haade, Phyllis Barry.

*Mr. Wong Detective* (1938) Director: William Nigh. Producer: Scott R. Dunlap. Associate Producer: William T. Lackey. Screenplay: Houston Branch. Based on the stories by Hugh Wiley. Photography: Harry Neumann. Editor: Russell Schoengarth. Musical Director: Art Meyer. Make-up: Gordon Bau. Released by Monogram Pictures. Cast: Boris Karloff, Grant Withers, Maxine Jennings, Evelyn Brent, Lucien Prival, William Gould, John Hamilton, John St. Polis, Frank Bruno, Hooper Atchley, George Lloyd.

*Son of Frankenstein* (1939) Director and Producer: Rowland V. Lee. Screenplay: Willis Cooper. Suggested by the novel *Frankenstein* by Mary Wollstonecraft Shelley. Photography: George Robinson. Editor: Ted Kent. Special Effects: John P. Fulton. Art Director: Jack Otterson. Associate Art Director: Russell Gausman. Make-up: Jack P. Pierce. Music: Frank Skinner. Musical Arrangements: Hans J. Salter. Musical Director: Lionel Newman. Costumes: Vera West. Released by Universal Pictures. Cast: Basil Rathbone, Boris Karloff, Bela Lugosi, Lionel Atwill, Josephine Hutchinson, Donnie Dunagan, Emma Dunn, Edgar Norton, Perry Ivins, Lawrence Grant, Lionel Belmore, Michael Mark, Caroline Cook, Gustav Von Seyffertitz.

*The Mystery of Mr. Wong* (1939) Director: William Nigh. Producer: Scott R. Dunlap. Associate Producer: William T. Lackey. Screenplay: W. Scott Darling. Based on a story by Hugh Wiley. Photography:

Harry Neumann. Editor: Russell Schoengarth. Make-up: Gordon Bau. Released by Monogram Pictures. Cast: Boris Karloff, Grant Withers, Dorothy Tree, Craig Reynolds, Lotus Long, Morgan Wallace, Holmes Herbert, Ivan Lebedoff, Hooper Atchley, Bruce Wong.

*Mr. Wong in Chinatown* (1939) Director: William Nigh. Producer: Scott R. Dunlap. Supervised by William T. Lackey. Screenplay: W. Scott Darling. Based on a story by Hugh Wiley. Photography: Harry Neumann. Editor: Russell Schoengarth. Make-up: Gordon Bau. Released by Monogram Pictures. Cast: Boris Karloff, Grant Withers, Marjorie Reynolds, Peter George Lynn, William Royle, Huntley Gordon, James Flavin, Lotus Long, Richard Loo, Bessie Loo, Lee Tong Foo, Guy Usher.

*Tower of London* (1939) Director and Producer: Rowland V. Lee. Script and story: Robert N. Lee. Photography: George Robinson. Editor: Edward Curtiss. Art Director: Jack Otterson. Associate Art Director: Richard H. Riedel. Orchestrations: Frank Skinner. Musical Director: Charles Previn. Costumes: Vera West. Make-up: Jack P. Pierce. Released by Universal Pictures. Cast: Basil Rathbone, Boris Karloff, Barbara O'Neil, Ian Hunter, Vincent Price, Nan Grey, John Sutton, Leo G. Carroll, Miles Mander, Lionel Belmore, Rose Hobart, Ralph Forbes, Frances Robinson, Ernest Cossart, G.P. Huntley, John Rodion, Ronald Sinclair.

*The Fatal Hour* (1940) Director: William Nigh. Producer: William T. Lackey. Script: W. Scott Darling. Based on a story by Hugh Wiley. Adaptation: Joseph West. Photography: Harry Neumann. Editor: Russell Schoengarth. Make up: Gordon Bau. Released by Monogram Pictures. Cast: Boris Karloff, Grant Withers, Marjorie Reynolds, Charles Trowbridge, John Hamilton, Craig Reynolds, Jack Kennedy, Lita Chevret, Frank Puglia, I. Stanford Jolley, Jason Robards, Sr.

*British Intelligence* (1940) Director: Terry Morse. Script: Lee Katz. Based on the play *Three Faces East* by Anthony Paul Kelly. Additional Dialogue: John Langan. Photography: Sid Hickox. Editor: Thomas Pratt. Musical Score: Heinz Roemheld. Make-up: Perc Westmore. Released by Warner Brothers--First National Pictures. Cast: Boris Karloff, Margaret Lindsay, Maris Wrixon, Leonard Mudie, Holmes Herbert,

Winifred Harris, Lester Matthews, John Graham, Austin Fairman, Clarence Derwent, Louis Brien, Frederick Vogeding.

*Black Friday* (1940) Director: Arthur Lubin. Producer: Burt Kelly. Script and story: Curt Siodmak and Eric Taylor. Photography: Elwood Bredell. Editor: Phillip Cahn. Special Effects: John P. Fulton. Art Director: Jack Otterson. Associate Art Director: Harold MacArthur. Set Decorator: Russell Gausman. Musical Director: Hans J. Salter. Costumes: Vera West. Make-up: Jack P. Pierce. Released by Universal Pictures. Cast: Boris Karloff, Bela Lugosi, Stanley Ridges, Anne Nagel, Anne Gwynne, Virginia Brissac, Edmund MacDonald, Paul Fix, Murray Alper, Jack Mulhall, Joe King

*The Man With Nine Lives* (1940) Director: Nick Grinde. Producer: Wallace McDonald. Script: Karl Brown. Based on a story by Harold Shumate. Photography: Benjamin Kline. Editor: Al Clark. Art Director: Lionel Banks. Musical Director: Morris W. Stoloff. Released by Columbia Pictures. Cast: Boris Karloff, Roger Pryor, Jo Ann Sayers, Stanley Brown, Hal Taliaferro, Byron Foulger, Charles Trowbrudge, Ernie Adams, Lee Willard, Ivan Miller, Bruce Bennett, John Dilson.

*Devil's Island* (1940) Director: William Clemens. Producer: Bryan Foy. Script: Don Ryan and Kenneth Gamet. Original story by Anthony Coldeway and Raymond L. Schrock. Photography: George Barnes. Editor: Frank Magee. Art Director: Max Parker. Technical Advisor: Louis Van Den Ecker. Released by Warner Brothers—First National Pictures. Cast: Boris Karloff, Nedda Harrigan, James Stephenson, Adia Kuznetzoff, Rolla Gourvitch, Will Stanton, Edward Keane, Robert Warwick, Pedro de Cordoba, Tom Wilson, John Harmond, Richard Bond, Earl Gunn.

*Doomed To Die* (1940) (Alternate title: *The Mystery of Wentworth Castle*) Director: William Nigh. Producer: Paul Malvern. Script: Ralph G. Bettinson and Michael Jacoby. Based on the short stories by Hugh Wiley. Photography: Harry Neumann. Editor: Robert Golden. Make-up: Gordon Bau. Cast: Boris Karloff, Grant Withers, Marjorie Reynolds, Melvin Lang, Guy Usher, Catherine Craig, William Sterling, Kenneth Harlan, Wilbur Mack, Henry Brandon.

*Before I Hang* (1940) Director: Nick Grinde. Producer: Wallace MacDonald. Script: Robert D. Andrews. Based on a story by Karl Brown and Robert D. Andrews. Photography: Benjamin Kline. Editor: Charles Nelson. Art Director: Lionel Banks. Musical Director: Morris W. Stoloff. Released by Columbia Pictures. Cast: Boris Karloff, Evelyn Keyes, Bruce Bennett, Edward Van Sloan, Ben Taggart, Pedro de Cordoba, Wright Kramer, Barton Yarborough, Don Beddoe, Robert Fiske, Kenneth McDonald, Frank Richards.

*The Ape* (1940) Director: William Nigh. Producer: Scott R. Dunlap. Associate Producer: William T. Lackey. Assistant Director: Allen Wood. Script: Curt Siodmak and Richard Carroll. Based on the play by Adam Hull Shirk. Photography: Harry Neumann. Editor: Russell Schoengarth. Art Director: E.R. Hickson. Musical Director: Robert Kay. Released by Monogram Pictures. Cast: Boris Karloff, Maris Wrixon, Gertrude Hoffman, Henry Hall, Gene O'Donnell, Dorothy Vaughn, Jack Kennedy, Jessie Arnold, Selmer Jackson, Philo McCullough, George Cleveland.

*You'll Find Out* (1940) Director and Producer: David Butler. Script: James V. Kern, Monte Brice, Andrew Bennison, and R.T.M. Scott. Based on a story by David Butler and James V. Kern. Photography: Frank Redman. Editor: Irene Morra. Special Effects: Vernon L. Walker. Art Director: Van Nest Polglase. Musical Director: Roy Webb. Music and Lyrics: Jimmy McHugh and Johnny Mercer. Costumes: Edward Stevenson. Released by RKO--Radio Pictures. Cast: Kay Kyser, Peter Lorre, Boris Karloff, Bela Lugosi, Helen Parrish, Dennis O'Keefe, Alma Kruger, Joseph Eggenton, Ginny Simms, Harry Babbitt, Sully Mason, Ish Kabibble, Kay Kyser's Band.

*The Devil Commands* (1941) Director: Edward Dmytryk. Producer: Wallace MacDonald. Script: Robert D. Andrews and Milton Guzberg. Based on the novel *The Edge of Running Water* by William Sloane. Photography: Allen G. Siegler. Editor: Al Clark. Art Director: Lionel Banks. Musical Director: Morris W. Stoloff. Released by Columbia Pictures. Cast: Boris Karloff, Richard Fiske, Amanda Duff, Anne Revere, Ralph Penney, Dorothy Adams, Walter Baldwin, Kenneth McDonald, Shirley Warde.

*The Boogie Man Will Get You* (1942) Director: Lew Landers. Producer: Colbert Clark. Script: Edwin Blum. Adaptation: Paul Gangelin. Photography: Henry Freulich. Editor: Richard Fantl. Art Director: Lionel Banks. Associate Art Director: Robert Peterson. Musical Director: Morris W. Stoloff. Released by Columbia Pictures. Cast: Boris Karloff, Peter Lorre, Maxie Rosenbloom, Larry Parks, Jeff Donnell, Maude Eburne, Don Beddow, George McKay, Frank Puglia, Eddie Laughton, Frank Sully, James Morton.

*The Climax* (1944) Director and Producer: George Waggner. Script: Curt Siodmak and Lynn Starling. Adaptation: Curt Siodmak. Based on the play by Edward Locke. Photography: Hal Mohr and W. Howard Greene. Editor: Russell Schoengarth. Special Effects: John P. Fulton. Art Directors: John B. Goodman and Howard Golitzen. Set Decorators: Russell A. Gausman and Ira S. Webb. Musical Score: Edward Ward. Musical Director: Don George. Libretto: George Waggner. Assistant Director: Seymour Friedman. Costumes: Vera West. Make-up: Jack P. Pierce. Released by Universal Pictures. Cast: Boris Karloff, Susanna Foster, Turhan Bey, Gale Sondergaard, Thomas Gomez, June Vincent, George Dolenz, Ludwig Stossel, Jane Farrar, Erno Verebes, Lotte Stein, Scotty Beckett, William Edmunds, Maxwell Hayes, Dorothy Lawrence.

*House of Frankenstein* (1944) Director: Erle C. Kenton. Producer: Paul Malvern. Executive Producer: Joseph Gershenson. Script: Edward T. Lowe. Based on a story by Curt Siodmak. Assistant Director: William Tummell. Photography: George Robinson. Editor: Philip Cahn. Special Photography: John P. Fulton. Art Directors: John B. Goodman and Martin Obzina. Musical Score: Hans J. Salter, Paul Desau, Frank Skinner, and Charles Previn. Make-up: Jack P. Pierce. Released by Universal Pictures. Cast: Boris Karloff, Lon Chaney, Jr., John Carradine, J. Carrol Naish, Anne Gwynne, Peter Coe, Lionel Atwill, George Zucco, Elena Verdugo, Glenn Strange, Sig Rumann, William Edmunds, Charles Miller, Philip Van Zandt, Julius Tannen, Hans Herbert, Dick Dickinson, George Lynn, Michael Mark, Olaf Hytten, Frank Reicher, Brandon Hurst.

*The Body Snatcher* (1945) Director: Robert Wise. Producer: Val Lewton. Executive Producer: Jack J. Gross. Script: Philip MacDonald and Carlos

Keith (Val Lewton). Based on the story by Robert Louis Stevenson. Assistant Director: Harry Scott. Photography: Robert De Grasse. Editor: J.R. Whittredge. Art Directors: Albert S. D'Agostino and Walter Keller. Musical Score: Roy Webb. Musical Director: Constantin Bakaleinikoff. Costumes: Renee. Released by RKO-Radio Pictures. Cast: Boris Karloff, Bela Lugosi, Henry Daniell, Edith Atwater, Russell Wade, Rita Corday, Sharyn Moffett, Donna Lee, Robert Clarke, Carl Kent, Jack Welch, Larry Wheat, Mary Gordon, Jim Moran, Ina Constant, Bill Williams.

*Isle of the Dead* (1945) Director: Mark Robson. Producer: Val Lewton. Executive Producer: Jack J. Gross. Script: Ardel Wray and Josef Mischel. Suggested by the painting by Arnold Bocklin. Assistant Director: Harry Scott. Photography: Jack MacKenzie. Editor: Lyle Boyer. Art Directors: Albert S. D'Agostino and Walter Keller. Musical Score: Leigh Harline. Musical Director: Constantin Bakaleinikoff. Costumes: Edward Stevenson. Released by RKO--Radio Pictures. Cast: Boris Karloff, Ellen Drew, Marc Cramer, Katherine Emery, Helene Thimig, Alan Napier, Jason Robards, Sr., Skelton Knaggs, Sherry Hall, Ernst Dorian, Erick Hanson.

*Bedlam* (1946) Director: Mark Robson. Producer: Val Lewton. Executive Producer: Jack J. Gross. Script: Mark Robson and Carlos Keith (Val Lewton). Suggested by the painting "Bedlam" by William Hogarth. Assistant Director: Dorian Cox. Photography: Nicholas Musuraca. Special Photographic Effects: Vernon L. Walker. Art Directors: Albert S. D'Agostino and Walter E. Keller. Musical Score: Roy Webb. Musical Director: Constantin Bakaleinikoff. Costumes: Edward Stevenson. Released by RKO--Radio Pictures. Cast: Boris Karloff, Anna Lee, Billy House, Richard Fraser, Glenn Vernon, Ian Wolfe, Jason Robards, Sr., Leland Hodgson, Joan Newton, Elizabeth Russell, Ellen Corby, Robert Clarke, Victor Holbrook, Larry Wheat, Bruce Edwards, John Meredith.

*The Secret Life of Walter Mitty* (1947) Director: Norman Z. McLeod. Producer: Samuel Goldwyn. Script: Ken Englund and Everett Freeman. Based on the story by James Thurber. Assistant Director: Rollie Asher. Photography: Lee Garmes. Special Effects: John P. Fulton. Art Directors: George Jenkins and Perry Ferguson. Musical

Score: David Raskin. Musical Director: Emil Newman. Songs: Sylvia Fine. Costumes: Irene Sharoff. Released by RKO--Radio Pictures. Cast: Danny Kaye, Virginia Mayo, Boris Karloff, Fay Bainter, Ann Rutherford, Thurston Hall, Konstantin Shayne, Florence Bates, Gordon Jones, Reginald Denny, Henry Corden, Doris Lloyd, Fritz Feld, Frank Reicher, Milton Parsons, Mary Brewer, Betty Carlyle, Lorraine De Rome, Jackie Jordan, Martha Montgomery, Sue Casey, Pat Patrick, Irene Vernon.

*Lured* (1947) (British title: *Personal Column*) Director: Douglas Sirk. Producer: James Nasser. Executive Producer: Hunt Stromberg. Associate Producer: Henry S. Kessler. Script: Leo Rosten. Based on a story by Jacques Companeez, Ernest Neuville, and Simon Gentillon. Assistant Director: Clarence Eurist. Photography: William Daniels. Editors: John M. Foley and James E. Newcom. Art Director: Nicolai Remisoff. Musical Score: Michel Michelet. Musical Director: David Chudnow. Make-up: Don Cash. Released by United Artists. Cast: George Sanders, Lucille Ball, Charles Coburn, Boris Karloff, Alan Mowbray, Cedric Hardwicke, George Zucco, Joseph Calleia, Tanis Chandler, Alan Napier, Robert Coote, Jimmie Aubrey, Dorothy Vaughan, Sam Harris.

*Unconquered* (1947) Director and Producer: Cecil B. DeMille. Script: Charles Bennett, Frederic M. Frank, and Jesse Lasky, Jr. Based on the novel *The Judas Tree* by Neil H. Swanson. Photography: Ray Rennahan. Editor: Anne Bauchens. Make-up: Wally Westmore. Special Effects: Gordon Jennings. Art Direction: Hans Dreier and Walter Tyler. Musical Score: Victor Young. Cast: Gary Cooper, Paulette Goddard, Howard da Silva, Boris Karloff, Cecil Kellaway, Ward Bond, Virginia Campbell, Katherine DeMille, Henry Wilcoxon, C. Aubrey Smith, Virginia Grey, Mark Lawrence, Richard Gaines, Alan Napier, Gavin Muir, Nan Sutherland, Lloyd Bridges, Oliver Thorndike.

*Dick Tracy Meets Gruesome* (1947) Director: George Marshall. Producer: Herman Schlom. Script: Robertson White and Eric Taylor. Based on a story by William H. Graffis and Robert E. Kent and the comic strip by Chester Gould. Photography: Frank Redman. Editor: Elmo Williams. Special Effects: Russell A. Cully. Art Directors: Albert

S. D'Agostino and Walter Keller. Musical Score: Paul Sawtell. Musical Director: Constantin Bakaleinikoff. Released by RKO-Radio Pictures. Cast: Boris Karloff, Ralph Byrd, Anne Gwynne, Edward Ashley, June Clayworth, Lyle Latell, Tony Barrett, Skelton Knaggs, Jim Nolan, Joseph Crehan, Milton Parsons.

*Tap Roots* (1948) Director: George Marshall. Producer: Walter Wanger. Script: Alan Le May. Based on a novel by James Street. Additional Dialogue: Lionel Wiggam. Photography: Lionel Lindon and Winton C. Hoch. Editor: Milton Carruth. Art Director: Frank A. Richards. Musical Score: Frank Skinner. Costumes: Yvonne Wood. Make-up: Bud Westmore. Released by Universal-International Pictures. Cast: Van Heflin, Susan Hayward, Boris Karloff, Julie London, Whitfield Connor, Ward Bond, Richard Long, Arthur Shields, Griff Barnett, Sondra Rogers, Ruby Dandridge, Russell Simpson, Jack Davis, Gregg Barton, George Hamilton, Jonathan Hale.

*Abbott and Costello Meet the Killer, Boris Karloff* (1949) Director: Charles T. Barton, Jr. Producer: Robert Arthur. Script: Hugh Wedlock, Jr., Howard Snyder, and John Grant. Based on a story by Hugh Wedlock, Jr. and Howard Snyder. Assistant Director: Joe Kenny. Photography: Charles Van Enger. Editor: Edward Curtiss. Special Effects: David S. Horsley. Art Directors: Bernard Herzbrun and Richard H. Reidel. Musical Score: Milton Schwarzwald. Costumes: Rosemary Odell. Make-up: Bud Westmore. Released by Universal-International Pictures. Cast: Bud Abbott, Lou Costello, Boris Karloff, Lenore Aubert, Gar Moore, Donna Martell, Alan Mowbray, James Flavin, Roland Winters, Nicholas Joy, Mikel Conrad, Morgan Farley, Percy Helton, Victoria Horne, Clair Du Brey, Vincent Renno, Harry Hayden, Murray Alper, Patricia Hall.

*The Strange Door* (1951) Director: Joseph Pevney. Producer: Ted Richmond. Script: Jerry Sackheim. Based on the story *The Sire de Maletroit's Door* by Robert Louis Stevenson. Assistant Director: Jesse Hibbs. Photography: Irving Glassberg. Editor: Edward Curtiss. Special Effects: David S. Horsley. Art Directors: Bernard Herzbrun and Eric Orbom. Musical Director: Joseph Gershenson. Costumes: Rosemary Odell. Make-up: Bud Westmore. Released by Universal-International

Pictures. Cast: Charles Laughton, Boris Karloff, Sally Forrest, Richard Stapley, Michael Pate, Paul Cavanagh, Alan Napier, William Cottrell, Morgan Farley, Charles Horvath, Edwin Harker.

*The Emperor's Nightingale* (1951) Directors: Milos Makovec (live action) and Jiri Trnka (animation). Script: Jiri Trnka and Jiri Drdecka. Based on a story by Hans Christian Andersen. English Narrative: Phyllis McGinley. Photography: Ferdinand Pecenka. Musical Score: Vaclav Trajan. Released in the U.S. by Rembrandt Films. Cast: Jaramir Sobota, Helena Patockova, Boris Karloff (Narrator).

*The Black Castle* (1951) Director: Nathan Juran. Producer: William Alland. Script and story: Jerry Sackheim. Assistant Director: William Holland. Photography: Irving Glassburg. Editor: Russell Schoengarth. Special Effects: David S. Horsley. Art Directors: Bernard Herzbrun and Alfred Sweeney. Musical Director: Joseph Gershenson. Costumes: Bill Thomas. Make-up: Bud Westmore. Released by Universal-International Pictures. Cast: Richard Greene, Boris Karloff, Stephen McNally, Paula Corday, Lon Chaney, Jr., John Hoyt, Michael Pate, Nancy Valentine, Tudor Owen, Otto Waldis.

*Abbott and Costello Meet Dr. Jekyll and Mr. Hyde* (1953). Director: Charles Lamont. Producer: Howard Christie. Script: Lee Loeb and John Grant. Based on the screen story by Sidney Fields and Grant Garrett and the novel by Robert Louis Stevenson. Photography: George Robinson. Editor: Russell Schoengarth. Special Effects: David S. Horsley. Art Directors: Bernard Herzbrun and Eric Orbom. Musical Director: Joseph Gershenson. Costumes: Rosemary Odell. Make-up: Bud Westmore. Release by Universal-International Pictures. Cast: Bud Abbott, Lou Costello, Boris Karloff, Helen Westcott, Craig Stevens, John Dierkes, Reginald Denny, Patti McKaye, Lucille Lamarr, Harry Corden, Marjorie Bennett, Carmen de Lavallade.

*Monster of the Island* (1953) Directors: Roberto Montero and Alberto Vecchietti. Producer: Fortunato Mislano. Script: Roberto Montero and Albert Vecchietti. Based on a story by Carlo Lombardo. Photography: Augusto Tiezzi. Editor: Iolanda Benvenuti. Musical Score: Carlo Innocenzi. Released by Romano Films. Cast: Boris Karloff, Franca Marzi,

Renato Vicario, Germana Paolieril, Patrizi Remiddi, Jose Fierro, Carlo Duse. Released by Romana Films.

*The Hindu* (1953) (Re-released in the U.S.in 1955 as *Sabaka*). Director and Producer: Frank Ferrin. Script and Story: Frank Ferrin. Photography: Allen Svensvold and Jack McCoskey. Editor: Jack Foley. Art Director: Ralph Ferrin. Musical Score: Daksnamurti. Released by United Artists. Cast: Boris Karloff, Nino Marcel, Lou Krugman, Reginald Denny, Victor Jory, June Foray, Jay Novello, Lisa Howard, Peter Coe, Paul Marion, Vito Scotti, Lou Merrill.

*Colonel March Investigates* (1953) Director: Cyril Endfield. Producer: Donald Ginsberg. Script: Leo Davis. Based on the stories by Carter Dickson (John Dickson Carr). Photography: Jonah Jones. Editor: Stan Willis. Art Director: George Paterson. Musical Score: John Lanchberry. Musical Director: Eric Robinson. Released by Criterion Films. Cast: Boris Karloff, Ewan Roberts, Richard Wattis, Sheila Burrell, Anthony Forwood, John Hewer, Joan Sims, Ronald Leigh Hunt, Roger Maxwell, Patricia Owens, Dana Wynter, Sonya Hana, Bernard Rebel.

*Voodoo Island* (1957) (Re-released as *Silent Death*). Director: Reginald LeBorg. Producer: Howard W. Koch. Executive Producer: Aubrey Schenck. Script and Story: Richard Landau. Assistant Director: Paul Wurtzel. Photography: William Marguiles. Editor: John F. Schreyer. Special Effects: Jack Rabin and Louis De Witt. Musical Score: Les Baxter. Make-up: Ted Coodley. Released by United Artists. Cast: Boris Karloff, Beverly Tyler, Murvyn Vye, Elisha Cook, Jr., Rhodes Reason, Jean Engstrom, Frederick Ledebur, Glenn Dixon, Gwen Cunningham, Herbert Patterson, Jerome Frank.

*The Haunted Strangler* (1958) (British title: *Grip of the Strangler*) Director: Robert Day. Producer: John Croydon. Executive Producer: Richard Gordon. Script: Jan Read and John C. Cooper. Based on a story by Jan Read. Photography: Lionel Banes. Editor: Peter Mayhew. Special Effects: Les Bowie. Art Director: John Elphick. Musical Score: Buxton Orr. Musical Director: Frederick Lewis. Released by MGM. Cast: Boris Karloff, Jean Kent, Elizabeth Allan, Anthony Dawson, Vera Day, Tim Turner, Diane Aubrey, Dorothy Gordon, Peggy Ann Clifford,

Leslie Perrins, Michael Atkinson, Desmond Roberts, Jesse Cairns, Roy Russell, Derek Birch, George Hirste.

*Frankenstein 1970* (1958) Director: Howard W. Koch. Producer: Aubrey Schenck. Script: Richard Landau and George Worthing Yates. Based on a story by Aubrey Schenck and Charles A. Moses. Assistant Director: George Vieira. Photography: Carl E. Guthrie. Editor: John A. Bushelman. Art Director: Jack T. Collins. Set Decorator: Jerry Welch. Musical Score: Paul A. Dunlap. Make-up: Gordon Bau. Released by Allied Artists. Cast: Boris Karloff, Tom Duggan, Jana Lund, Donald Barry, Charlotte Austin, Irwin Berke, Rudolph Anders, John Dennis, Norbert Schiller, Mike Lane.

*The Raven* (1963) Director and Producer: Roger Corman. Executive Producers: James H. Nicholson and Samuel Z. Arkoff. Script: Richard Matheson. Suggested by the poem by Edgar Allan Poe. Assistant Director: Peter Bolton. Photography: Floyd Crosby. Editor: Ronald Sinclair. Special Effects: Pat Dinga. Art Director: Daniel Haller. Musical Score: Les Baxter. Costumes: Marjorie Corso. Make-up: Ted Coodley. Released by American International Pictures. Cast: Vincent Price, Peter Lorre, Boris Karloff, Hazel Court, Olive Sturgess, Jack Nicholson, Connie Wallace, William Baskin, Aaron Saxon.

*Corridors of Blood* (1963) Director: Robert Day. Producers: John Croydon and Charles Vetter. Executive Producer: Richard Gordon. Associate Producer: Peter Mayhew. Script and story: Jean Scott Rogers. Assistant Director: Peter Bolton. Photography: Geoffrey Faithfull. Editor: Peter Mayhew. Art Director: Anthony Masters. Musical Score: Buxton Orr. Musical Director: Frederick Lewis. Makeup: Walter Schneiderman. Released by MGM. Cast: Boris Karloff, Betta St. John, Finlay Currie, Christopher Lee, Francis Matthews, Adrienne Corri, Francis De Wolff, Basil Dignam, Frank Pettingell, Marian Spencer, Carl Bernard, Yvonne Warren, Charles Lloyd Pack, Robert Raglan, John Gabriel, Nigel Green, Howard Lang.

*The Terror* (1963) Director and Producer: Roger Corman. Executive Producer: Harvey Jacobson. Associate Producer: Francis Ford Coppola. Script and story: Leo Gordon and Jack Hill. Assistant Director: Monte Hellman. Photography: John Nicholaus. Editor: Stuart O'Brien.

Art Director: Daniel Haller. Musical Score: Les Baxter. Costumes: Marjorie Corso. Released by American International Pictures. Cast: Boris Karloff, Jack Nicholson, Sandra Knight, Richard Miller, Dorothy Neumann, Jonathan Haze.

*The Comedy of Terrors* (1964) (Re-released as *The Graveside Story*) Director: Jacques Tourneur. Producers: Anthony Carras and Richard Matheson. Executive Producers: James H. Nicholson and Samuel Z. Arkoff. Screenplay and Story: Richard Matheson. Assistant Director: Robert Agnew. Photography: Floyd Crosby. Special Effects: Pat Dinga. Art Director: Daniel Haller. Musical Score: Les Baxter. Costumes: Marjorie Corso.. Make-up: Charlie Taylor. Released by American International Pictures. Cast: Vincent Price, Peter Lorre, Boris Karloff, Basil Rathbone, Joyce Jameson, Joe E. Brown, Beverly Hills, Paul Barsolow, Linda Rogers, Luree Nicholson, Buddy Mason.

*Black Sabbath* (1964) Director: Mario Bava. Producer: Salvatore Billitteri. Presented in the U.S. by James H. Nicholson and Samuel Z. Arkoff. Script: Marcello Fondato, Alberto Bevilacqua, and Mario Bava. Based on the stories "The Drop of Water" by Anton Chekhov, "The Telephone" by F.G. Snyder, and "The Wurdalak" by Alexei Tolstoy. Photography: Ubaldo Terzano. Editor: Mario Serandrei. Art Director: Georgio Giovannini. Musical Score: Les Baxter (U.S.) and Roberto Nicolosi (Italy). Make-up: Otello Fava. Released by Emmepi/Galatea/Lyre Films (Italy) and American International Pictures (U.S.). Cast: Boris Karloff, Mark Damon, Susy Andersen, Michele Mercier, Lidia Alfonsi, Jacqueline Perrieux, Milli Monti, Glauco Onorato, Rika Dialina, Massino Righi.

*Bikini Beach* (1964) Director: William Asher. Producer: Anthony Carras. Executive Producers: James H. Nicholson and Samuel Z. Arkoff. Script: William Asher, Leo Townsend, and Robert Dillon. Photography: Floyd Crosby. Editor: Fred Feitshans. Special Effects: Roger and Joe Zonar. Art Director: Daniel Haller. Musical Score: Les Baxter. Songs by Guy Hemric, Jerry Styner, Gary Usher, Roger Christian, Jack Merrill, and Red Gilson. Released by American International Pictures. Cast: Frankie Avalon, Annette Funicello, Martha Hyer, John Ashley, Don Rickles, Harvey Lembeck, Keenan Wynn, Jody McCrea, Candy

Johnson, Danielle Aubry, Meredith MacRae, Dolores Welles, Janos Prohaska, Timothy Carrey, Val Warren, Donna Loren, Little Stevie Wonder, the Pyramids, Boris Karloff.

*Die, Monster, Die* (1965) (British title: *Monster of Terror*) Director: Daniel Haller. Producer: Pat Green. Executive Producers: James H. Nicholson and Samuel Z. Arkoff. Script: Jerry Sohl. Based on the story "The Colour Out of Space" by H.P. Lovecraft. Assistant Director: Dennis Hall. Photography: Paul Beeson. Editor: Alfred Cox. Special Effects: Wally Veevers and Ernest Sullivan. Art Director: Colin Southcott. Musical Score: Don Banks. Make-up: Jimmy Evans. Released by American International Pictures. Cast: Boris Karloff, Nick Adams, Freda Jackson, Suzan Farmer, Terence De Marney, Patrick Magee, Paul Farrell, George Moon, Gretchen Franklin, Sydney Bromley, Billy Milton, Leslie Dwyer.

*The Ghost in the Invisible Bikini* (1966) Director: Don Weis. Producer: Anthony Carras. Executive Producers: James H. Nicholson and Samuel Z. Arkoff. Script: Louis M. Heyward and Ellwood Ullman. Based on a story by Louis M. Hayward. Photography: Stanley Cortez. Editors: Fred Feitshans and Eve Newman. Special Effects: Roger George. Art Director: Daniel Haller. Musical Score: Les Baxter. Songs: Guy Hemric and Jerry Styner. Make-up: Ted Coodley. Released by American International Pictures. Cast: Tommy Kirk, Deborah Walley, Aron Kincaid, Quinn O'Hara, Jesse White, Harvey Lembeck, Nancy Sinatra, Claudia Martin, Boris Karloff, Basil Rathbone, Patsy Kelly, Susan Hart, Francis X. Bushman, Luree Holmes, Benny Rubin, Alberta Nelson, George Barrows.

*The Daydreamer* (1966) Director: Jules Bass. Produced and scripted by Arthur Rankin, Jr. Executive Producer: Joseph E. Levine. Based on the stories *The Little Mermaid*, *The Emperor's New Clothes*, *Thumbelina*, and *The Garden of Paradise*. Animagic Sequences: Don Duga. Anamagic Photography: Tad Mochinga. Live Action Sequences Photography: Daniel Cavelli. Art Director: Maurice Gordon. Music and Lyrics: Maury Laws and Jules Bass. Released by Embassy Pictures. Cast: Paul O'Keefe, Jack Gilford, Ray Bolger, Margaret Hamilton, Robert Harter. Voices: Cyril Ritchard, Hayley Mills, Burl Ives, Tallulah

Bankhead, Terry-Thomas, Victor Borge, Patty Duke, Robert Goulet, Sessue Hayakawa, Boris Karloff, Ed Wynn.

*The Venetian Affair* (1967) Director: Jerry Thorpe. Producers: Jerry Thorpe and E. Jack Neuman. Script: E. Jack Neuman. Based on the novel by Helen MacInnes. Photography: Milton Krasner and Enzo Serafin. Editor: Henry Berman. Special Effects: Carroll L. Shepphird. Art Directors: George W. Davis and Leroy Coleman. Music and Lyrics: Lalo Schifrin and Hall Winn. Make-up: William Tuttle. Released by MGM. Cast: Robert Vaughn, Elke Sommer, Felicia Farr, Karl Boehm, Edward Asner, Boris Karloff, Roger C. Carmel, Joe De Santis, Fabrizio Mioni, Wesley Lau, Luciana Paluzzi, Bill Weiss.

*Mondo Balordo* (1967) Director: Robert Bianchi Montero. Narrative: Castaldo and Tori. American version: Ted Weiss. Photography: Giuseppe la Torre. Editor: Enzio Alfonsi. American version: Fred von Bernewitz. Musical Score: Lallo Gori and Nani Rossi. Narrator: Boris Karloff. A Cine Produzioni Film (Italy) and an Ivanhoe Production (U.S.). Released by Crown International.

*The Sorcerers* (1967) Director: Michael Reeves. Producers: Tony Tenser and Patrick Curtis. Executive Producer: Arnold Louis Miller. Script: Michael Reeves and Tom Baker. Based on a story by John Burke. Photography: Stanley Long. Editor: David Woodward and Ralph Sheldon. Art Director: Tony Curtis. Musical Score: Paul Ferris. Released by Tigon-Curtwell-Global (Great Britain) and Allied Artists (U.S.). Cast: Boris Karloff, Catherine Lacey, Ian Ogilvy, Elizabeth Ercy, Victor Henry, Susan George, Dani Sheridan, Ivor Dean, Peter Fraser, Meier Tzelniker, Bill Barnsley, Martin Terry, Gerald Campion, Alf Joint.

*Mad Monster Party?* (1967) Director: Jules Bass. Producer: Arthur Rankin, Jr. Executive Producer: Joseph E. Levine. Script: Harvey Kurtzman, Len Lorobkin, and Forrest J. Ackerman. Based on a story by Arthur Rankin, Jr. Music and Lyrics: Maury Laws and Jules Bass. Puppet Design: Jack Davis. Released by Embassy Pictures. Voices: Boris Karloff, Phyllis Diller, Ethel Ennis, Gale Garnett, Alan Swift.

*Targets* (1968) Director and Producer: Peter Bogdanovich. Script: Peter Bogdanovich. Based on a story by Peter Bogdanovich and Polly Platt. Photography: Laszlo Kovacs. Editor: Peter Bogdanovich. Art Director: Polly Platt. Associate Producer: Daniel Selznick. Assistant to the Director: Frank Marshall. Make-up: Scott Hamilton. Released by Paramount Pictures. Cast: Boris Karloff, Tim O'Kelly, Nancy Hsueh, James Brown, Mary Jackson, Tanya Morgan, Peter Bogdanovich, Sandy Baron, Arthur Peterson, Monty Landis, Paul Condylis, Mark Dennis, Stafford Morgan, Daniel Ades, Timothy Burns, Warren White, Geraldine Baron, Gary Kent, Ellie Wood Walker, Frank Marshall, Byron Betz, Mike Farrell, Jay Daniel, Carol Samuels, James Morris.

*The Crimson Cult* (1970) (British title: *Curse of the Crimson Altar*) Director: Vernon Sewell. Producer: Louis M. Heyward. Executive Producer: Tony Tenser. Script and story: Mervyn Haisman and Henry Lincoln. Based on the story *Dreams in the Witch House* by H.P. Lovecraft. Additional Material: Gerry Levy. Photography: Johnny Coquillon. Editor: Howard Lanning. Art Director: Derek Bannington. Musical Score: Peter Knight. Make-up: Pauline Worden and Elizabeth Blattner. Costumes: Michael Southgate. Released by Tigon Pictures (Great Britain) and American International Pictures (U.S.). Cast: Boris Karloff, Christopher Lee, Mark Eden, Barbara Steele, Michael Gough, Virginia Wetherell, Rupert Davies, Rosemarie Reede, Derek Tasnsey, Michael Warren, Ron Pomber, Denys Peek, Nita Lorraine, Carol Anne, Jenny Shaw, Vivienne Carlton.

*Isle of the Snake People* (1971) (Alternate titles: *Snake People* and *Cult of the Dead*) Directors: Juan Ibanez and Jack Hill. Producers: Luis Enrique Vergara and Juan Ibanez. Script: Jack Hill. Photography: Austin McKinney and Raul Dominguez. Musical Score: Alice Uretta. Released by Azteca Pictures (Mexico) and Columbia Pictures (U.S.). Cast: Boris Karloff, Julissa, Charles East, Rafael Bertrand, Judy Carmichael, Tongolee, Quentin Miller, Santanon, Quinton Bulnes.

*The Incredible Invasion* (1971) (Alternate titles: *Sinister Invasion* and *Alien Terror*) Directors: Luis Enrique Vergara and Jack Hill. Producers:

Luis Enrique Vergara and Juan Ibanez. Script: Karl Schranzer and Luis Enrique Vergara. Photography: Austin McKinney and Raul Dominquez. Special Effects: Jack Tannenbaum. Musical Score: Alice Uretta. Released by Azteca Pictures (Mexico) and Columbia Pictures (U.S.). Cast: Boris Karloff, Enrique Guzman, Christa Linder, Maura Monti, Yerye Beirute, Tere Valdez, Sangro Alemez, Sergio Kleiner, Mareila Flores, Greselda Mejia.

*Cauldron of Blood* (1971) (Alternate titles: *Blind Man's Bluff* and *The Shrinking Corpse*) Director and story: Edward Mann (Santos Alcocer). Producer: Robert D. Wienbach. Script: John Melson, Jose Luis Bayonas, and Edward Mann. Photography: Francisco Sempere. Editor: J. Antonio Rojo. Art Director: Gil Parrando. Musical Score: Jose Luis Navarro and Ray Ellis. Songs: Edward Mann and Bob Harris. Make-up: Manolita Garcia Fraile. Released by Hispamer Films (Spain) and Cannon Films (U.S.). Cast: Boris Karloff, Viveca Lindfors, Jean-Pierre Aumont, Jacqui Speed, Rosenda Monteros, Ruven Rojo, Dianik Zurakowska, Milo Quesada, Mercedes Rojo, Mary Lou Palermo, Manuel de Blas, Eduardo Coutelen.

*The Fear Chamber* (1971) Directors: Juan Ibanez and Jack Hill. Producers: Luis Enrique Vergara and Jack Hill. Script: Jack Hill. Photography: Austin McKinney and Raul Dominguez. Musical Score: Alice Uretta. Special Effects: Enrique Gordillo. Released by Azteca Pictures (Mexico) and Columbia-Pictures (U.S.). Cast: Boris Karloff, Yerye Beirute, Julissa, Santanon, Carlos East.

*House of Evil* (1972) (Alternate titles: *Dance of Death* and *Macabre Serenade*) Directors: Luis Enrique Vergara and Jack Hill. Producers: Luis Enrique Vergara and Juan Ibanez. Script: Jack Hill. Photography: Austin McKinney and Raul Dominguez. Musical Score: Alice Uretta. Special Effects: Enrique Gordillo. Released by Azteca Films (Mexico) and Columbia Pictures (U.S.). Cast: Boris Karloff, Julissa, Andres Garcia, Angel Espinoza, Beatriz Baz, Quinton Bulnes, Manuel Alvarado, Carmen Vega, Felipe Flores, Fernando Saucedo.

## SHORT FILMS

*Screen Snapshots, No. 11.* (1934) Released by Columbia Pictures. Cast: Boris Karloff, Bela Lugosi, James Cagney, Eddie Cantor, Pat O'Brien, Maureen O'Sullivan, Genevieve Tobin.

*Universal Newsreel.* (1934) Released by Universal Pictures. Cast: Boris Karloff, Bela Lugosi.

*Hollywood Hobbies.* (1935) Cast: Richard Arlen, Buster Crabbe, Clark Gable, Boris Karloff.

*Breakdowns of 1937.* (1937) Released by Warner Brothers. Cast: Humphrey Bogart, Bette Davis, George Brent, Ricardo Cortez, Glenda Farrell, Errol Flynn, Dick Foran, Kay Francis, Boris Karloff, Margaret Lindsay, Pat O'Brien, Dick Powell, Claude Rains, Jane Wyman.

*Cinema Circus.* (1937) Released by Metro-Goldwyn-Mayer Pictures. Director: Roy Rowland. Producer: Louis Lewyn. Cast: Rex Bell, Leo Carrillo, Chester Conklin, Cliff Edwards, James Gleason, William S. Hart, Boris Karloff, Pert Kelton, Olsen and Johnson, Martha Raye, Mickey Rooney, Lee Tracy, Ben Turpin, Rudy Vallee, others.

*Information Please No. 8.* (1941) Released by RKO-Pathe Pictures. Host: Clifton Fadiman. Panelists: John P. Kieran, Franklin P. Adams, Boris Karloff.

*Information Please No. 12.* (1941) Released by RKO-Pathe Pictures. Host: Clifton Fadiman. Panelists: John P. Kieran, Franklin P. Adams, Boris Karloff, Oscar Levant.

*Hedda Hopper's Hollywood No. 6.* (1942) Released by Paramount Pictures. Producers: Herbert Moulton and Whitney Williams. Cinematographer: Robert C. Bruce. Narrator: Hedda Hopper. Cast: Joan Bennett, Claudette Colbert, Joan Davis, Reginald Denny, June Havoc, Hedda Hopper, Ian Hunter, Boris Karloff, Adolphe Menjou, Mary Pickford, Basil Rathbone, Mack Sennett, Rudy Vallee, Dame May Whitty.

*The Juggler of Our Lady.* (1957) Released by Twentieth-Century Fox/Terrytoons. Director: Al Kousel. Producer: Bill Weiss. Supervisor: Gene Deitch. Screenplay and story: R.O. Blechman. Animation: Gene Deitch and Al Kousel. Musical Score: Philip Scheib. Narrator: Boris Karloff.

*Today's Teens.* (1964) Released by Twentieth Century-Fox/Movietone Pictures. Narrator: Boris Karloff.

# RADIO

During his career, Karloff made many appearances on radio, some of which may not be accounted for. Therefore, the following is a close approximation of his radio credits.

*Hollywood on the Air* Jan. 27, 1934
*Fleischmann Hour* Oct. 11, 1934
*Shell Chateau* Aug. 31, 1935
*Fleischmann Hour* Feb. 6, 1936
*Lights Out* "Cat Wife". June 17, 1936
*Royal Gelatin Hour* Sept. 3, 1936
*Royal Gelatin Hour* Nov. 11, 1937
*Lights Out* "Uninhabited". Dec. 22, 1937
*Chase & Sanborn Hour* Jan. 1938
*Baker's Broadcast* Feg Murray, Ozzie Nelson, Harriet Hilliard, Boris
    Karloff, Bela Lugosi.
March 13, 1938
*Lights Out* "The Dream". March 23, 1938
*Lights Out* "Valse Triste." March 30, 1938
*Lights Out* "Cat Wife". April 6, 1938
*For Men Only* April 10, 1938
*Lights Out* "Three Matches". April 13, 1938
*Lights Out* "Night on the Mountain" . April 20, 1938
*Royal Gelatin Hour* May 5, 1938
*Fleischmann Hour* Jan. 5, 1939
*Royal Gelatin Hour* April 6, 1939
*Kay Kyser's Kollege of Musical Knowledge* Dec. 25, 1940

*Stars On Parade* "The Big Man". 1941
*Information Please* Jan. 24, 1941
*Inner Sanctum Mysteries* March 6, 1941
*Kate Smith Hour* March 7, 1941
*Inner Sanctum Mysteries* "The Man of Steel". March 16, 1941
*Hollywood News Girl* March 22, 1941
*Inner Sanctum Mysteries* "The Man Who Hated Death". March 23, 1941
*Bundles For Britain* April 14, 1941
*Inner Sanctum Mysteries* "Death in the Zoo". April 16, 1941
*The Voice of Broadway* April 19, 1941
*Inner Sanctum Mysteries* "The Fog". April 20, 1941
*Inner Sanctum Mysteries* "Imperfect Crime". May 11, 1941
*Inner Sanctum Mysteries* "The Fall of the House of Usher". June 1, 1941
*Inner Sanctum Mysteries* "The Green-Eyed Bat". June 22, 1941
*Inner Sanctum Mysteries* "The Man Who Painted Death". June 29, 1941
*Friendship Bridge* July 3, 1941
*United Press Is On the Air* July 11, 1941
*Inner Sanctum Mysteries* "Death Is A Murderer". July 13, 1941
*Inner Sanctum Mysteries* "The Tell-Tale Heart". August 3, 1941
*The Gloria Whitney Show* Aug. 13, 1941
*Inner Sanctum Mysteries* "The Terror on Bailey Street". October 26, 1941
*Best Plays* "Arsenic and Old Lace". Boris Karloff, Jean Adair, Donald Cook, Edgar Stehli, Evelyn Varden, Wendell Holmes, Joan Tompkins. 1941
*Special USO Program* Nov. 23, 1941
*Time To Smile* Eddie Cantor, Dinah Shore, Boris Karloff. Dec. 17, 1941
*Keep 'em Rolling* Morton Gould, Clifton Fadiman, Boris Karloff. Feb. 8, 1942
*Information Please* Feb. 20, 1942
*Listen, Please* March 22, 1942
*Inner Sanctum Mysteries* "The Fall of the House of Usher". April 5, 1942
*War Bond Show* April 9, 1942
*Inner Sanctum Mysteries* "Blackstone". April 19, 1942
*Inner Sanctum Mysteries* "Study For Murder". May 3, 1942
*Inner Sanctum Mysteries* "The Man of Steel". May 24, 1942
*Inner Sanctum Mysteries* "Death Wears My Face". May 31, 1942
*The Charlie McCarthy Show* Edgar Bergen, Charlie McCarthy, Boris Karloff.

*Information Please* May 17, 1943
*Blue Ribbon Town* Groucho Marx, Virginia O'Brien, Fay MacKenzie, Boris Karloff. June 3, 1944
*Inner Sanctum Mysteries* "Strange Request". June 7, 1942
*Inner Sanctum Mysteries* "The Grey Wolf". June 21, 1942
*Creeps By Night* Host: Boris Karloff. Feb. 15, 1944 to August 15 1944. Karloff departed the show after twelve episodes.
*Information Please* Nov. 20, 1944
*Camel Comedy Caravan* 1944
*Duffy's Tavern* Jan. 12, 1945
*Suspense* "Drury's Bones". Jan. 25, 1945
*The Fred Allen Show* Oct. 14, 1945
*Those Websters* Oct. 19, 1945
*Hildegarde's Radio Room* Oct. 23, 1945
*Inner Sanctum Mysteries* "The Corridor of Doom". Oct. 23, 1945
*The Charlie McCarthy Show* Oct. 28, 1945
*Inner Sanctum Mysteries* "Death For Sale". Oct. 30, 1945.
*Report to the Nation* John Daly, Boris Karloff, Alan Young, Maxine Sullivan. Nov. 4, 1945
*Information Please* Nov. 5, 1945
*Inner Sanctum Mysteries* "The Wailing Wall". Nov. 6, 1945
*The Theatre Guild On The Air* "Where the Cross Is Made". Nov. 11, 1945. Canada Lee, Boris Karloff, Everett Sloane, Margaret Phillips, James Monks.
*The Helen Hayes Show* "Angel Street". Cast: Helen Hayes, Boris Karloff, Cedric Hardwicke. Dec. 8, 1945
*Exploring the Unknown* "The Baffled Genie". Dec. 23, 1945
*Information Please* Dec. 24, 1945
*The Kate Smith Show* Jan. 4, 1946
*The Chesterfield Supper Club* Jan. 16, 1946
*Request Performance* "The Reconversion of Karloff". Boris Karloff, Frank Morgan, Roy Rogers, Janet Blair, Allan Jones. Feb. 3, 1946
*The Sealtest Village Store* Feb. 14, 1946
*Fitch Bandwagon* March 24, 1946
*The Ginny Simms Show* April 5, 1946
*Show Stoppers* June 9, 1946
*Truth or Consequences* Oct. 26, 1946

*That's Life* Nov. 8, 1946

*The Lady Esther Screen Guild Playhouse* "Arsenic and Old Lace". Boris Karloff, Eddie Albert, Verna Felton, Jane Morgan, Joseph Kearns. Nov. 25, 1946

*Show Stoppers* 1946

*The Jack Benny Show* "I Stand Condemned". Jan. 19, 1947

*Kay Kyser's Kollege of Musical Knowledge* March 12, 1947

*Duffy's Tavern* May 21, 1947

*Lights Out* "Death Robbery". July 16, 1947

*Lights Out* July 23, 1947

*Lights Out* "The Ring". July 30, 1947

*Lights Out* August 6, 1947

*Philco Radio Time* Oct. 29, 1947

*The Jimmy Durante Show* Boris Karloff, Arthur Treacher, Peggy Lee. Dec. 10, 1947

*Suspense* "Wet Saturday". Dec. 19, 1947

*Kraft Music Hall* Al Jolson, Boris Karloff, Oscar Levant. Dec. 25, 1947

*Information Please* Jan. 16, 1948

*We, the People* Jan. 27, 1948

*Skippy Hollywood Theater* Feb. 24, 1948

*Hi! Jinx* Aug. 13, 1948

*Guest Star* "The Babysitter". Sept. 12, 1948

*NBC University Theatre* "The History of Mr. Polly". Oct. 17, 1948

*The Sealtest Dorothy Lamour Show* Oct. 28, 1948

*Great Scenes From Great Plays* "On Borrowed Time". Boris Karloff, Parker Fennelly. Oct. 29, 1948

*Truth or Consequences* Oct. 30, 1948

*Stars Over Hollywood* Nov. 6, 1948

*Theater USA* Feb. 3, 1949

*Spike Jones Spotlight Review* April 9, 1949

*The Theatre Guild On the Air* "Perfect Alibi". Boris Karloff, Joan Lorring. May 29, 1949

*The Sealtest Dorothy Lamour Show* June 23, 1949

*Starring Boris Karloff* Host: Boris Karloff. "Five Golden Guineas", "The Mask", "Mungahara", "Mad Illusion", "Perchance to Dream", "The Devil Takes A Bride", "The Moving Finger", "The Twisted Path", "False Face", "Cranky Bill", "Three

O'Clock", "The Shop at Sly Corner", "The Night Reveals". Sept. 21, 1949-Dec. 14, 1949
*This Is Your Life* Nov. 2, 1949
*Bill Stern's Sports Newsreel* Jan. 30, 1950
*Bill Stern's Sports Newsreel* July 21, 1950
*The Barbara Welles Show* Aug. 18, 1950
*Boris Karloff's Treasure Chest* September 17, 1950
*The Wayne Howell Show* Oct. 7, 1950
*The Theatre Guild On the Air* "David Copperfield". Richard Burton, Boris Karloff, Cyril Ritchard, Flora Robson. Dec. 24, 1950
*Stars On Parade* May 4, 1951
*Duffy's Tavern* Oct. 5, 1951
*The Ralph Edwards Show* Jan. 4, 1952
*Phillip Morris Playhouse* "Journey into Nowhere". Feb. 10, 1952
*The Paula Stone Show* Feb. 11, 1952
*The Theatre Guild On the Air* "Oliver Twist". Boris Karloff, Basil Rathbone, Melville Cooper. Feb. 24, 1952
*The Dean Martin and Jerry Lewis Show.* April 18, 1952
*The Theatre Guild On the Air* "The Sea Wolf". Boris Karloff, Edward G. Robinson. April 27, 1952
*What's My Line* May 27, 1952
*Phillip Morris Playhouse* "Outward Bound". Boris Karloff, Edward Hall. June 1, 1952
*Inner Sanctum Mysteries* "Birdsong For A Murderer". June 22, 1952
*Best Plays* "Arsenic and Old Lace". Boris Karloff, Donald Cook, Jean Adair, Edgar Stehli, Evelyn Varden, Wendell Holmes, Joan Tompkins, Arthur Matlin, Ted Osborne, Ed Latimer. July 6, 1952.
*Inner Sanctum Mysteries* "Death For Sale". July 13, 1952
*MGM Musical Comedy Theatre* "Yolanda and the Thief". Boris Karloff, Lisa Kirk, John Conte, John Griggs, Wendell Holmes, Eileen Heckart. Nov. 16, 1952.
*Phillip Morris Playhouse* "Man Against Town". Dec. 10, 1952
*The Theatre Guild On the Air* "Great Expectations". Tom Helmore, Boris Karloff, Melville Cooper, Margaret Phillips, Estelle Winwood, Rex Thompson. April 5, 1953
*Phillip Morris Playhouse* "Dead Past". April 15, 1953

*Heritage* "Plague". April 23, 1953

*Phillip Morris Playhouse* "The Shop at Sly Corner". Boris Karloff, Charles Martin. June 17, 1953

*Reader's Digest* Dec. 16, 1953

*The Play of His Choice* BBC Radio. "The Hanging Judge" by Raymond Massey. Adaptation: John Richmond. Boris Karloff, Duncan McIntyre, Howieson Cuff, Robert Webber, Richard Williams, Norman Claridge, John T. St. Barry, Gabrielle Blunt, Richard Hutton. Dec. 1953.

*Sunday with Garroway* July 18, 1954

*The Nutrilite Show* Dec. 12, 1954

*Monitor* May 20, 1956

*Recollections at 30* Sept. 26, 1956

*Monitor* Feb. 17, 1957

*Monitor* Feb. 22, 1958

*Easy As ABC* "O Is For Old Wives Tales". Boris Karloff, Peter Lorre, Alfred Hitchcock. April 27, 1958.

*Reader's Digest* Host: Boris Karloff. Syndicated. 1956-1969

*The Bob Hope Christmas Show* BBC Radio. Bob Hope, Peter Sellers, Jeannie Carson, Michael Holliday, Boris Karloff, Warren Mitchell, Johnny Desmond, Billy Tement and His Orchestra. Dec. 25, 1961

*The Barry Gray Show* Jan. 26, 1963. Karloff and Peter Lorre were guests on this New York program.

*Flair* April 1963. Host: Dick Van Dyke. Boris Karloff, Orson Bean.

*This Time of Day* BBC Radio. 1965.

## TELEVISION

*We, the People* (July 27, 1948)
NBC
Boris Karloff, Everett Sloane. Director: James Sheldon.

*Winner Take All* (1949)
CBS

*Chevrolet Tele-Theatre* (Feb. 7, 1949)
NBC
"Expert Opinion". Boris Karloff, Dennis King, Vicki Cummings.

*Ford Theater* (April 11, 1949)
CBS
"Arsenic and Old Lace". Boris Karloff, Josephine Hull, Ruth McDevitt, William Prince, Bert Freed, Edgar Stehli, Anthony Ross. Producer: Garth Montgomery. Director: Marc Daniels.

*Texaco Star Theater* (April 12, 1949)
NBC
Milton Berle, Boris Karloff, Richard Tucker.

*Preview* (April 25, 1949)
CBS
Tex McCrary, Jinx Falkenburg, Boris Karloff.

*Suspense* (April 26, 1949)
CBS
"A Night at an Inn". Boris Karloff, Anthony Ross, Jack Manning, Barry Macollum, Joan Stanley. Writer: Halsted Welles. Director: Robert Stevens.

*Chevrolet Tele-Theatre* (May 9, 1949)
NBC
"A Passenger to Bali". Boris Karloff, Vicki Cummings, Stanley Ridges.

*Suspense* (May 17, 1949)
CBS
"The Monkey's Paw". Boris Karloff, Mildred Natwick. Writer: Frank Gabrielson. Director: Robert Stevens.

*Suspense* (June 7, 1949)
CBS
Boris Karloff, Felicia Montealegre, Russell Collins, Douglas Watson. Writer: Halsted Welles. Director: Robert Stevens.

*Starring Boris Karloff* (Sept 22-Dec. 15, 1949)
ABC
Producer: Alex Segal. Karloff appeared each week in this series, which was retitled *Mystery Playhouse Starring Boris Karloff*. The episodes were "Five Golden Guineas", "The Mask", "Mungahara", "Mad Illusion", "Perchance to Dream", "The Devil Takes A Wife", "The Moving Finger", "The Twisted Path", "False Face", "Cranky Bill", "Three O'Clock", "The Shop at Sly Corner", "The Night Reveals".

*The Perry Como Show* (Feb. 19, 1950)
NBC

*Inside U.S.A. with Chevrolet* (March 2, 1950)
CBS

*Masterpiece Playhouse* (Sept. 3, 1950)
NBC
"Uncle Vanya". Boris Karloff, Eva Gabor, Walter Abel, Tod Andrews, Leora Dana, Isobel Elsom. Writer: H. Philip Minis. Director: Gordon Duff.

*Lights Out* (Sept. 18, 1950)
NBC
"The Leopard Lady". Boris Karloff, Martin Brandt, Ronald Long, Frank Gallop, A.J. Herbert, Sid Cassel. Writer: James Lee. Director: William Corrigan.

*Paul Whiteman Goodyear Revue* (Oct. 29, 1950)
ABC
"Mr. Preble Gets Rid of His Wife." Boris Karloff.

*Texaco Star Theater* (Dec. 12, 1950)
NBC

*The Jack Carter Show* (Dec, 30, 1950)
NBC

*Don McNeill TV Club* (April 11, 1951)
ABC
Karloff was a guest on this local show based in Chicago.

*Texaco Star Theater* (Oct. 9, 1951)
NBC

*The Fred Waring Show* (Oct. 21, 1951)
CBS

*Robert Montgomery Presents* (Nov. 19, 1951)
NBC
"The Kimballs". Boris Karloff, Vanessa Brown, Pat Malone, Ruth Maynard, Richard Waring. Writers: Agnes Eckhardt and Mitchell Wilson. Director: Norman Felton.

*Celebrity Time* (Nov. 25, 1951)
CBS

*Studio One* (Dec. 3, 1951)
CBS
"Mutiny on the Nicolette". Boris Karloff, Anthony Ross, Ralph Nelson, Dan Morgan, James Westerfield. Writer: Joseph Liss. Director: Franklin Schaffner.

*Suspense* (Dec. 25, 1951)
CBS
"The Lonely Place". Boris Karloff, Judith Evelyn, Robin Morgan.

*Lux Video Theatre* (Dec. 31, 1951)
CBS
"The Jest of Hahalaba". Boris Karloff, William MacDougall, Robin Craven, Sybil Baker. Writer: David Shaw. Director: Richard Goode.

*CBS Television Workshop* (Jan. 13, 1952)
CBS
"Don Quixote". Boris Karloff, Jimmy Savo, Grace Kelly. Writer: Alvin Sapinsley. Producer: Norris Houghton. Director: Sidney Lumet.

*Stork Club* (Jan. 30, 1952)
CBS

*Tales of Tomorrow* (Feb. 22, 1952)
ABC
"Memento." Boris Karloff, Barbara Joyce.

*Texaco Star Theater* (April 29, 1952)
NBC

*Studio One* (May 19, 1952)
CBS
"A Connecticut Yankee in King Arthur's Court". Boris Karloff, Thomas Mitchell, Barry Kroeger, Salem Ludwig, Loretta Daye, Robert Duke. Writer: Alvin Sapinsley. Director: Franklin Schaffner.

*Celebrity Time* (May 25, 1952)
CBS

*Curtain Call* (June 27, 1952)
NBC
"The Soul of the Great Bell". Boris Karloff, Raimondo Orselli, Robert Dale Martin, David Peffer, Richard Purdy. Writer: Worthington Miner. Director: Kirk Browning.

*Schlitz Playhouse of Stars* (July 4, 1952)
NBC
"The House of Death". Boris Karloff, Marjorie Bennett, John Dodsworth, Toni Gerry, Doris Lloyd, Ian Wolfe. Writer: Vincent O'Connor. Director: William Asher.

*I've Got A Secret* (Sept. 9, 1952)
CBS

*Lux Video Theater* (Dec. 8, 1952)
CBS
"Fear." Boris Karloff, Gene Lockhart, Ruth McDevitt, Bramwell Fletcher. Writer: Roland Winters. Director: Fielder Cook.

*Texaco Star Theater* (Dec. 16, 1952)
NBC

*Who's There* (1952)
CBS

*All Star Revue* (Jan. 17, 1953)
NBC
Boris Karloff, Peter Lorre, Martha Raye.

*Hollywood Opening Night* (March 2, 1953)
NBC
"The Invited Seven." Boris Karloff, Strother Martin, Marjorie Lord, John Qualen. Writer: Weldon Fane. Director: William Corrigan.

*Suspense* (March 17, 1953)
CBS
"The Black Prophet". Boris Karloff, Leslie Nielsen. Writer: Michael Dyne. Director: Robert Mulligan.

*Robert Montgomery Presents* (March 30, 1953)
NBC
"Burden of Proof". Boris Karloff. Writer: Gerald Savory.

*Tales of Tomorrow* (April 3, 1953)
ABC
"Past Tense". Boris Karloff, Robert F. Simon, Katherine Meskill, John McGovern. Writers: Willie Gilbert and Jack Weinstock. Director: Don Medford.

*Quick As A Flash* (May 7, 1953)
ABC
Laraine Day, Leo Durocher, Boris Karloff, June Lockhart. (Karloff made a second appearance on this show with Wendy Barrie.)

*Plymouth Playhouse* (also called *ABC Album*) (May 24, 1953)
ABC

"Four Stories". Boris Karloff, Kyle MacDonell, Philip Truex. Karloff made a second appearance on this series in "The Reticence of Lady Anne" with Donald Cook.

*Suspense* (June 23, 1953)
CBS
"The Signal Man". Writer: Ben Radin. Boris Karloff, Alan Webb.

*Colonel March of Scotland Yard*
(Premiered in syndication December 1953)
Boris Karloff, Ewan Roberts. Producer: Hannah Weinstein. Production Supervisor: Leslie Gilliat. Directors: Phil Brown, Arthur Crabtree, Paul Dickson, Cy Endfield, Terence Fisher, Donald Ginsberg, Bernard Knowles. 26 episodes based on the character by Carter Dickson (John Dickson Carr). "Death in the Dressing Room", "Death in Inner Space", "Error at Daybreak", "The Silver Curtain", "The Case of the Misguided Missal", "Hot Money", "Murder is Permanent", "The Case of the Kidnapped Poodle", "The Stolen Crime", "The New Invisible Man", "The Talking Head", "The Case of the Lively Ghost", "The Sorcerer", "Silent Vow", "Deadly Gift", "The Headless Hat", "Death and the Other Monkey", "The Second Mona Lisa", "The Strange Event at Roman Fall", "The Devil Sells His Soul", "At Night All Cats Are Grey", "The Abominable Snowman", "Present Tense", "The Invisible Knife", "The Missing Link", "Passage at Arms".

*I've Got A Secret* (1954)
CBS
The exact date of Karloff's appearance is unknown.

*I've Got A Secret* (Oct. 13, 1954)
CBS
Karloff was the surprise guest.

*Name's the Same* (Oct. 25, 1954)
ABC

*The George Gobel Show* (Nov. 6, 1954)
NBC

*Truih or Consequences* (Nov. 7, 1954)
NBC
Karloff was a guest on this game show.

*Climax!* (Dec. 17, 1954)
CBS
"White Carnations". Boris Karloff, Teresa Wright, Frank Wilcox, Vivi Janiss, Lester Matthews.

*Down You Go* (Dec. 1954--Feb. 1955)
Dumont
Karloff was a panelist on this game show. He was seen on Dec. 17th and 25th, Jan. 21st and 28th, and Feb. 10th and 24th.

*The Best of Broadway* (Jan. 5, 1955)
CBS
"Arsenic and Old Lace". Helen Hayes, Billie Burke, Boris Karloff, Peter Lorre, Orson Bean, Edward Everett Horton, John Alexander, Bruce Gordon. Writers: Howard Lindsay and Russel Crouse. Producer: Martin Manulis. Director: Herbert Bayard Swope, Jr.

*The Donald O'Connor Texaco Show* (Feb. 19, 1955)
NBC
Boris Karloff, Sid Miller, Joyce Smight.

*The Elgin TV Hour* (Feb. 22, 1955)
ABC
"The Sting of Death". Boris Karloff, Hermoinc Gingold, Martyn Green, Robert Flemyng. Writer: Alvin Sapinsley. Producer: Herbert Brodkin. Director: Daniel Petrie.

*Max Liebman Presents* (March 12, 1955)
NBC
"A Connecticut Yankee in King Arthur's Court". Eddie Albert, Janet Blair, Boris Karloff, Gale Sherwood, Leonard Elliott, John Conte. Writers: William Friedberg, Neil Simon, Will Glickman, Al Schwartz. Associate Producer and Director: Bill Hobin. Producer and Director: Max Liebman.

*Who Said That?* (April 30, 1955)
ABC
John K.M. McCaffrey, Jimmy Cannon, Boris Karloff, Harriet Van Horne.

*General Electric Theater* (May 1, 1955)
CBS
"Mr. Blue Ocean". Anthony Perkins, Susan Strasberg, Boris Karloff, Eli Wallach, Bramwell Fletcher, H.M. Wynant. Writer: Arthur Steuer.

*I've Got A Secret* (Aug. 24, 1955)
CBS
Karloff was the surprise guest.

*The U.S. Steel Hour* (Aug. 31, 1955)
CBS
"Counterfeit". Boris Karloff, John McGiver, Jessie Royce Landis, Edna Best, Sarah Marshall, Terence Rattigan. Writer: Ellen Violett.

*Alcoa Hour* (April 15, 1956)
NBC
"Even the Weariest River". Franchot Tone, Christopher Plummer, Lee Grant, Boris Karloff, Jason Robards, Jr., Milton Selzer. Writer: Alvin Sapinsley. Producer: Herbert Brodkin. Director: Robert Mulligan.

*The Amazing Dunninger* (July 18, 1956)
ABC
Karloff guest starred.

*Frankie Laine Time* (Aug. 8, 1956)
CBS
Boris Karloff, the Edith Barstow Dancers.

*The Ernie Kovacs Show* (Aug. 13, 1956)
NBC
Boris Karloff, Barbara Loden.

*Climax!* (Sept. 6, 1956)
CBS
"Bury Me Later". Boris Karloff, Angela Lansbury, Torin Thatcher, Henry Jones. Writers: Jean Holloway and John McGreevey. Director: Buzz Kulik.

*Playhouse 90* (Oct. 25, 1956)
CBS
"Rendezvous in Black". Franchot Tone, Laraine Day, Tom Drake, Boris Karloff, Viveca Lindfors, Elizabeth Patterson. Writer: James P. Cavanagh. Producer: Martin Manulis. Director: John Frankenheimer.

*The Red Skelton Show* (Nov. 27, 1956)
CBS
Boris Karloff, Eva Gabor.

*The $64,000 Question* (Dec. 11, 18, 25, 1956)
CBS
Karloff successfully answered questions in the category of children's stories.

*A To Z* (1957)
British TV.
Karloff guest starred.

*Hallmark Hall of Fame* (Feb. 10, 1957)
NBC
"The Lark". Julie Harris, Boris Karloff, Basil Rathbone, Eli Wallach, Denholm Elliott, Jack Warden, Bruce Gordon. Writer: James Costigan. Producer and Director: George Schaefer.

*Omnibus* (Feb. 24, 1957)
ABC
Boris Karloff, William Marshall, Lloyd Bochner, Henry Jones, Cleveland Amory, Jean-Louis Barrault.

*Lux Video Theatre* (April 25, 1957)
NBC
"The Man Who Played God". Boris Karloff, June Lockhart, Mary Astor, Ed Kemmer, Henry Hunter, Tom Laughlin, Doris Packer. Writer: Paul Franklin. Director: David McDearmon.

*Kate Smith Hour* (April 28, 1957)
ABC
Gertrude Berg, Edgar Bergen, Benny Goodman, Boris Karloff, Ed Wynn, Billy Williams Quartet. Producer: Ted Collins. Director: Greg Garrison.

*The Dinah Shore Chevy Show* (May 17, 1957)
NBC
Art Carney, Betty Hutton, Boris Karloff.

*The Lux Show Starring Rosemary Clooney* (Oct. 31, 1957)
NBC
Robert Cummings, Boris Karloff, Gale Storm.

*The Gisele MacKenzie Show* (Nov. 16, 1957)
NBC
Boris Karloff, Johnny Desmond.

*Suspicion* (Dec. 9, 1957)
NBC
"The Deadly Game". Gary Merrill, Joseph Wiseman, Boris Karloff, Harry Townes, Ian Wolfe, Frank Campanella. Writer: James Yaffe. Director: Don Medford.

*What's My Line?*
British TV.
The exact date of Karloff's appearance on England's version of this show is unknown.

*The Lux Show Starring Rosemary Clooney* (Jan. 8, 1958)
NBC
Karloff guest starred.

*The Betty White Show* (Feb. 12, 1958)
ABC
Buster Keaton, Boris Karloff.

*Telephone Time* (Feb. 25, 1958)
ABC
"Vestris". Boris Karloff, Torin Thatcher, Rita Lynn. Writer: David Evans. Producer: Jerry Stagg. Director: Arthur Hiller.

*Shirley Temple's Storybook* (March 5, 1958)
NBC
"The Legend of Sleepy Hollow". Shirley Temple, Boris Karloff, John Ericson, Jules Munshin, Russell Collins. Director: Paul Bogart.

*Studio One* (March 31, 1958)
CBS
"The Shadow of a Genius". Boris Karloff, Eva LeGallienne, Skip Homeier, Patricia Barry, Herbert Anderson, Morris Ankrum. Writer: Jerome Rise. Director: Ralph Nelson.

*The Jack Paar Show* (also called *The Tonight Show*) April 22, 1958
NBC
Diahann Carroll, Betty Garrett, Boris Karloff, Elsa Maxwell.

*Playhouse 90* (Nov. 6, 1958)
CBS
"Heart of Darkness". Roddy MacDowall, Richard Haydn, Oscar Homolka, Boris Karloff, Eartha Kitt, Cathleen Nesbitt, Inga Swenson, the Katharine Dunham Dancers. Writer: Stewart Stern. Producer: Fred Coe. Director: Ron Winston.

*This Is Your Life* (Nov. 13, 1958)
NBC
Karloff was the surprised guest of host Ralph Edwards, along with friends and family, including Evelyn Karloff, Sara Jane Karloff, Jack Pierce, and Frank Brink.

*The Veil* (December 1958)
Syndicated.
Karloff appeared in and hosted this pilot for an unsold anthology produced by Hal Roach, Jr. The episodes were "What Happened to Peggy", "Vision of Crime", "The Return of Madame Vernoy", "The Doctor", "The Crystal Ball", "Summer Heat", "Girl on the Road", "Genesis", "Food on the Table", "Destination Nightmare". They have been broadcast as TV movies titled *The Veil*, *Destination Nightmare*, and *Jack the Ripper*. Directors: Frank P. Bibas, Paul Landres, David McDonald, Herbert L. Strock, George Waggner.

*The Gale Storm Show* (Jan. 31, 1959)
CBS
"It's Murder, My Dear". Boris Karloff, Zasu Pitts, Roy Roberts, Frank Cady.

*General Electric Theater* (May 17, 1959)
CBS
"Indian Giver". Edgar Buchanan, Jackie Coogan, Boris Karloff, Carmen Mathews. Writer: Jackson Brewer. Director: Herschel Daugherty.

*Playhouse 90* (Feb. 9, 1960)
CBS
"To the Sound of Trumpets". Stephen Boyd, Dolores Hart, Dan O'Herlihy, Judith Anderson, Boris Karloff, Sam Jaffe, Robert Coote, Celia Lovsky. Writer: John Gay. Producer: Herbert Brodkin. Director: Buzz Kulik.

*DuPont Show of the Month* (March 5, 1960)
CBS
"Treasure Island". Hugh Griffith, Max Adrian, Michael Gough, Boris Karloff, Barry Morse, Tim O'Connor, Richard O'Sullivan, George Rose. Writer: Michael Dyne. Producer: David Susskind. Director: Daniel Petrie.

*Upgreen and At 'em Or A Maiden Nearly Over* (Spring 1960)
British TV.
Richard Attenborough, Jimmy Edwards, Boris Karloff.

*Breck Sunday Showcase* (April 3, 1960)
NBC
"Hollywood Sings". Eddie Albert, Tammy Grimes, Boris Karloff. Music: Franz Allers. Producer: Robert Saudek. Director: William A. Graham.

*The Secret World of Eddie Hodges* (June 23, 1960)
CBS
Eddie Hodges, Jackie Gleason, Margaret Hamilton, Boris Karloff, Bert Lahr, Hugh O'Brian, Janis Paige. Writers: John Aylesworth and Frank Peppiatt. Director: Norman Jewison.

*Thriller* (Sept. 13, 1960--July 9, 1962)
NBC
Karloff hosted all 67 episodes of this horror/suspense anthology. The five he acted in were "The Prediction" (Nov. 22, 1960) with Audrey Dalton and Alex Davion. Writer: Donald S. Sanford. Director: John Brahm. "The Premature Burial" (Oct. 2, 1961) with Sidney Blackmer, Patricia Medina, and Scott Marlowe. Writer: William D. Gordon. Director: Douglas Heyes. "The Last of the Sommervilles" (Nov. 6, 1961) with Martita Hunt, Phyllis Thaxter, and Peter Walker. Writer: R.M.H. Lupino and Ida Lupino. Director: Ida Lupino. "Dialogues with Death" (Dec. 4, 1961)—two half-hour-stories. "Friend of the Dead" with Ed Nelson, William Schallert, and George Kane.. Writer: Robert Arthur. Director: Herschel Daugherty. "Welcome Home" with Ed Nelson, Norma Crane, and Estelle Winwood. Writer: Robert Arthur. Director: Herschel Daugherty. "The Incredible Doktor Markesan" (Feb. 26, 1962) with Dick York and Carolyn Kearney. Writer: Donald S. Sanford. Director: Robert Florey. Producers: Fletcher Markle, William Frye. Associate Producers: Douglas Benton, James Wharton. Executive Producer: Hubbell Robinson.

*Here's Hollywood* (Nov. 7, 1960)
NBC
Karloff was interviewed by Dean Miller.

*Hallmark Hall of Fame* (Feb. 5, 1962)
NBC
"Arsenic and Old Lace". Tony Randall, Mildred Natwick, Dorothy Stickney, Boris Karloff, Tom Bosley, George Voskovec, Dodie Heath.

Writer: Robert Hartung. Producer and Director: George Schaefer.

*P.M. East—P.M. West* (Feb. 12, 1962)
Syndicated.
Mike Wallace and Joyce Davidson hosted a tribute to director George Schaefer with guests Maurice Evans, Julie Harris, Kim Hunter, Mildred Natwick, Boris Karloff, Tony Randall, Ed Wynn.

*Theatre '62* (March 11, 1962)
NBC
"The Paradine Case". Richard Basehart, Viveca Lindfors, Boris Karloff, Robert Webber, Tom Helmore, Bramwell Fletcher. Writer: Robert Goldman. Director: Alex March.

*The Dickie Henderson Show* (June 1962)
British TV.
Karloff guest starred.

*Route 66* (Oct. 26, 1962)
CBS
"Lizard's Leg and Owlet's Wing". George Maharis, Martin Milner, Boris Karloff, Peter Lorre, Lon Chaney, Jr., Conrad Nagel. Writer: Stirling Silliphant. Director: Robert Gist.

*Out of This World* (1962)
British TV.
Karloff hosted all 13 episodes of this science-fiction series.

*Wonderama* (Jan. 27, 1963)
WNEW
Karloff appeared on this local New York show hosted by Sonny Fox.

*I've Got A Secret* (Jan. 28, 1963)
CBS
Karloff guest starred.

*The Hy Gardner Show* (March 3, 1963)
WOR

Karloff and Peter Lorre guested on this New York talk show.

*The Jimmy Dean Show* (Oct. 31, 1963)
ABC
Karloff guest starred.

*The Today Show* (Nov. 8, 1963)
NBC
Karloff and Fay Wray appeared to discuss horror films.

*Chronicle* (Dec. 25, 1963)
CBS
Karloff narrated "A Danish Fairy Tale", a documentary on the life of Hans Christian Andersen.

*The Garry Moore Show* (April 21, 1964)
CBS
Boris Karloff, Alan King, Dorothy Loudon.

*The Entertainers* (Jan. 16, 1965)
CBS
Carol Burnett, Ruth Buzzi, John Davidson, Dom DeLuise, Chita Rivera, Boris Karloff, Caterina Valente.

*Shindig* (Oct. 30, 1965)
ABC
Jimmy O'Neill, Ted Cassidy, Boris Karloff, Bobby Sherman.

*The Wild, Wild West* (Sept. 23, 1966)
CBS
"Night of the Golden Cobra". Robert Conrad, Ross Martin, Boris Karloff, Audrey Dalton, Simon Scott. Writer: Henry Sharp. Director: Irving J. Moore.

*The Girl from U.N.C.L.E.* (Sept. 27, 1966)
NBC
"The Mother Muffin Affair". Stefanie Powers, Robert Vaughn, Boris Karloff, Bruce Gordon, Bernard Fox, Leo G. Carroll. Writer: Joseph Calvelli. Director: Sherman Marks.

*How the Grinch Stole Christmas* (Dec. 18, 1966)
CBS
Karloff narrated and provided the voice of the Grinch. Animation: Chuck Jones. Adaptation: Ted Geisel (Dr. Seuss) from his book. Music: Albert Hague.

*I Spy* (Feb. 22, 1967)
NBC
"Mainly on the Plains". Robert Culp, Bill Cosby, Boris Karloff, Carl Schell. Writers: Morton Fine and David Friedkin. Director: David Friedkin.

*Film Review* (March 15, 1968)
BBC
Boris Karloff, Christopher Lee, Tony Tenser.

*The Red Skelton Show* (Sept. 24, 1968)
CBS
Boris Karloff, Vincent Price. Producer: Bill Hobin. Director: Howard Quinn.

*The Jonathan Winters Show* (Oct. 30, 1968)
CBS
Boris Karloff, Agnes Moorehead. Director: Jorn Winther.

*The Name of the Game* (Nov. 29, 1968)
NBC
"The White Birch". Gene Barry, Susan Saint James, Jean-Pierre Aumont, Peter Deuel, Ben Gazzara, Richard Jaeckel, Boris Karloff, Bethel Leslie, Roddy MacDowall, Susan Oliver, Lilia Skala. Writers: Dean Hargrove and Luther Davis. Director: Lamont Johnson.

# COMMERCIALS

1966: Butternut Coffee, Schaeffer Pens.
1967: Volkswagen
1968: A-1 Sauce, Ronson Lighters.
1960's: Karloff did a British ad for beer.

# DISCOGRAPHY

1. *Aesop's Fables.* Caedmon TC 1221. Karloff read the following: "The Ant and the Grasshopper", "The Fox and the Lion", "The Oak and the Reed", "The Wolf and the Crane", "The Vain Jackdaw", "The Mountain in Labor", "The Old Hound", "The Cock and the Jewel", "The Man and the Satyr", "The Flies and the Honey-Pot", "Mercury and the Woodman", "The Tortoise and the Eagle", "The Shepherd Boy and the Wolf", "The Ass and the Grasshopper", "The Fox and the Goat", "The Hare and the Tortoise", "The Frog and the Ox", "The Fox and the Grapes", "The Dog and the Shadow", "The Crow and the Pitcher", "The Country Mouse and the Town Mouse", "The Travellers and the Bear", "The Gnat and the Bull", "The Lion and His Three Counsellors", "The Eagle and the Arrow", "The Wind and the Sun", "The Mice in Council", "The Lion in Love". "The Hare and the Hound", "The One-Eyed Doe", "Hercules and the Wagoner", "The Lioness", "The Angler and the Little Fish", "The Farmer and His Sons", "The Country Maid and Her Milk Can", "The Thief and His Mother", "The Goose with the Golden Eggs", "The Old Man and Death", "The Boy Bathing", "Venus and the Cat", "The Boys and the Frogs", "The Miller, His Son, and Their Ass".

2. *Best-Loved Fairy Tales.* Childcraft CLP 1206.

3. *Classics of English Poetry for the Elementary Curriculum.* Caedmon TC 1301. Read by Jeremy Brett, Katharine Cornell, Ronald Fraser, George Grizzard, Boris Karloff, James Mason, Frederick O'Neal, Ralph Richardson, Cyril Ritchard. "The Rime of the Ancient Mariner", "The Lay of the Last Minstrel", "Breathes There a Man", "Lochinvar", "How They Brought the Good News from Ghent to Aix", "Incident of the French Camp", "My Last Duchess", "The Owl and the Pussycat", "How Do I Love Thee?", "The Charge of the Light Brigade", "Gunga Din", "The Law of the Jungle", "The Highwaymen".

4. *Come My Laurie With Me/He Is There.* MOL (45 rpm)

5. *Cymbeline* by William Shakespeare. Caedmon SRS 236. (1962) Read by Boris Karloff, Claire Bloom, Pamela Brown, John Fraser,

Alan Dobie, Paul Daneman, Walter Hudd, John Dane, Robin Palmer, Wallas Eaton, James Cairncross, Stephen Moore, Harold Lang, Eric House, Eric Jones, Douglas Muir, Richard Dare, Derek Godfrey, Judith South.

6. *The Daydreamer.* Columbia OL-6540/05-2940. (1966) Soundtrack from the animated feature.

7. *Dr. Seuss: How the Grinch Stole Christmas.* Leo the Lion S-901. (1967) Soundtrack from the TV special.

8. *An Evening with Boris Karloff and His Friends.* Decca DL-4833. (1967) Karloff narrated and introduced scenes from Universal's horror classics. Written and produced by Verne Langdon, Milt Larsen, and Forrest J. Ackerman. Original Background by William Loose.

9. *Rudyard Kipling: Gunga Din and Other Poems.* Caedmon TC 1193. Read by Nigel Davenport, Ronald Fraser, Boris Karloff, Murray Melvin, Edward Woodward. "The Law of the Jungle", "Recessional", "Song of the Galley-Slaves", "To Thomas Atkins", "The Way Through the Woods", "The White Man's Burden", "A Song of the English", "The Song of the Dead, II", "The Ballad of East and West", "Gunga Din", "The Ladies", "Fuzzy-Wuzzy", "Mandalay", "Tommy", "Danny Deever".

10. *Rudyard Kipling: How the Alphabet Was Made and Other Just So Stories.* Caedmon TC 1361 Karloff read "How the First Letter Was Written" and "The Crab That Played with the Sea". Anthony Quayle read "How the Alphabet Was Made."

11. *Rudyard Kipling: The Cat That Walked By Himself and Other Just So Stories.* Caedmon TC 1139. Karloff read "The Cat That Walked By Himself", "The Butterfly That Stamped" and "How the First Letter Was Written".

12. *Rudyard Kipling: The Elephant's Child and Other Just So Stories.* Caedmon TC 1088. Karloff read "The Elephant's Child", "The Sing-Song of Old Man Kangaroo", "The Beginning of the Armadillos" and "How the Leopard Got His Spots".

13. *Rudyard Kipling: How Fear Came.* Caedmon TC 1100.

14. *Rudyard Kipling: Toomai of the Elephants.* Caedmon TC 1176.

15. *The Legend of Sleepy Hollow* and *Rip Van Winkle* by Washington Irving. Pickwick CR-32/reissue SPC-5156. Arranged and produced by Ralph Stein. Script by Sid and Helen Frank. Words and music by Frank and Judy Stein.

16. *Let's Listen.* Caedmon TC 1182 Read by Julie Harris, Boris Karloff, Gwen Verdon. Karloff read "Petunia, Beware" and "The Pony Engine".

17. *The Little Match Girl and Other Tales* by Hans Christian Andersen. Caedmon TC 1117. Karloff read "The Little Match Girl", "Thumbelina", "The Swineherd", "The Top and the Ball", and "The Red Shoes". Translated by Reginald Spink.

18. *Mad Monster Party.* RCA Soundtrack from the animated feature.

19. *Mother Goose.* Caedmon TC 1091. Read by Celeste Holm, Boris Karloff, and Cyril Ritchard. Music by Hershy Kay.

20. *Peter and the Wolf* by Prokofiev. Childcraft CLP 13, also on Vanguard VRS-1208/VSP-2010/reissue SRV-174. Karloff narrated.

21. *Peter Pan* by James M. Barrie. Columbia AOL 4312. Soundtrack from the Broadway. Musical. Presented by Peter Lawrence and Roger L. Stevens. Director: John Burrell. Associate Director: Wendy Toye. Recording Director: Robert Lewis Shayon. Incidental Music: Alec Wilder. Musical Conductor: Ben Steinberg. Record Adaptation: Henry Walsh. Narrator: Torin Thatcher. Songs and Lyrics: Leonard Bernstein. Karloff sang "The Pirate Song" and "The Plank". Cast: Jean Arthur, Boris Karloff, Peg Hillias, Marcia Henderson, Jack Dimond, Charles Taylor, Norman Shelly, Lee Barnet, Richard Knox, Philip Hepburn, Charles Brill, Edward Benjamin, Buzzy Martin, Joe E. Marks, David Kurlan, Will Scholz, Nehemiah Persoff, Harry Allen, John Dennis, William Marshall, Vincent Beck.

22. *The Pickwick Papers* by Charles Dickens. Caedmon TC 1121. Karloff read "The Story of the Goblin Who Stole A Sexton" and Sir Lewis Casson read "Mr. Pickwick's Christmas".

23. *The Pied Piper* and *The Hunting of the Snark*. Caedmon TC 1075. Karloff read the stories by Robert Browning and Lewis Carroll.

24. *The Pony Engine and Other Stories For Children*. Caedmon TC 1355, CP-1355. Julie Harris, Boris Karloff, David Wayne. Karloff read "The Pony Engine", "The Old Woman and Her Pig", and "The Country Mouse and the Town Mouse".

25. *The Reluctant Dragon* by Kenneth Grahame. Caedmon TC 1074.

26. *Tales of the Frightened, Vol. 1*. Mercury MG 20815/Stereo 60815. (1963) Karloff read "The Man in the Raincoat", "The Deadly Dress", "The Hand of Fate", "Don't Lose Your Head", "Call at Midnight", "Just Inside the Cemetery", "The Fortune Teller". Writer: Michael Avallone. Producer: Lyle Kenyon Engel. Assistant Producer: Marla Ray. Editor: George S. Engel.

27. *Tales of the Frightened, Vol. 2*. Mercury 60816. (1963) Karloff read "The Vampire Sleeps", "Mirror of Death", "Never Kick a Black Cat", "The Ladder", "Nightmare!". "Voice From the Grave", "Theda Is Death", "The Barking Dog", "Defilers of the Tombs", "Terror in the Window", "Tom, Dick, and Horror", "Portrait in Hell", "The Graveyard Nine", "Say Goodnight to Mr. Sporko", "Beware the Bird", "The Phantom Soldier", "Some Things Shouldn't Be Seen", "You Can Take It With You", "Children of the Devil". Writer: Michael Avallone. Producer: Lyle Kenyon Engel.

28. *The Three Little Pigs and Other Fairy Tales*. Caedmon TC 1129. Karloff read "The Three Little Pigs", "The Three Bears", "Jack and the Beanstalk", "The Old Woman And Her Pig", "Henny Penny", "Hereafterthis", "The Three Sillies" and "King of The Cats".

29. *The Ugly Duckling and Other Tales* by Hans Christian Andersen. Caedmon TC 1109. Karloff read "The Ugly Duckling", "The

Shepherdess and the Chimney Sweep", "The Princess and the Pea", "The Collar", "Clod-Poll", and "The Fir Tree".

30. *The United States Air Force Band Presents Christmas.* (1967) Karloff read "Timmy Discovers Christmas", an original story written by Master Sgt. Ed Dawkins. Original music composed by Chief Master Sgt. Floyd Werle and performed by the U.S. Air Force Band. Conductor: Lt. Col. Arnald D. Gabriel. Also featured was singer Nancy Wilson with the Doodletown Pipers performing "It's Christmas Time". Executive Producer: Maj. Jack Oswald. This album, not released commercially, was distributed to radio stations nationwide.

31. *The Year Without A Santa Claus.* Capitol SL 6588. (1968) Narrator: Boris Karloff. Writer: Phyllis McGinley.

# BROADWAY

*Arsenic and Old Lace*
Author: Joseph Kesselring. Producers: Howard Lindsay and Russel Crouse. Director: Bretaigne Windust. Settings and Costumes: Raymond Sovey. Opened Jan. 10, 1941 at the Fulton. Closed June 1942 after 1,444 performances. National tour. Cast: Josephine Hull (Abby Brewster), Jean Adair (Martha Brewster), Boris Karloff (Jonathan Brewster), Allyn Joslyn (Mortimer Brewster), John Alexander (Teddy Brewster), Helen Brooks (Elaine Harper), Edgar Stehli (Dr. Einstein), Wyrley Birch (the Reverend Dr. Harper), John Quigg (Officer Brophy), Bruce Gordon (Officer Klein), Anthony Ross (Officer O'Hara), Victor Sutherland (Lieutenant Rooney), Henry Herbert (Mr. Gibbs), William Parke (Mr. Witherspoon).

*The Linden Tree*
Author: J.B. Priestley. Producer: Maurice Evans. Director: George Schaefer. Settings: Peter Wolf. Costumes: Frank Thompson. Opened March 2, 1948 at the Music Box. Closed March 6, 1948 after 7 performances. Cast: Boris Karloff (Professor Robert Linden), Una O'Connor (Mrs. Colton), Noel Leslie (Alfred Lockhart), Barbara Everest (Mrs.

Linden), Halliwell Hobbes, Jr. (Rex Linden), Viola Keats (Jean Linden), Cathleen Cordell (Marion Linden), Mary Kimber (Edith Westmore), Marilyn Erskine (Dinah Linden), Emmett Rogers (Bernard Fawcett).

*The Shop at Sly Corner*
Author: Edward Percy. Producer: Grant Gaither. Director: Margaret Perry. Settings and Costumes: Willis Knighton. Opened Jan. 18, 1949 at the Booth. Closed Jan. 22, 1949 after 7 performances. Cast: Boris Karloff (Descius Heiss), Jay Robinson (Archie Fellowes), Mary MacLeod (Margaret Heiss), Jane Lloyd-Jones (Joan Deal), Ethel Griffies (Mathilde Heiss), Una O'Connor (Mrs. Catt), Philip Saville (Robert Graham), Emmett Rogers (Corder Morris), Alfred Hyslop (Steve Hubbard), Reginald Mason (John Elliot).

*Peter Pan*
Author: James M. Barrie. Producers: Peter Lawrence and Roger L. Stevens. Director: John Burrell. Assistant Director: Wendy Toye. Music and Lyrics: Leonard Bernstein. Orchestrations: Hershy Kay. Music Coordination and Arrangements: Trude Rittman. Incidental Music: Alec Wilder. Musical Conductor: Ben Steinberg. Settings: Ralph Alswang. Costumes: Motley. Opened April 24, 1950 at the Imperial. Closed Jan. 27, 1951 after 321 performances. National tour. Cast: Jean Arthur (Peter Pan), Boris Karloff (Mr.Darling/Captain Hook), Peg Hillias (Mrs. Darling), Marcia Henderson (Wendy), Jack Dimond (John), Charles Taylor (Michael), Norman Shelly (Nana/The Crocodile), Gloria Patrice (Liza/Tiger Lily), Lee Barnett (Tootles), Richard Knox (Slightly), Philip Hepburn (Curly), Charles Brill and Edward Benjamin (The Twins), Buzzy Martin (Nibs), Joe E. Marks (Smee), David Kurlan (Starkey), Will Scholz (Jukes), Nehemiah Persoff (Cecco), Harry Allen (Mullins), John Dennis (Noodler), William Marshall (Cookson), Vincent Beck (Whibbles).

*The Lark*
Author: Lillian Hellman. Based on the play *L'Alouette* by Jean Anouilh. Producer: Kermit Bloomgarden. Director: Joseph Anthony. Music: Leonard Bernstein. Settings and Lighting: Jo Mielziner. Costumes: Alvin Colt. Opened Nov. 17, 1955 at the Longacre. Closed June 1956 after 229 performances. National tour. Cast: Julie Harris (Joan of Arc),

Boris Karloff (Bishop Cauchon), Christopher Plummer (Warwick), Ward Costello (Joan's Father), Lois Holmes (Joan's Mother), John Reese (Joan's Brother), Roger De Koven (The Promoter), Joseph Wiseman (The Inquisitor), Michael Higgins (Brother Ladvenu), Theodore Bikel (Robert De Beaudricourt), Ann Hillary (Agnes Sorel), Joan Elan (The Young Queen), Paul Roebling (The Dauphin), Rita Vale (Queen Yolande), Bruce Gordon (Monsieur de la Tremouielle/ Captain La Hire), Richard Nicholls (Archbishop of Rheims), Ralph Roberts (Executioner), Leonard Knight (English Soldier), Joe Bernard (Scribe).

# Bibliography

Ackerman, Forrest J., ed. *The Frankenscience Monster*. Ace Publishing Co., 1969.
"A Fiery Particle". *Time*, Nov. 28, 1955.
American Theatre Wing. *The Tony Award*. 1980
Arliss, George. *My Ten Years in the Studios*. Little, Brown, & Co., 1940
"Being A Monster Is Really A Game". *TV Guide*. Sept. 13, 1960.
Bennetts, Leslie. "A '40's Classic Returns to Broadway". *The New York Times*, June 22, 1986.
Bogdanovich, Peter. *Pieces of Time*. Arbor House/Esquire, 1973.
Bojarski, Richard and Beals, Kenneth. *The Films of Boris Karloff*. The Citadel Press, 1974.
"Boris Karloff". *Current Biography 1941*
Bronner, Edwin. *The Encyclopedia of the American Theater 1900-1975*. A.S. Barnes & Co., 1976.
Brooks, Tim and Marsh, Earle. *The Complete Directory to Prime-Time Network TV Shows 1946-Present*. Ballantine Books, 1979.
Burns, Aleene. "Karloff Runs Thriller Biz". *Los Angeles Times*, Sept. 10, 1960.
Crist, Judith. "In the First Time Out". *New York*, Aug. 19, 1968
Dunning, John. *Tune In Yesterday*. Published by the author, 1976.
Eames, John Douglas. *The MGM Story*. Crown Publishers, Inc., 1979.
Evans, Maurice. *All This....and Evans Too!*. University of South Carolina Press, 1987.
Everson, William K. *Classics of the Horror Film*. The Citadel Press, 1974.

"Frankenstein Finished.". *The New York Times*, Oct. 11, 1931.

Gerani, Gary with Schulman, Paul. *Fantastic Television*. Harmony Books, 1977.

Gifford, Denis. *Karloff: The Man, The Monster, The Movies*. Curtis Books, 1973.

Gingold, Hermoine. *How To Grow Old Disgracefully*. St. Martin's Press, 1988.

Ginnakos, Larry James. *Television Drama Series Programming: A Comprehensive Chronicle 1947-1959*. The Scarecrow Press, 1980.

Grams, Jr., Martin. *Inner Sanctum Mysteries: Behind the Creaking Door*. OTR Publishing. 2002.

Hirschorn, Clive. *The Universal Story*. Crown Publishers, Inc., 1983.

"How They Sweated Out The Chills". *TV Guide*, May 6, 1961.

Humphrey, Hal. "Curtain Call For Mr. Frankenstein". *Los Angeles Times*, Oct. 24, 1962.

"James Whale and 'Frankenstein'". *The New York Times*, Dec. 20, 1961.

Jensen, Paul M. *Boris Karloff and His Films*. A.S. Barnes & Co., 1974.

Kaplan, Mike, ed. *Variety Presents the Complete Book of Major U.S. Show Business Awards*. Garland Publishing Inc., 1985.

Karloff, Boris. "Houses I Have Haunted". *Liberty*, Oct. 4, 1941.

Karloff, Boris. "I Hate The Word Horror". *Film Weekly*, April 18, 1936.

Karloff, Boris, with Eisenberg, Arlene and Howard. "Memoirs Of A Monster". *The Saturday Evening Post*, Nov. 3, 1962.

Karloff, Boris. "Oaks From Acorns". *Screen Actor*, October/November 1960.

Karloff, Boris. *Tales of Terror*. World Publishing Co., 1943.

Karloff, Boris. "Young Folks On The Stage". *The Book of Knowledge*, 1952.

Katz, Ephraim. *The Film Encyclopedia.*. Thomas Y. Crowell Publishers, 1994.

Lanchester, Elsa. *Elsa Lanchester Herself*. St. Martin's Press, 1983.

Lee, Christopher. *Tall, Dark, and Gruesome*. W.H. Allen, 1977.

Lenning, Arthur. *The Count: The Life and Films of Bela "Dracula" Lugosi*. G.P. Putnam's Sons, 1974.

Lentz, III, Harris M., compiled by. *Science Fiction, Horror, and Fantasy Film and Television Credits*. McFarland and Co., 1983.

Leonard, William Torbert. *Broadway Bound: A Guide to Shows That Died Aborning*. The Scarecrow Press, 1980.
Lindsay, Cynthia. *Dear Boris*. Alfred A. Knopf, 1975.
"Love That Monster". *TV Guide*, Jan. 11, 1958.
Mandell, Paul. "Edgar Ulmer and 'The Black Cat'". *American Cinematographer*, October 1984.
Mank, Gregory William. *It's Alive! The Classic Cinema Saga of Frankenstein*. A.S. Barnes & Co., 1981.
Mantle, Burns. *The Best Plays of 1946-47*. Dodd, Mead, & Co.,1947.
McNeil, Alex. *Total Television: A Comprehensive Guide to Programming From 1946 To the Present*. Penguin Books, 1984.
Meyers, Richard. *TV Detectives*. A.S. Barnes & Co., 1981.
Miller, Don. *B Movies: An Informal Survey of the American Low-Budget Film 1933-1945*. Curtis Books, 1973.
Moss, Robert F. *Karloff and Company: The Horror Film*. Pyramid Communications, Inc., 1974
"Mr. Boris Karloff On Horror Films". *The Times*, Aug. 6, 1962.
Nevins, Jr., Francis M. "Cornell Woolrich on the Small Screen", *The Armchair Detective*, Spring 1985.
Nolan, Jack Edmund. "Karloff On TV". *Film Fan Monthly*, December 1969.
Parish, James Robert and Whitney, Steven. *Vincent Price Unmasked*. Drake Publishers, 1974.
Pendo, Stephen. "The Golden Age of Horror". *Films in Review*, March 1975.
Perry, Jeb H. *Universal Television: The Studio and Its Programs 1950-1980.*. The Scarecrow Press, 1983.
Price, Vincent. *Vincent Price: His Movies, His Plays, His Life*. Doubleday & Co., 1978.
Singer, Michael, ed. *Directors: A Complete Guide*. Lone Eagle Productions, Inc., 1982.
Skinner, Cornelia Otis. *Life with Lindsay & Crouse*. Houghton Mifflin Co., 1976.
Smith, Cecil. "Karloff--Arsenic, Very Old Lace". *Los Angeles Times*, Oct. 5, 1962.
Stickney, Dorothy. *Openings and Closings*. Doubleday & Co., 1979.
Swartz, Jon D. and Reinehr, Robert C. *Handbook of Old -Time Radio: A Comprehensive Guide to Golden Age Radio Listening and Collecting*. The Scarecrow Press, 1993.

Taves, Brian. "Universal's Horror Tradition". *American Cinematographer*, April 1987.

Taylor, Frank. "Jack Pierce--Forgotten Make-Up Genius", *American Cinematographer*, January 1985.

Terrace, Vincent. *Radio's Golden Years: The Encyclopedia of Radio Programs*. A.S. Barnes & Co., 1981.

Underwood, Peter. *Karloff*. Drake Publishers, 1972.

Wright, Gene. *Horrorshows: The A-To-Z of Horror in Film, Television, Radio, and Theater*. Facts on File Publications, 1986.

www.ingramcontent.com/pod-product-compliance
Lightning Source LLC
Chambersburg PA
CBHW071949160426
43198CB00011B/1610